Children's Language and Multilingualism

Children's Language and Multilingualism

Indigenous Language Use at Home and School

Edited by

Jane Simpson and
Gillian Wigglesworth

continuum

Continuum International Publishing Group
The Tower Building   80 Maiden Lane, Suite 704
11 York Road   New York
London SE1 7NX   NY 10038

British Library Cataloguing-in-Publication Data
A catalogue record for this book is available from the British Library.

ISBN: 978-08264-9516-7 (hardback)
        978-08264-9517-4 (paperback)

Library of Congress Cataloguing-in-Publication Data
The Publisher has applied for CIP data

Typeset by Newgen Imaging Pvt Ltd, Chennai, India
Printed and bound in Great Britain by MPG Books, Cornwall

In memory of our mothers:
Joanna Erlistoun Simpson
Agnes Ruth Wigglesworth

and

to the late Dr R. Marika, who encouraged us in this
work but sadly did not live to see it to fruition

Contents

viii   Contents

Foreword
Shirley Brice Heath

Language socialisation in Indigenous families has been burdened by both ignorance and myth for decades. Few anthropologists and linguists working in Indigenous communities have studied how children learn not only the language of their own households but also, as is so often the case, several other languages of their community and surrounding neighbourhoods. In communities in Indigenous Australia, social scientists have often had to undertake writing the grammars of these languages. As a consequence, the focus of scholars has been on their own language-learning rather than that of the children around them. Aside from the few brief comments or notes of anthropologists such as Diane Bell and other social scientists with specific research interests (e.g. Annette Hamilton with a focus on child-rearing or Stephen Harris with an emphasis on educational adaptation), we know few hard facts about language socialisation among young Indigenous children. Even less is known of how older children learn language, though the work of Annie Langlois and Ute Eickelkamp in the first decade of the twenty-first century has begun to fill this void. Both of these scholars contextualise later language development, as well as changes in language structures and uses of other modes of communication along with spoken language.

The current volume is therefore a seminal work that pulls together case studies that advance our understanding of theories of language-learning and research methods for language socialisation research. This work locates language socialisation within the processes of co-participation and also enables us to grasp something of what must go on in the heads of individual learners. Set forth here are several provocative positions that will be of significance to practice theory (de Certeau, 1984; Lave and Wenger, 1991; Rogoff, 2003; Ortner, 2006). Practice in the head, as well as in social interaction, grounds learning. The fact that practice is also critical to creativity and to the means by which individuals manage to be both tactical and strategic in using all kinds of situations to advance their own learning is often overlooked. Rituals of daily care with young children that engage them with play and *bricolage*, as well as manipulations of space, food, household objects, shape the degree and extent of receptive and productive opportunities the young have to learn the language(s) of their immediate surroundings. Technologies, whether primarily for spectatorship (e.g. television) or communicative interaction (e.g. telephones), also play an increasingly important role in the everyday language-learning of both young children and adolescents.

Contributions from this book are abundant, but three offer particularly promising launch pads for further work. First is the matter of envisionment or the use of images in the head as well as focused visual attention on learning language. In the first decade of the twenty-first century, neuroscientists and cognitive theorists have given considerable attention to 'the cognitive work of images' (Stafford, 2007), but they have not addressed language socialisation as such. However, reports within this volume may stir an interest in just how self-regulatory private speech, dramatic play and visuo-spatial working memory relate to verbal knowledge. Visual discernment needs extensive modelling and reinforcement; only through practice does one become a truly discriminating observer. Neuro-scientific research forces attention on how that which is observed visually ties to that which we can recapture verbally and remember in our meaning-making through symbol systems. Cognitive scientists have, through experimental work and modelling or 'mindware', shown the extent to which imagination works in the 'extended mind' (Clark, 1996, 2007). The studies of language socialisation here do not directly address these questions, but they offer ample suggestions on how Indigenous language socialisation offers a natural laboratory for further investigation into how visual learning relates to verbal acquisition.

A second contribution of this work links to cultures' different ways of judging 'intelligence'. Of key importance in such judgments is the extent to which language habits will figure in the ways that locals judge how 'smart', 'sharp' or 'quick' an individual is in one or another kind of task. Such judgments have, with the growing importance of schooling and 'information societies', been subject to assessments of the facility of individuals when they interact with means of communication other than oral language (e.g. by drawing, dancing, creating music or representing other modes of performance). Since many patterns of work in everyday life among Indigenous peoples around the world depend on observation and imitation by young children and not on verbal instruction from elders, the matter of how well young learners link their seeing to doing is highly significant in the acceptance of individuals within communities where manual and craft labour have mattered greatly and may still matter during certain seasons of the year or preparation for rites of intensification or rites of passage.

A third contribution of this book is the enlivenment of interest in dramatic play or the taking on of roles by children. Role-playing and its significance within language-learning can tell scholars much about relationships that hold between agency and language-learning. We must remember that through the work of Bambi Schieffelin and Don Kulick, in vastly different communities of Papua New Guinea, linguists and anthropologists learned a great deal about role-play among children and between parents and children. These works called our attention to the importance of outward-directed visual viewing by children during adults' narratives of the current scene. Co-participation of toddlers in care of infants and animals indicated ways that language worked while children were in the midst of their own seemingly independent exploration of imitating adult behaviours in everyday tasks. Visual focus, motivated by the intention to take up roles, enables the viewer to take on a sense of *agency* critical for putting roles into play. When called for frequently, and within a developing sense of agency, sustained visual focus and perception of detail correlate with a gain in fluency in later language development, particularly in forms and genres related to envisioning a future (e.g. knowing how to lay out a plan verbally, develop a scenario or sketch a series of actions through to an imagined outcome) (see Heath, 2000, 2006; Turner, 2006).

Beyond these three areas of contribution to theories of learning or cognitive and linguistic control is a critical theme in the book's case studies: displacement, change, and a wrenching from externally driven altered life circumstances. Accounts of Australian Indigenous language-learning from anthropologists and linguists have, for the most part, been carried out in relatively intact communities – either in co-dependence with the pastoral industry or as part of community life in relatively inaccessible geographic regions of Australia.

However, by the 1990s, much had changed, particularly for Indigenous communities that had for most of the twentieth century lived with bush tucker, some degree of seasonal migration, and with varying degrees of access to health-care, education and arts promotion through association with the pastoral industry and the legacies of the nearby residence of missionaries. To be sure, horrific inequities and disrespect for the sacred nature of land, animals and traditional rituals characterise much of what occurred for the first three-quarters of the twentieth century. But by the 1990s in certain areas, such as the central desert, the rapid removal of access to the familiar routines of food-gathering, family and community ceremonies, and regular work for men and women brought disruptions across communities. Adult–child interactions altered radically in a sedentary life that turned to shops for food and provided no gender-based divisions of labour and means of gaining status and respect. Gone were the vital infrastructures of parent–child interaction, as well as relationships with kin, decision-making regarding selection of suitable marriage partners and modelling of work and creativity towards achievement of a project or goal.

Policymakers focused, to a large extent, on increased control of children's education in schools and adult behaviours with relation to spousal abuse, alcohol prohibition and vehicle access. These externally enforced rules and forms of punishment collided with traditional patterns of family interaction. Without a coherent encircling structuring of language socialisation, children were left with fragments of former ideologies of learning, such as independence, wilful risk-taking on one's own, and habits of resistance to authority, regimen and decontextualised input. Accounts within this volume give us stories of the consequences of fragmented socialisation of children as well as narratives of the development of alternative patterns of peer adaptation and socialisation that avoid the culturally and personally destructive consequences of dislocation in so many communities.

Thus we are left after reading this volume with a keen sense first and foremost of just how central language socialisation is to child-rearing and to cognitive control. The ability to resist temptations, distractions, destructive high-risk situations, as well as the facility for holding information and skills in working memory, matter while making adjustments to change (Diamond et al., 2007). Children need to have sustained focused situations in which their attentions are held visually, hear directive talk that enables them to develop self-regulatory private speech, play roles and see themselves in future scenarios. Development of the hypothetical, the conditional and a sense of consequences that result from the march of cause and effect have to be in place for children by the end of toddlerhood and these have to be consistently modelled thereafter. Children have to grow up with a sense of something for them to do and be in the future. This vision of future possibilities depends in large part on language input of 'quality and quantity'. Sufficient language modelling and interaction that includes a range of syntactic structures critical to planful thinking enable internal regulation and the envisionment of a future. Stories of the past and the future build a mindful sense of what one can be as an individual and as a community member. Some degree of apprenticing and participatory role-playing has to come from being a co-participant in some kind of project or event that demonstrates order, plan and purpose, and not from undirected chaos. As language learners grow older, they need increased access to participating roles with experts, guides and caring models. Some kind of regimentation of interactions is critical to language-learning and indeed to human development. This regimentation need not dictate how parties to an interaction must take only certain roles. Instead, ways of engaging need to offer possibilities for multiple roles and stances that individuals can take up for experiment within scaffolded situations. Models also need to play different roles, simultaneously guiding young learners to grasp the potential of situations for individuals to gain skills, information and a sense of the socially responsible membership.

Language socialisation, perhaps more than any other aspect of growing up, frames our way of being in the social worlds in which we will live. It is curious that so few scholars, relatively speaking, have seen the importance of this aspect of human development. This book comes at a time when this long neglect is being rectified. Several books have either recently been published (Hornberger and Duff, 2007) or are being planned (Duranti et al., forthcoming) on this topic. No area of the world offers such rich cases as Australia, and Indigenous Australians provide unique opportunities to understand the intertwining of language loss as well as language maintenance and change with drastic and rapid cultural changes. The diverse and rich contributions within this provocative volume will inspire not only new research but also the refinement of current theories of language, learning and culture across a range of human sciences.

References

Clark, A. (1996). *Being There: Putting Brain, Body, and World Together Again*. Cambridge, MA: MIT Press.

Clark, A. (2007). *Magic Words: How Language Augments Human Computation*. http://www.nyu.edu/gsas/dept/philo/courses/concepts/magicwords.html.

de Certeau, M. (1984). *The Practice of Everyday Life*. Steven Rendall (Trans.). Berkeley, CA: University of California Press.

Diamond, A., Barnett, W. S., Thomas, J. and Munro, S. (2007). Preschool program improves cognitive control. *Science, 318*, 1387–88.

Duranti, A., Ochs, E. and Schieffelin, B. B. (eds) (Forthcoming). *Handbook of Language Socialization*. London: Blackwell.

Heath, S. B. (2000). Seeing our way into learning. *Cambridge Journal of Education, 30*(1), 121–32.

Heath, S. B. (2006). Dynamics of completion: gaps, blanks, and improvisation. In M. Turner (ed.), *The Artful Mind* (pp. 133–52).Oxford: Oxford University Press.

Hornberger, N. and Duff, P. (eds) (2007). Language socialization. *Encyclopedia of Language and Education* (Vol. 8; Second edn). New York: Springer.

Lave, J. and Wenger, E. (1991). *Situated Learning: Legitimate Peripheral Participation*. Cambridge: Cambridge University Press.

Ortner, S. (2006). *Anthropology and Social Theory: Culture, Power, and the Acting Subject*. Durham, NC: Duke University Press.

Rogoff, B. (2003). *The Cultural Nature of Human Development*. Oxford: Oxford University Press.

Stafford, B. M. (2007). *Echo Objects: The Cognitive Work of Images*. Chicago: University of Chicago Press.

Turner, M. (ed.) (2006). The *Artful Mind: Cognitive Science and the Riddle of Human Creativity*. Oxford: Oxford University Press.

Acknowledgements

The impetus for this book came from our work on the Aboriginal Child Language Acquisition Project with Patrick McConvell, Samantha Disbray, Felicity Meakins, Betty Nakkamarra Morrison, Karin Moses, Carmel O'Shannessy, Samantha Smiler Nangala-Nanaku and Colin Yallop. The work was funded by a discovery grant from the Australian Research Council (DP0343189), and the University of Melbourne. We would like to thank Jo Caffery, Cathie Elder, Jenny Green, Barb Kelly and Julie Robinson for their helpful comments on the manuscript, Joshua Clothier for formatting the manuscript, Deborah Loakes, Rachel Nordlinger and Rebecca Pressing for help with the indices, and Hannah Gason for the maps.

List of contributors

Samantha Disbray works as a linguist for the Northern Territory Department of Employment, Education and Training. She is about to submit her PhD in Linguistics at the University of Melbourne. She researches child language development. s.disbray@pgrad.unimelb.edu.au

Ute Eickelkamp is ARC Research Fellow in the School for Social and Policy Research at Charles Darwin University. She studies Aboriginal children's play and meaning-making, and is interested in child-focused anthropology and psychoanalytic perspectives. Ute.Eickelkamp@cdu.edu.au

Elizabeth 'Lizzie' Marrkilyi Ellis is a Ngaatjatjarra/Ngaanyatjarra woman. She is an interpreter/translator, language teacher and language consultant and is completing her BA (Language and Linguistics). marrkilyi@yahoo.com.au

Ann Galloway is Director of Centre for Indigenous Australian Knowledges at Edith Cowan University. Ann researches in language in education and Indigenous education. a.galloway@ecu.edu.au

Judy Gould is a Speech Pathologist and PhD student in Applied Linguistics currently studying first language and literacy development and communication disorders among Aboriginal children. jgbg@ozemail.com.au

Shirley Brice Heath is Professor at Large at Watson Institute for International Studies, Brown University and Professor of English and Linguistics, Emerita, Stanford University.

Caroline Jones is Senior Lecturer in Education at University of Wollongong. She works on Ngarinyman language and in child language development especially phonology. caroline_jones@uow.edu.au

Inge Kral is an ARC Post-Doctoral Research Fellow at the Centre for Aboriginal Economic Policy Research at the Australian National University researching non-formal youth learning and literacy. inge.kral@anu.edu.au

Patrick McConvell is Research Fellow, Language and Society at the Australian Institute of Aboriginal & Torres Strait Islander Studies, Canberra. He works on Aboriginal languages and language change, mainly in north western Australia. patrick.mcconvell@aiatsis.gov.au

Felicity Meakins just completed her PhD at the University of Melbourne. She is continuing documentation work on Gurindji Kriol, Bilinarra and Gurindji through the University of Manchester. Felicity.Meakins@manchester.ac.uk

Karin Moses is Co-ordinator of the Academic Skills Unit at Latrobe University, Bendigo. She has worked with Aboriginal people as a teacher, lecturer and researcher. k.moses@latrobe.edu.au

Joy Campbell Nangari is Tutor at Yarralin School. She has Ngarinyman from her father and Gurindji from her mother. She wants to keep language strong for the kids.

Carmel O'Shannessy is Assistant Professor in Linguistics at the University of Michigan. She works on language contact and shift and first and second language acquisition. carmelos@umich.edu

Elanor Reeders is a Linguist with the Aboriginal Resource and Development Service. She works on the Yolngu languages of north-east Arnhem Land. elanor. reeders@yahoo.com.au

Jane Simpson is a Senior Lecturer in linguistics at the University of Sydney. She works on the Warumungu language of Tennant Creek. jhs@mail.usyd.edu.au

Gillian Wigglesworth is Head of the School of Languages and Linguistics at the University of Melbourne and researches first and second language acquisition. gillianw@unimelb.edu.au

Colin Yallop is an Honorary Fellow in Linguistics at the University of Melbourne. He worked previously at Macquarie University and was Editor-in-Chief of the Macquarie Dictionary. cyallop@unimelb.edu.au

List of abbreviations

1	first person
2	second person
3	third person
ABC Test	Alchini Bizaad Comprehension Test
-ABL	ablative (from)
ACLA	Aboriginal Child Language Acquisition Project
AE	Aboriginal English
-ALL	allative (to)
CAT	catalyst (auxiliary)
CHL	conductive hearing loss
-COM	comitative
-DAT	dative (for)
DIM	diminutive
-DIS	discourse marker
DUR	durative
EPEN	epenthetic syllable
-ERG	ergative (agent)
-FOC	focus
-FUT	future
-GROUP	group
H	high
HOLT	Hualapai Oral Language Test
IELTS	International English Language Testing System
-IMP	imperative
ing	like the English verb ending '-ing'
L	Low
-LOC	locative (at, in, on)
-NF	non-future tense
-NOM	nominaliser
NPST	non-past tense
NT	Northern Territory
OM	otitis media
-ONLY	only
-PA	epenthetic syllable
-PAUC	paucal (a number of)
PERF	Perfect
PL	plural
PROG	progressive
-PRS	present tense

-PST	past tense
REDUP	reduplication
SAE	Standard Australian English
SG	singular
TIL	Traditional Indigenous Language
-TRN	transitive
WE	Wumpurrarni English
WROLT	Window Rock Oral Language Test

List of maps and figures

Maps

Figures

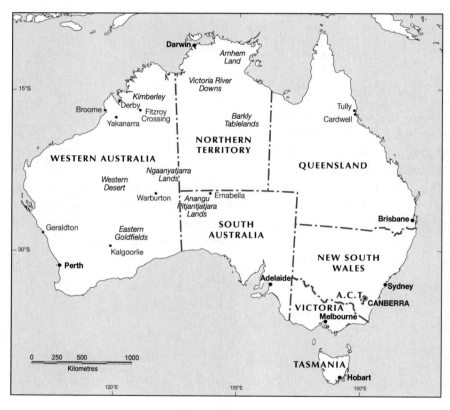

Map of Australia

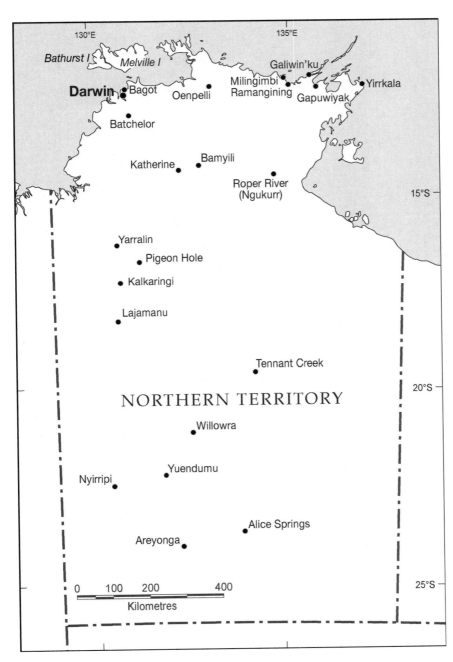

Map of the Northern Territory

Introduction
Jane Simpson and Gillian Wigglesworth

Across Australia, Indigenous children are growing up in many different situations. Some are growing up with parents who grew up in the bush and can remember the first white man they saw. Some are growing up in cities with families on country from which their ancestors were dispossessed over 200 years ago. Some are growing up in comfortable middle-class settings. Others are growing up in country towns with parents who have bitter memories of state-sponsored racism. Diversity of experience leads to diversity of expectations among Indigenous families.

One of the areas of greatest diversity to confront teachers, speech pathologists and language professionals are the 'language landscapes' surrounding the children. What languages do they hear in everyday life? What languages do they speak? What are the language practices of the communities they are growing up in? How do they learn to speak and use language?

There has been surprisingly little work done on Indigenous child-rearing practices generally, and even less on how people talk to children and in what languages, and on the process or route the children take as they learn to talk and to understand. Glimpses are found in ethnographic writings, such as Phyllis Kaberry's work in the Kimberley in the 1930s (Kaberry, 2004). The first detailed study of child rearing, by Annette Hamilton, discusses both traditional child-rearing practices (gleaned from conversations and extrapolations) and practices among the semi-sedentary Anbarra at Maningrida from 1968–1969 where she lived as an anthropology student with a young child (Hamilton, 1981). At the time of her fieldwork, Maningrida was a multilingual community with speakers from at least 13 language groups living there. The Anbarra people she was working with mostly married within the same language group, and the women and young children had not adopted English as a lingua franca. She spent much of her time with the women as they looked after their children and she looked after hers, and she surveyed the ways people interacted with children under five. Hamilton provides a revealing glimpse into how the expectations of outsiders can be confounded when observing the child-rearing practices of another group:

> I had never thought it possible for children to have so few restraints and their parents so few anxieties about them. (Hamilton, 1981, p. 120)

Gender played a major role in the division of labour. It is likely that children learned this gender division early, given Hamilton's observation that Anbarra women gave more warnings and instructions to their daughters, and that from 5 years or so on, girls were expected to help around the camp much more than their brothers. There were strong ideas on propriety about sexual and reproductive matters, and constraints on what could be talked about between men and women. However, Anbarra women would gently abuse and tease children with sexual swearing, and we have found the same patterns in Kalkaringi and Tennant Creek. This is distinct from the widely attested 'obscene joking relation' (Garde, 1996), a type of playful joking which can take place throughout the whole lives of the pairs of people in these relationships; for example, a grandmother or her brother may use sexual swearing to the grandmother's daughter's child. This can be confronting for non-Indigenous Australians, but it is essential to recognise that it is playful and has nothing to do with child abuse.

Hamilton noted how restrained Anbarra people were with young children, how they distracted them rather than punish them, or else used stereotyped threat gestures. Children were encouraged to defend themselves, however. She also noticed that young children often formed quite large groups (one large group consisted of 16 children all under 5, 8 from 5 families, 3 from families which regularly visited, 5 from irregularly visiting families, as well as 6 children between 6 and 9). This peer group determined most of the play, as well as some things like washing and wearing clothes which non-Indigenous Australians often take to be the job of parents.

These observations reflect the value that Anbarra people placed on the autonomy of the child. This is understandable when one considers the demands of hunter–gatherer life; children must learn to feed and look after themselves. Equally important for the survival of small societies is that along with autonomy comes the importance of group membership and group responsibility – older children and older brothers and sisters take on much more responsibility for younger children.

A similar finding about the emphasis on the child's autonomy features in Hamilton's later work among the Yankunytjatjara and Pitjantjatjara in Everard

Park (Mimili, northern South Australia; Hamilton, 1982). We do not know how widespread the methods of child rearing described by Hamilton were in traditional Indigenous Australia, and how much they are affected by the rapid and painful changes that have taken place since contact. But much of what she says is echoed in recent work by Gillian Shaw at Warburton in 2002, where she carried out both observation and interviews of Ngaanyatjarra (Western Desert) women of different ages and backgrounds about their child-rearing practices (Shaw, 2002). Shaw concludes that Ngaanyatjarra child rearing has not changed over 70 years of contact. The living conditions have changed – the Ngaanyatjarra are now settled in communities and most of their food comes from shops. But child rearing is still based on the principle that:

> children know themselves and what they need, and that they will grow up in their own way. An adult's role in this is to meet the child's demands where possible, and to hold the child as a part of family. (Shaw, 2002, p. 96)

Sedentary life has had major effects on what children learn. No longer are they exposed as a matter of daily life to the demands of hunting and gathering, of moving through the country, of learning about where resources are to be found. As Hamilton writes:

> The tragedy of children today is that so much of their understanding of the world, and their intellectual stimulus, has been curtailed without any replacement in the settlement situation. (Hamilton, 1981, p. 667)

While self-reliance and group responsibility are valuable attributes, they have unexpected bad consequences in modern societies (Pocock, 2003). If children can choose for themselves what, when and how much to eat, that can easily lead to malnutrition if healthy food is not easily available. If children can choose for themselves what to do, they may well decide not to go to school. They may decide to speak the language of their peers, rather than the language of their parents, or the standard English being taught at school. The fear of being shamed by other members of the group can lead to children under-achieving in school (Kamien, 1978, p. 171) or not attending school at all. The families' respect for the children's autonomy can lead to confrontation with non-Aboriginal people who may perceive this as a failure of discipline and as neglect. Shaw concludes that:

> The findings of this study suggest that putting pressure on [Ngaanyatjarra] parents to ensure their children attend school will not be a successful strategy. It is likely that a person from outside of the immediate cultural system would be more successful in ensuring that children go to school. (Shaw, 2002, p. 95)

Differences in child-rearing practices and in expectations about children's behaviour make it vitally important that teachers and other professionals working with Indigenous children and their families come with an open mind, prepared to learn and work with the families and the children to ensure that they can recognise and respect the expectations and values that the families may have, but reduce the unintended negative consequences following from these values. This is not an easy task. Strategies which punish parents for sticking to a major, if partly unconscious value, without giving them good reason to modify that value, are unlikely to be successful. Indeed they may cause the situation in which parents covertly support their children's resistance to school; in Bourke (New South Wales) in the early 1970s Max Kamien noted that Indigenous people 'who had been institutionalised as children could not abide supervision of even the most benign form' (Kamien, 1978, p. 169).

We turn now to the language landscapes. Table 1 shows the Australian Indigenous languages with the most speakers. The numbers are very small, and it is clear that the largest are the new Indigenous languages Kriol and Torres Strait Creole. Indigenous people in many parts of the world are struggling to keep their languages alive in the face of the dominant colonising languages. It is much harder for them to do this in countries like Australia, Canada and the United States, where there are many Indigenous languages, and limited resources which are hard to share, than in countries like New Zealand/ Aotearoa where there is only one major Indigenous language. Generally Indigenous languages survive best in remote areas where social structures have remained to some extent, although remarkable survivals around towns are known. Arnhem Land and the Western Desert and Tanami Desert are places in Australia where children still grow up speaking traditional Indigenous languages. In this book Western Desert languages are discussed – Ngaanyatjarra in the chapter by Kral and Ellis, and Pitjantjatjara in the chapter by Eickelkamp, while Reeders discusses Djambarrpuyngu, a language spoken in Arnhem Land. In the Tanami Desert, Warlpiri is strong in some communities, but, as O'Shannessy shows in her chapter, this is changing in other communities. On the eastern edge of the Tanami Desert Arrandic languages are spoken, and one, Alyawarr, was quite strong until the early 1990s. The chapter by Moses and Wigglesworth provides a snapshot of children in a community which was on the verge of shifting from the traditional language.

Many of these communities are multilingual, and often the language landscape is a rapidly changing one. New languages are being developed based on the interaction of traditional languages and English. These new languages vary

Table 1 2006 Census: people speaking major Indigenous languages at home

Language name	Where spoken	2006 Census
Alyawarr	NT: Central Australia	1,664
Anindilyakwa	NT: Groote Eylandt	1,283
Anmatyerr	NT: Central Australia	1,002
Arrernte	NT: Central Australia	2,835
Burarra	NT: Arnhem Land	1,074
Djambarrpuyngu	NT: Arnhem Land	2,766
Kalaw Kawaw Ya/Kalaw Lagaw Ya	Torres Strait	1,216
Luritja	NT: Central Australia	1,480
Murrinh Patha	NT: Wadeye, Port Keats	1,832
Ngaanyatjarra	WA: Western Desert	1,000
Pitjantjatjara	NT, SA: Central Australia	2,657
Tiwi	NT: Tiwi Islands	1,716
Warlpiri	NT: Central Australia	2,507
Wik Mungkan	Qld: Cape York	1,050
Kriol	Northern Australia	4,213
Aboriginal English	Australia	488
Torres Strait Creole (Yumpla Tok)	Torres Strait	6,042
Speakers of other Australian Indigenous languages with fewer than 1,000 speakers		**20,870**
Total number of people speaking Indigenous languages at home		55,695

Source: ABS and our calculations. ABS 2006 Cat. No. 2068.0 – 2006 Census Tables 2006 Census of Population and Housing Australia, Language spoken at home (Australian Indigenous languages only) by sex.

along a continuum. At one end, the way of talking is close to the way some people in Australia talk (we'll call this an 'acrolectal' variety). They might say *He come yesterday* and *He done it* for the past tense instead of standard English *came* and *did*. At the other end are mixed languages, in which the structure of the new language contains words and features of several languages. These are discussed by Meakins, and O'Shannessy, in this book (Chapters 13 and 12, respectively).

In the middle of the range are varieties of an English-based creole (we'll call this a 'basilectal' variety) which differ from community to community. The best-known variety (spoken around Katherine, Ngukurr) is called 'Kriol', that is the word 'creole' written using the spelling system that has been devised for this particular variety. Speakers might say *Yu bin kam* instead of *you came*. Kriol spread throughout the northern part of the NT from late in the nineteenth century, with a major spread point being Roper River Mission (now Ngukurr), east of Katherine (Sandefur, 1985; Harris, 1993). Today it is the first language of many thousands of people (the Census figures given in Table 1 are undoubtedly an underestimate), and the second language of many others (Munro, 2004). Varieties include Barkly Kriol (Barkly Tablelands), Fitzroy Valley Kriol (Fitzroy Crossing) and Torres Strait Creole (Yumpla Tok). Disbray, and Moses and Yallop describe communities in which varieties of this English-based creole are the main home language for most Indigenous children. In general, then, the language situation in these communities is highly variable and complex, and clearly multilingual.

In this book we tread a path through this complex linguistic environment, which children in many Indigenous communities encounter on a daily basis and must negotiate. In the preschool years, the children learn to talk and communicate in their home languages; when they enter the school system, the language situation becomes more complex as they encounter Standard Australian English.

The book is divided into four parts. The first section focuses on the early development of language and language-related activities at home. Wigglesworth and Simpson (Chapter 1) provide an overview of the language landscapes in three communities which are part of the Aboriginal Child Language Acquisition (ACLA) project[1] – Kalkaringi, Tennant Creek and Yakanarra. In these communities, the traditional languages of the area are not being acquired by the current generation of children, who are instead acquiring creoles or a new mixed language. The next two chapters are also part of the ACLA project; Moses and Yallop (Chapter 2) examine the range and variety of questioning techniques used to children in Yakanarra, and point out that, in contrast to the widely held view to the contrary, children are constantly engaged by their caregivers in question and answer routines, and encounter a wide range of question types during their play and other activities. Disbray's focus (Chapter 3) is on the use of narrative by caregivers telling stories to their children from a picture book. She finds that different techniques are adopted by different caregivers, and with children of different ages, with greater expectations of older children to participate and be actively involved. Her study also demonstrates the ways in which the story styles of the traditional language of the area, Warumungu, are incorporated into the storytelling activity. Continuing with the theme of storytelling, Eickelkamp (Chapter 4) examines the ways in which children use traditional sand stories to illustrate their feeling and thoughts. The ability to do this is a cultural milestone in children's language development, and understanding the role of sand stories in the community is important for teachers because they can build the children's formal learning on these skills.

The second section of the book focuses on language and learning in the classroom context. Most Indigenous communities have primary schools, and in these schools, children learn standard English. Very few Indigenous communities have secondary schools, and children who want a secondary education must go away to subsidised private boarding schools, which vary greatly as to the provision of Indigenous language and culture education.

A major problem with education in Australia has been the way Indigenous families move. People travel a great deal, for mourning, to access services in towns, to visit relations, to conduct business and, being concerned for their children's well-being, they usually take their children with them. This sometimes results in the children missing school, and this may result in children failing to learn to read and write.

Almost all Indigenous children are taught in standard English, even if they come to school, as many of them do, not knowing standard English. In a handful of government schools in the Northern Territory and South Australia, and a few independent schools in Western Australia, children have some Indigenous teachers who can explain ideas to them in their first language. But adequately funded bilingual education has mostly been abandoned in Australia (Hoogenraad, 2001), without proper trials, and without being replaced by well-resourced English-as-a-second-language programmes. The disparity between home language and school language inevitably leads to difficulties for the children.

The three chapters in the second section address a variety of different educational issues. Reeder's Chapter 5 is a detailed discourse analysis study of learning in traditional Yolngu society. In this context, children are recognised as independent and autonomous beings, and while they are encouraged to participate, this is not forced on them. These findings have important implications for teachers working with Indigenous children in the formal educational context. The next chapter also focuses on discourse, but this time examines the discourse of the classroom, in an English-only context where a new and relatively inexperienced teacher encounters her Indigenous primary students. Moses and Wigglesworth (Chapter 6) outline the difficulties that may be encountered owing to the lack of cross-cultural understanding and illustrate some of the factors that may contribute to lack of school success. The focus of Kral and Ellis (Chapter 7) is the acquisition of literacy and factors which impact on literacy. The chapter focuses on the acquisition of literacy in Ngaanyatjarra culture, and illustrates the extent to which literacy practices have been adopted in the community, and shows how important it is that literacy practices are adopted into the daily life of the community.

The third section is concerned with assessment. Jones and Nangari (Chapter 8) discuss the problems inherent in devising an assessment instrument for identifying the receptive skills of children in the traditional languages of the communities in which they live. This is a very under-researched area, and such instruments are likely to be valuable in language revival and revitalisation contexts. The assessment of children with potential speech disorders is the focus of Chapter 9 by Gould who focuses on the complex issue of evaluating Indigenous children's language abilities with instruments which are standardised on different groups, and she describes a methodology which allows appropriate assessment of the children's language development. The final chapter in this section (Chapter 10) is concerned with the widespread problem of ear infections which abound in Indigenous children and Galloway discusses a range of measures which teachers can take to counteract the potential problems associated with hearing loss in the classroom.

The three chapters in the fourth and final section of the book are concerned with language landscapes, language shift and multilingualism. McConvell (Chapter 11) provides an overview of the kinds of factors which impact on the language ecology of a region, and how they may affect the health of the language. This is followed by chapters detailing two studies which focus on communities in which language shift has taken place, but in rather different ways. O'Shannessy (Chapter 12) describes the languages the children are acquiring in Lajamanu where they begin by learning Light Warlpiri and then at a later age start to use Warlpiri. Meakins (Chapter 13) describes the complex language situation in Kalkaringi where older people speak Gurindji, while a mixed language is emerging among younger speakers, which combines elements from both Gurindji and Kriol in a systematic way.

Each chapter in the book presents a case study approach to a particular problem, encapsulated within a broader international framework. The challenges faced in Australia by Indigenous communities, and those working with Indigenous communities, are very similar to those faced by Indigenous communities across the world. It is our hope that this book will contribute to opening up the discussion.

Note

1. We are grateful to the Australian Research Council for funding this project through two grants to the editors, DP0343189 (2003–2006) and DP0770488 (2008–2012).

References

Garde, M. J. (1996). '"Saying nothing": the language of joking relationships in Aboriginal Australia'. Unpublished Graduation Diploma Arts thesis, Northern Territory University, NT.

Hamilton, A. (1981). *Nature and Nurture: Aboriginal Child-Rearing in North-Central Arnhem Land*. Canberra: Australian Institute of Aboriginal Studies.

Hamilton, A. (1982). Child health and child care in a desert community 1970–71. In J. Reid (ed.), *Body, Land and Spirit: Health and Healing in Aboriginal Society* (pp. 48–71). Brisbane: University of Queensland Press.

Hoogenraad, R. (2001). Critical reflections on the history of bilingual education in Central Australia. In J. Simpson, D. Nash, M. Laughren, P. Austin and B. Alpher (eds), *Forty Years On: Ken Hale and Australian Languages* (pp. 123–50). Canberra: Pacific Linguistics.

Kaberry, P. (2004). *Aboriginal Woman: Sacred and Profane*. London; New York: Routledge.

Kamien, M. (1978). *The Dark People of Bourke: A Study of Planned Social Change*. Canberra: Australian Institute of Aboriginal Studies; Humanities Press.

Munro, J. M. (2004). 'Substrate language influence in Kriol: the application of transfer constraints to language contact in Northern Australia'. Unpublished PhD thesis, University of New England, Armidale, NSW.

Pocock, J. (2003). *State of Denial: The Neglect and Abuse of Indigenous Children in the Northern Territory*. Melbourne: Secretariat of National Aboriginal and Islander Child Care, SNAICC.

Sandefur, J. (1985). English-based languages and dialects currently spoken by Aboriginal people: suggestions towards a consensus on terminology. *Australian Journal of Linguistics, 5*, 67–78.

Shaw, G. (2002). 'An ethnographic exploration of the development in child rearing style among the Ngaanyatjarra people from the pre-contact era to the present'. Unpublished Masters thesis, University of New South Wales, Sydney.

Section 1

section1

The language learning environment of preschool children in Indigenous communities

Gillian Wigglesworth and Jane Simpson

1

Chapter Outline

Very little is known about the languages spoken to children in multilingual communities where language use is rapidly changing. Nor is it clear how the languages heard by children affect changes in language use in such communities. This paper summarises the findings of a longitudinal study focusing on the languages input provided to children in three remote Australian Aboriginal communities. In each community, between six and eight focus children were recorded interacting with a variety of caregivers over a 4-year period. We examine differences in the proportion of traditional language use across the three communities, and, within each community, with interlocutors of different ages. We conclude with a discussion of the processes of language shift that appear to be in progress in all the three communities, and discuss the differences in the directions in which these shifts are moving.

Introduction

Children learn the language, or languages, of the community they grow up in, and they learn language apparently with very little effort. They also appear to learn language largely without any very specific teaching, and in a vast range of circumstances, some of which appear far more attuned to the task of language learning than others. However, regardless of the varying circumstances in which children find themselves learning language, they almost always end up speaking, in terms of their community, a language which is accurate, fluent, complex and which reflects the language, or languages, they hear around them.

Learning a first language, or languages, and the myriad functions of language, are crucial to the child's ability to successfully function in society. Language is used for education, for work and for social relations; it plays a vital role in learning how to think, and how to behave appropriately towards other people. Language is the means through which children learn to make sense of their world and to make sense of what other people are doing, and why they are doing it.

We now know a great deal about how children growing up in monolingual communities learn language. There have been numerous studies of children learning their first language – diary studies which detail each minute step, and every new word spoken or understood by a single child; longitudinal sampling studies which follow small groups of children learning language over a long period of time by collecting language samples; experimental studies which may focus on cross-sectional comparisons of children at various ages. We also know increasing amounts about children growing up in bilingual situations, although these studies by their nature tend to be individual case studies since children being raised bilingually tend to grow up in a unique environment. However, despite the fact that most children grow up in multilingual societies, learning more than one language as a matter-of-course, we know very little about how children learn languages in such societies (but see Genesee and Nicoladis (2007), and references therein).

As we mentioned in the Introduction, little work has been done in remote Indigenous communities on how children learn to talk and to understand. This means that we know little about the language or languages the children speak, how competent they are in those languages, or how their caregivers impart language knowledge to them, and what environmental factors affect how they learn language. In this chapter, we begin to address some of the issues in this highly complex and rapidly changing language environment in which the children find themselves, and in which they must acquire their first language.

Background

Hamilton's work on child-rearing practices among the semi-sedentary Anbarra at Maningrida from 1968 to 1969 (Hamilton, 1981) was discussed in the Introduction. As part of her study, she carried out quite detailed observations of language practices: noting who talked to children; how they talked to them; and what kinds of things they said. She surveyed the ways in which people interacted with children under five. One analysis was based on 30 hours of observation of people in one area. Another was based on two 5-minute records each of 31 children aged under five, and the results were tabulated. However, she does not give many examples of utterances used in context, and consequently her work does not detail how the children's language develops as they learn. But she has some findings of great interest to understanding language practices. They include:

Language practices

- Infants have a very sociable time. However, Anbarra people did not talk very much to babies under 6 months old, but used certain stereotyped gestures very frequently. These gestures were also used to children aged 6 to 18 months.
- 25 per cent of verbal utterances to babies consisted of mothers uttering abuse but 'in a quiet, amused way' (p.41); 13.6 per cent of verbal utterances to children aged 6 to 18 months also consisted of playful abuse.
- 44 per cent of verbal utterances to children aged 6 to 18 months consisted of comments, warnings and instructions; for boys aged between 18 months and 3 years the figure drops to 23 per cent, while for girls of the same age the figure is 39 per cent.
- 15 per cent of verbal utterances to children aged 6 to 18 months were commands, and 39 per cent consisted of calling their names.
- For children aged between 18 months and 3 years, mothers talked more to their daughters than their sons, and the difference was in giving far more warnings and instructions. Instructing children in kin-relations was very common.
- Mothers pointed things out to children when carrying them around on their shoulders and travelling, but not when they were sitting at home.

Language acquisition

- Anbarra children aged 6 to 18 months used the term for 'mother', and perhaps 'father', but otherwise communicated non-verbally.
- A vocabulary test of naming parts of the body showed that not until around 43 months were children correctly naming basic parts of the body such as hands, while a vocabulary test of name and status of kin suggested that by 43 months they were correctly identifying most basic kin terms (mother, father, sister, mother's mother, mother's brother, mother's sister and father's brother).

- Three- and four-year-olds asked very few questions; 'where' was used, but 'why', 'when' and 'how' were seldom used; Hamilton suggests that one reason for this lies in the uninformative answers that adults gave to 'when' questions, such as 'later'.
- Gillian Shaw's work at Warburton in 2002 with Ngaanyatjarra (Western Desert) children (Shaw, 2002) is also focused on child rearing, but she too makes observations about language practices, describing different ways of trying to change children's behaviour through talk, shouting at children; and two of these are perhaps more applicable to older children: a stylised exhortation about desired behaviour spoken 'slowly and rhythmically', and 'growling', which is a public statement of displeasure. She makes an important point about the expectations of Ngaanyatjarra mothers in contrast to many non-Indigenous Australian mothers:

> However this does not mean that mothers are not cross with their children. On the contrary they are often annoyed, and shout instructions to their children to behave. What is different is that they do not expect that these instructions will necessarily be obeyed, or even that they should be obeyed – they are simply putting in their bid for what the child should do. (Shaw, 2002, p. 76)

Some studies in the 1980s and 1990s have focused on child language acquisition. Ann Jacobs attempted to link child-rearing practices, greater use of non-verbal communication and language development among Indigenous children in the Kalgoorlie area of Western Australia (Jacobs, 1988, 1990). Laughren (1984) published the first linguistic account of baby talk in an Indigenous community. Working with the Warlpiri at Yuendumu in Central Australia, Laughren found a stylised way of talking that was used for the benefit of children from new born to around 5 years.

Working with the same community, Edith Bavin and Tim Shopen conducted a series of studies on how the children were acquiring Warlpiri (Bavin, 1987, 1990, 1991, 1992, 1993, 1995, 1998, 2000; Bavin and Shopen, 1985). These studies not only involved careful detailing of which forms and structures were produced at what ages, but they also observed the effect of contact with English. Bavin and Shopen (1991, p. 106) note the importance of input from older children, and suggest that this input was the source for some innovations in child language.

More recent work by Anne Lowell and others (Lowell et al., 1996) on language socialisation among the Yolngu at Galiwin'ku described the high level of verbal interaction which children were exposed to. Some of their findings echoed those of Hamilton and Jacobs – for example, the use of signs and of non-verbal cues, the instructional element in teaching children about kinship. Other findings included question strategies, scaffolding and repetition.

They noted that emphasis was placed on children's quickness at noticing things (whether it was seeing or hearing).

All these studies have involved communities whose traditional languages are strong, and where they were, at least at the time of study, the dominant languages heard by children. However, as was mentioned in the Introduction, many Indigenous communities are multilingual communities where new languages are being developed based on the interaction of traditional languages with English. In such communities, children are simultaneously learning and creating these new languages. It is these communities that are the focus of our study in the Aboriginal Child Language Acquisition project (ACLA).

Recent work on child language acquisition world-wide

Children's early language development is strongly influenced by what they hear around them, their 'language input'. In many societies, children hear several languages from birth onwards. These languages may be separated, as when each person speaks one language, or they may be mixed as when a speaker changes language within a conversational turn (inter-sentential code-switching) or even uses two languages within one sentence (intra-sentential code-switching). For children growing up in bilingual environments, the latter input type is the most common, although it is not proportionally represented in the bilingual first language acquisition literature, which focuses largely on middle-class children of professional parents, often themselves linguists (Romaine, 1995).

Most of the published studies of how bilingual children learn their first language, and how they learn to use it appropriately, have involved single children, often growing up in a 'one parent, one language' environment (Döpke, 1992). Such children encounter social situations which are either predominantly monolingual, or where there is clear functional separation of the two languages, for example, on the basis of person (mother speaks French and father speaks English) or situation (English is spoken at home and French is spoken at child care). Often the focus has been on the child's cognitive development, particularly with respect to when and how a child who is exposed to more than one language learns to differentiate between them. Research suggests that children growing up in bilingual situations develop both languages at a similar rate to their monolingual peers (Oller et al., 1997) and are able to clearly separate the different languages from an early age (Genesee, 1989, 2001).

Much less attention has been paid to how children acquire language when they hear a variety of languages in multilingual contexts, and when they may hear speakers switching from one language to another in the course of a sentence. But in many bilingual and multilingual communities, such variable input is very common; it may include several languages and/or dialects, in addition to considerable code-switching (McConvell, Chapter 11). Thus the input these children receive is different from those children growing up in 'one parent, one language' environments receive, where the language input is much more 'sanitised'.

In the communities in Central Australia and the Kimberley, the areas of our study, the children are growing up in communities where the people spoke Traditional Indigenous languages (often several), as well as new languages (creoles and mixed languages), varieties of English, and other introduced languages. While the focus of our study is on the language input the children receive from their various caregivers and peers, there are a number of other input factors which need to be borne in mind. One of these is literacy. Many child language acquisition studies have focused on children growing up in households where reading and writing are important and where the written material is usually in a standardised form of the language. Thus from an early age such children are receiving a lot of input in the standard language. Few language acquisition studies have involved children in societies with no tradition of literacy, exceptions being work on language socialisation in Papua New Guinea (Kulick, 1992; Schieffelin, 1990) and Samoa (Ochs, 1988). While in the past Indigenous Australian societies had no tradition of literacy (although they do have symbol systems), colonisation has brought with it mass education in reading and writing standard Australian English, and the parents of the children in our study have all been to school. As Kral and Ellis (Chapter 7) show, while the exposure to reading and writing is probably less than in most middle-class households, it cannot be ignored. Another factor is exposure to radio, television and videos; these are widespread in these communities and are kept on much of the time. They serve to increase the children's exposure to standard Australian English, as well as to other dialects, such as varieties of American English.

Essential to the understanding of how children acquire two or more languages in any bilingual environment is detailed documentation of the kind of input the child is receiving in the languages he or she is exposed to. For example we need to know if one or other of the languages is dominant, whether the codes are mixed or separated in the input, and how much, and in what circumstances the different languages are spoken, and by whom. We also need to describe the languages they hear, because those will be the languages they acquire. These may differ from the languages described in formal grammars. If most of the language the children are hearing is in a non-standard variety of English, or a creole, then standard English is not the children's target. For example, if the child rarely hears a regular past tense such as 'He talked', but frequently hears 'I bin tok' with the creole past tense marker 'bin', then we cannot say that because the child doesn't use the '-ed' form, that child hasn't learned how to express events in the past. Instead, we must look at when the child starts using 'bin'.

The project

In this project we have documented over 4 years the language input provided to Indigenous children from the age of approximately 18 months. We have done this in three communities, with comparisons made to a fourth (Lajumanu), over the period 2003-2006. We are detailing the language input received by the children in the following three communities:

- Kalkaringi, a small town in the Victoria River District on Gurindji country, of about 700 people, most of whom identify as Gurindji;
- Tennant Creek, a town in Warumungu country, of about 3,000 people, some of whom identify as Warumungu, and some of whom identify with other language groups and
- Yakanarra, a community of about 150 people, in an area of the Kimberley where most older people speak Walmajarri.

Some comparisons have been made with Lajamanu, a community of northern Warlpiri people living in traditional Gurindji country where O'Shannessy (Chapter 12) has been documenting children's language acquisition.

The documentation of the language input to the children was done by Felicity Meakins and Samantha Smiler Nangala-Nanaku at Kalkaringi, Samantha Disbray and Betty Nakamarra Morrison in Tennant Creek, and Karin Moses in Yakanarra, all of whom had close relationships with the communities in which they worked.

At the beginning of the study, eight to ten children between the ages of 12 months and 2 years of age were identified as focus children in each community. The aim was to video record each child several times on two trips per year, over a 3-year period. In the event, and because the budget allowed it, an additional recording session was conducted in the fourth year of the project.

Three to five recordings of each child were made on each visit, as they interacted with caregivers of different ages, in smaller and larger groups, and in more and less structured situations. The more structured sessions involved activities such as the caregiver telling the child a story from a picture book; the semi-structured sessions included playing with toys and other items provided by the project for the children, such as toy mobile phones, building blocks, or toy cars; the naturalistic data sessions were those where, for example, children and caregivers went on fishing trips or were playing at a water hole. All data were recorded on digital video, and transcribed.

Languages used in the three communities

Each community has a school in which children are taught in standard English, and businesses (private and Government) in which standard English is the main language. People living in these communities speak a range of languages, as summarised in Table 1.1. These may include more or less knowledge of one or more traditional languages, standard Australian English, and varieties of creoles and mixed languages which vary along a continuum. Speakers may not have specific names for the varieties they use. Thus the Gurindji use the term 'Gurindji' both for the traditional language, and for the new mixed language, which we will call 'Gurindji Kriol' (Meakins, 2007). Some speakers may call both the acrolectal and basilectal varieties 'English', or 'Camp English', or 'Pidgin English', or, in the case of Tennant Creek, 'Wumpurrarni English' (Disbray, Forthcoming). Speakers may also firmly say that they do not speak

Table 1.1 Overview of language situation in the three communities

Community	Traditional languages	New languages	Standard Australian English
Kalkaringi	Gurindji, Warlpiri	A range of varieties including **Gurindji Kriol**, a mixed language	Spoken in more formal contexts (e.g. school) and with non-Indigenous people
Tennant Creek	Warumungu country, but speakers of other languages have moved there	A range of varieties often called **Wumpurrarni English**, and including **Barkly Kriol**	Spoken in more formal contexts (e.g. school) and with non-Indigenous people
Yakanarra	Walmajarri	A range of varieties including **Kimberley Kriol**, a creole	Spoken in more formal contexts (e.g. school) and with non-Indigenous people

'Kriol', because they identify 'Kriol' as being the way of talking around the Roper River, and thus as different from their own ways of talking.

Social background

The three communities differ in their access to services. Tennant Creek has many services, Kalkaringi has fewer services and Yakanarra is a small community with even more limited services. In all the three communities, most of the Indigenous families are poor. In some families people have jobs; other families live on social security pensions of different types. People in all communities tend to suffer from poor health and from the constant mourning for people dying too young. The main causes of untimely death are the diseases of poverty: heart failure owing to rheumatic fever, kidney failure and complications resulting from diabetes. However, deaths due to violence, especially alcohol-fuelled violence, are too common.

In the face of these health and social issues, family life is important, and children are very much loved. Adults, as well as older children, spend time with both their children, and the children of their kin. Children enjoy close and loving relationships with a wide range of kin and are generally well cared for.

In Tennant Creek Aboriginal people associate with non-Indigenous people in workplaces, sports clubs and pubs, but there are few long-term relationships between non-Indigenous and Aboriginal people and mostly the two do not mix. The communities lead overlapping but separate lives. Much the same is true in Kalkaringi and Yakanarra.

In all the three communities, during the period of our study, people travelled a good deal; in Kalkaringi there was a tendency for the people without jobs to move. The most mobile people were probably people in the most remote of the three communities – Yakanarra. Access to services was one reason for moving around – for example, Tennant Creek people had to move to Alice Springs in the event of kidney failure. 'Sorry business' (funerals and associated mourning ceremonies) was another reason why people moved. Some people also moved to escape violent situations.

Family backgrounds

The children in our study have loving caregivers, and are part of large networks of siblings and cousins who play with them, and take great responsibility for younger children. Young children usually sleep with their mothers or grandmothers, as caregivers prefer to have their babies with them (as Hamilton observed for the Anbarra), and in fact the idea of making their babies sleep in a separate room, as non-Indigenous Australian mothers often do, was disturbing to some Gurindji mothers (Meakins, personal communication).

In Kalkaringi, the most common family grouping is a family living with grandmother who takes care of the children when mothers are working or studying. In Tennant Creek children spend time with grandmothers and great grandmothers when the mothers are working or studying. In Yakanarra, there is no common family grouping; some people live in nuclear families (although there is a lot of interaction between families) and some people live in extended family groups.

The findings

Our preliminary findings are discussed in Disbray and Wigglesworth (Forthcoming), and are summarised in Table 1.2. It is already clear that communities vary as to the range and type of varieties of language used to and around the children, and that children are exposed to considerable code-switching in the languages they hear around them.

The children in these communities have to deal with complex multilingual input. In none of the three communities, involved in this study, are people speaking straight Traditional Indigenous Languages (TILs) to the children. However, this is not universally the case in all Indigenous communities. For example, in Lajamanu – our comparator community – the children are acquiring the traditional language of the area, Warlpiri, to a much greater extent than is the case in Kalkaringi, Tennant Creek or Yakanarra. The interlocutors with whom the children in these three communities are interacting are using a broad range of language varieties which range from mixed languages through a variety of more or less basilectal Kriol to Standard Australian English.

Not only are the children receiving input from different people in a variety of different codes, they are also receiving variable input from the same person through 'code-switching'. Code-switching is a very common phenomenon in the language of bilinguals where speakers are competent in two or more languages (or dialects) and have the ability to alternate between the different languages, dialects or registers during conversations, storytellings or narratives – in other words through a range of discourse activities. Code-switching is common in communities where there is widespread competence in two or more languages (or dialects) in the community. Code-switching may involve a single word, or a phrase, a sentence or a series of sentences (see Meakins, Chapter13; McConvell, Chapter 11; and Meakins, 2007).

Table 1.2 Variation as to varieties observed across communities

	Kalkaringi	Tennant Creek	Yakanarra
Input directed to children is . . .	In Gurindji Kriol, a mixed language	In varieties of WE, and/or English, with a little Warumungu and/or other traditional languages (TILs)	Largely in Kimberley Kriol and/or standard Australian English with a limited number of Walmajarri words
Children may hear . . .	Older adults using Gurindji among themselves	Some Warumungu and other TILs from older (grandparent age) people talking among themselves with a lot of code-switching	Adults using Walmajarri, Kriol and English, and code-switching between them.
Input to children is determined by situational factors including location, purpose, participants and language skills, and age of interlocutor	Only partially	Only partially	Mostly
Children understand . . .	Predominantly Gurindji Kriol, and have some understanding of Gurindji	WE and English	Kriol and English
Children's production is . . .	Only in Gurindji Kriol	Mostly in WE, but can switch (e.g. role-plays) to speaking close to standard English	Largely in Kriol

Example 1 below is a good example of the kind of input a child might receive and illustrates code switching between acrolectal (*italics*) and basilectal (**bold**) forms of Kriol in Tennant Creek:

Example 1

Mother: *Did you come today?* **Yu bin kam fo plei? Baby yu bin kam for plei?**
'Did you come today? You came to play? Baby you came to play?'

The next example is similar, but comes from Yakanarra. In this example, the speakers are once again code-switching between acrolectal (*italics*) and basilectal (***bold italics***) varieties of Kriol, but note additionally the insertion of a Walmajarri word (**bold**) into the discourse:

Example 2

Mother: ***wat i doing did man?***
'what's that man doing?'

Child: ***i silipin iya.***
'he's sleeping.'

Mother: ***a i silipin.***
'ah he's sleeping.'

Mother: *en wat is* **kunyarr** *doing?*
'and what's the dog doing?'

The next example is more complex and illustrates code-switching between Warumungu (**bold**), acrolectal Wumpurrarni English (*italics*) and basilectal Wumpurrarni English (***bold italics***), together with some indeterminate forms (plain):

Example 3 (Tennant Creek)

Adult 1: ***da*** Rita, ***da*** Rita
'That's Rita, that's Rita'

Adult 2: she's *deya o* **partirranyi ama**?
leave. past she
'Is she there or **has she gone**?'

Adult 3: **apurtu** *im deya o* **warraku** taun **kana**?
FM   nothing to
'Father's mother, is she there or **not – in** town?'

im deya o im gown taun?
'Is she there or has she gone to town?'

The proportion of language, therefore, that the children hear which is code-switched can be very high. Single speakers demonstrate great variability across a single text, sentence, or speech event and this variability may occur at different levels. This may occur at the syntactic level, with whole phrases being code-switched as in Example 3; it may occur with single lexical items inserted into a sentence structure in a different language as can be seen in Example 2, where the Walmajarri word for 'dog' is inserted into an acrolectal sentence. Alternatively it may occur at the morphological level as shown in the Warumungu example below, in which a speaker first uses the Kriol preposition 'gad', and then rephrases the ideas using the Warumungu suffix '-jangu':

Example 4 (Tennant Creek)

Adult: *kam yu luk yu garra plei gad toi-s.*
'Come, have a look, you should play with the toys.'

Adult: *luk toi-s-jangu yu plei.*
        -having
'Look, you play WITH THE TOYS.¹'

As can be seen from these examples, the input the children in these communities are receiving is linguistically highly complex, and there is either little or no functional separation of the languages. Thus the children need to understand all these structures, even if they do not use the same variety themselves, since these are commonly used structures not only in the community, but also by single individuals in the community. Consider the following examples of variation collected during the project (mostly from a single speaker):

Example 5 (Tennant Creek)

Form	'im'	Determiner
1. weip yo nos 'wipe your nose'	no	possessive pronoun
2. weip nos iya 'wipe (your) nose here'	no	no article
3. wap that nos deya 'wipe that nose there'	no	demonstrative adjective
4. wun weipim da nos, deya? 'want to wipe the nose there?'	yes	definite article
5. sidan na, weipim a nose 'sit down, wipe her nose'	yes	possessive pronoun
6. weipim nos yaki 'wipe your yucky nose'	yes	no article

These utterances illustrate how variable the input is that the child may receive. In this case, the adult varies between using the creole transitive marker '-im' on the verb (4, 5, 6), and between kinds of determiner used on the inalienably possessed noun. These range from the standard English use of a possessive pronoun (1, 5) or demonstrative adjective (3), to Warumungu use of a null determiner (2, 6), to a definite article (4), which is not used in either language. Note that the creole transitive marker '-im' can occur with a possessive pronoun '-a', 'her' in (5), and the English verb form 'wipe' can occur with the absence of a definite article as in Warumungu, as in (2). Hence there is mixing of acrolectal and basilectal creole within a single utterance.

This example illustrates quite nicely the problem for the child who must work out what linguistic devices to use where, and how appropriate they are in different circumstances. That children do recognise variation, and employ it themselves, is shown in example 6 from Kalkaringi. The mother and child are using the mixed language Gurindji Kriol. This language, as Meakins (Chapter 13; 2007) and McConvell (Chapter 11) argue is the result of code-switching at an earlier generation. It contains words of Gurindji and Kriol origin; about 63 per cent of the vocabulary is fixed, that is, the speakers have settled on using one word for a concept, either Kriol or Gurindji, and the equivalents from the other language are never used. However, speakers are more flexible with the remaining 37 per cent, using words of Gurindji and Kriol origin apparently interchangeably.

Example 6 (Kalkaringi)

*Mother (ca 21):	dat guana garra kom gedim yu baitim yu-mob.
	'That goanna's going to come and get you and bite you all.'
	i garra kom **rarraj** dijei **nyawa kankula**.
	'It'll come running this way, this one above.'
*Mother:	i garra baitim yu-mob binij.
	'It'll really bite you all.'
*Child (ca. 4?):	i-l be **katurl** im inti Mam?
	'It'll really bite won't it Mum?'
*Mother:	hmm yu-rra **katurl** im.
	'Hmm you'll bite it.'

(Gurindji source words in bold)

The mother starts by using only words shared between Kriol and Gurindji Kriol, but then introduces words shared with Gurindji 'rarraj' ('running'), 'nyawa' ('this') and 'kankula' ('above'). Her next utterance has no Gurindji words and she uses the Kriol verb 'baitim'. The child repeats the idea, switching to a Gurindji word 'katurl' for 'biting'. The mother responds using 'katurl'. What is interesting is the child's deliberate choice of a partial synonym shared with Gurindji but not Kriol, for words the mother uses which are shared with Kriol. It shows that the child has mastery of the synonyms, and, at least on this occasion, is experimenting with the Gurindji source form. Meakins discussed this example with the mother, who noticed that her child used the Gurindji word, and suggested that this was because the child was spending more time with her grandmothers.

Conclusion

It is clear from the findings of the ACLA project that there are substantive differences in both the nature of the languages being learned (from more to less acrolectal creoles) and the type of languages being learned (from Kriol to mixed language) in the three communities. The children's access to the traditional languages of their communities also varies from one community to another, and with the age of the interlocutor (McConvell et al., 2005).

The children in these communities are learning language from very variable input, both at the community level and the individual level. The next stage of the project will be to look in detail at the language the children are producing, and then to consider the implications of this – the language with which they commence schooling – for their successful education.

Notes

1. Putting a word or phrase at the front of a sentence is like emphasising a word with stress in English.

References

Bavin, E. (1987). Anaphora in children's Warlpiri. *Australian Review of Applied Linguistics, 10* (2), 1–11.

Bavin, E. (1990). Socialization and the acquisition of Warlpiri kin terms. *Papers in Pragmatics, 1,* 319–44.

Bavin, E. (1991). *Some Remarks on the Acquisition of Functional Categories with Data from Warlpiri.* Paper presented at the workshop: Theoretical Linguistics and Australian Aboriginal Languages, University of Queensland, Queensland.

Bavin, E. (1992). The acquisition of Warlpiri. In D. Slobin (ed.), *Crosslinguistic Study of Language Acquisition* (pp. 309–71). Hillsdale, NJ: Lawrence Erlbaum Associates.

Bavin, E. (1993). Language and culture: socialisation in a Warlpiri community. In M. Walsh and C. Yallop (eds), *Language and Culture in Aboriginal Australia* (pp. 85–96). Canberra: Aboriginal Studies Press.

Bavin, E. (1995). Inflections and lexical organisation: some evidence from Warlpiri. In H. Pishwa and K. Marold (eds), *The Development of Morphological Systematicity* (pp. 39–53). Tübingen: Narr.

Bavin, E. (1998). Factors of typology in language acquisition: some examples from Warlpiri. In A. Siewierska and J. J. Song (eds), *Case, Typology and Grammar: In Honor of Barry J. Blake [Typological Studies in Language, 38]* (pp. 37–55). Amsterdam: John Benjamins.

Bavin, E. (2000). Ellipsis in Warlpiri children's narratives: an analysis of frog stories. *Linguistics, 38*(3), 569–88.

Bavin, E. and Shopen, T. (1985). Warlpiri and English: languages in contact. In M. Clyne (ed.), *Australia, Meeting Place of Languages* (Vol. Series C - No. 92, pp. 81–94). Canberra: Pacific Linguistics.

Bavin, E. and Shopen, T. (1991). Warlpiri in the '80s: an overview of research into language variation and child language. In S. Romaine (ed.) *Language in Australia* (pp.104–17). Cambridge: Cambridge University Press.

Disbray, S. (Forthcoming). 'More than one way to catch a frog: children's discourse in a contact setting'. Unpublished PhD thesis, University of Melbourne, Melbourne.

Disbray, S. and Wigglesworth, G. (Forthcoming). Variability in children's language input in three communities in Aboriginal Australia. In G. Robinson, J. Goodnow, I. Katz and U. Eickelkamp (eds), *Contexts of Child Development: Culture, Policy and Intervention.* Alice Springs, NT: Charles Darwin University Press.

Döpke, S. (1992). *One Parent One Language: An Interactional Approach.* Amsterdam: Benjamins.

Genesee, F. (1989). Early bilingual development: one language or two? *Journal of Child Language, 16,* 161–79.

Genesee, F. (2001). Bilingual first language acquisition: exploring the limits of the language faculty. *Annual Review of Applied Linguistics: Language and Psychology, 21,* 153–68.

Genesee, F. and Nicoladis, E. (2007). Bilingual first language acquisition. In E. Hoff and M. Shatz (eds), *Handbook of Language Development* (pp. 324–42). Oxford, England: Blackwell Publishers.

Hamilton, A. (1981). *Nature and Nurture: Aboriginal Child-rearing in North-Central Arnhem Land.* Canberra: Australian Institute of Aboriginal Studies.

Jacobs, A. M. (1988). A descriptive study of the bilingual language development of Aboriginal children in the goldfields of Western Australia. *Australian Journal of Human Communications Disorders, 16*(82), 3–15.

Jacobs, A. M. (1990). The natural language development of Aboriginal children. In C. Walton and W. Eggington (eds), *Language: Maintenance, Power and Education in Australian Aboriginal Contexts* (pp. 75–82). Darwin, NT: Northern Territory University Press.

Kulick, D. (1992). *Language Shift and Cultural Reproduction: Socialization, Self and Syncretism in a Papua New Guinean village.* Cambridge: Cambridge University Press.

Laughren, M. (1984). Warlpiri baby talk. *Australian Journal of Linguistics*, 4(1), 73–88.

Lowell, A., Gurimangu, Nyomba, and Ningi. (1996). Communication and learning at home: a preliminary report on Yolngu language socialisation. In M. Cooke (ed.), *Aboriginal Languages in Contemporary Contexts: Yolngu Matha at Galiwin'ku (DEETYA Project Report)* (pp. 109–52). Batchelor, NT: Batchelor College.

McConvell, P., Simpson, J. and Wigglesworth, G. 2005. *Mixed Codes: A Comparison across Four Field Sites*. Seminar presented at Max Planck Institute, Nijmegen, 18 April 2005.

Meakins, F. (2007). 'Case-marking in contact: the development and function of case morphology in Gurindji Kriol, an Australian mixed language'. Unpublished PhD thesis, University of Melbourne, Melbourne.

Ochs, E. (1988). *Culture and Language Development: Language Acquisition and Language Socialization in a Samoan Villa*. Cambridge; New York: Cambridge University Press.

Oller, D., Eilers, R., Urbano, R. and Cobo-Lewis, A. (1997). Development of precursors to speech in infants exposed to two languages. *Journal of Child Language*, 24, 407–25.

Romaine, S. (1995). *Bilingualism* (Second edn). London: Blackwell Publishers.

Schieffelin, B. B. (1990). *The Give and Take of Everyday Life: Language Socialization of Kaluli Children*. Cambridge: Cambridge University Press.

Shaw, G. (2002). 'An ethnographic exploration of the development in child rearing style among the Ngaanyatjarra people from the pre-contact era to the present'. Unpublished Masters thesis, University of New South Wales, Sydney.

2

Questions about questions

Karin Moses and Colin Yallop

Educationists sometimes seek to explain differences in classroom behaviour between Indigenous and non-Indigenous children by appealing to the relationship between language, culture and learning. One of the most common observations made of Australian Aboriginal children in classrooms is that they are reticent and have only limited verbal interaction with their non-Aboriginal teachers. In particular, influential studies in the 1970s and 1980s suggested that this was because Aboriginal people do not ask many questions and do not make use of questions as a teaching or learning tool. The data collected from a longitudinal study of preschool age children and their caregivers in a Walmajarri community in the Kimberley suggests that the way in which Aboriginal adults use questions with their young children is far more complex than the earlier studies suggest; indeed, many of the earlier claims are not supported by the Yakanarra data.

Introduction

In 1995, in a small one-teacher school in the Northern Territory, Australia, Indigenous children sat with their heads cast down avoiding the questions that were directed at them. Their well-meaning and well-liked teacher tried hard to get a response, but the children seemed uncomfortable with the routine, and from an outsider's perspective, appeared to be actively resisting. One older child would stuff tissues into her mouth whenever the questioning routine became protracted (Moses, 1995). At the time, this reticence was attributed to the differences between Aboriginal and non-Aboriginal styles of interaction and learning. In the United States, Philips (1972) and others had accounted for the often-reported phenomenon of the 'silent Indian child' in terms of the cultural inappropriateness of non-Indian teachers' questioning and directing strategies. In Australia, Harris (1980) had applied the same ethnographic approach to the problems encountered by Yolngu children in Northeast Arnhem Land. Like his American counterparts, Harris concluded that there was little cultural congruence between the school and the community. In particular, he argued a case for a distinct Aboriginal learning paradigm that was based on observation and imitation rather than verbal instruction and demonstration (Harris, 1984, p. 4), a learning style that was at odds with the non-Aboriginal teachers' expectations of classroom behaviour.

Although Harris was not the first to characterise the Aboriginal child as an action-oriented, largely non-verbal learner (see Grey, 1973, p. 33; Watts, 1973, p. 177), his anthropological approach resulted in a far more detailed study of Yolngu teaching and learning practices, and his work was far more influential. Subsequently, researchers have continued to stress that 'typical Aboriginal learning takes place without recourse to any verbalisations' (Christie, 1985, p. 15) and that 'there is little verbal interaction for the deliberate and conscious purpose of teaching and learning' (Nichol, 2005, p. 412). The Indigenous child was cast as an 'imaginal' learner relying more on 'visual images, symbols [and] diagrams', and as a 'kinaesthetic' learner for whom 'information is taken in more easily through hands and movement' (Nichol, 2005, p. 413). Since questions are so fundamental to traditional western pedagogy, they have been part of almost every discussion about Aboriginal verbal behaviour and its relationship to education (Christie, 1985; Harris, 1984; Malcolm, 1982).

Aboriginal people's use of questions

The research on which this chapter is based is part of a larger study of the occurrence of questions in the discourse of Aboriginal people at Yakanarra, Western Australia, which is in turn part of a larger ARC-funded Aboriginal child language project (see Wigglesworth and Simpson, Chapter 1; Meakins, Chapter 13; Disbray, Chapter 3). This chapter will address two claims: first, that Aboriginal children are not encouraged to ask and answer questions; and secondly, that they are unfamiliar both with *why* questions and *display* questions.

While no one claims that Aboriginal children never ask questions, the point is often made that they are discouraged from doing so. Harris (1984, p. 15) provides an example of a Yolngu assistant teacher who in response to the children asking a lot of questions in a maths lesson admonishes them, 'Don't ask so many questions – you're not balanda [non-Aboriginal] children'. A number of researchers from diverse fields have commented on Aboriginal children's tendency to use non-verbal rather than verbal information-seeking strategies. Drinkwater (1981, p. 133) cites psychologists who commented that children tended to search their interlocutors' faces rather than ask questions when they were unsure how to respond in a testing situation. Similarly, in her anthropological study of Anbarra child-rearing practices in Arnhem Land, Hamilton (1981, p. 80) noted that 'a striking feature of Anbarra 3- and 4-year-olds is the lack of questions they ask'.

It has also been claimed that Aboriginal people rarely make use of 'why' questions, whereas non-Aboriginal people regularly use them to determine and explain reasons and causes. For Eades (1982, p. 230), this is 'the most striking aspect of language use concerning reason in SEQAB conversations', that is, conversations in South East Queensland Aboriginal English. She notes that

> [I]n the three years I have worked in South East Queensland I have never heard an Aboriginal person ask a why-information question. I have heard why questions used as complaints (usually what-for), e.g. 'What are you going there for?' . . . but never a direct question to find out the reason. (Eades, 1985, p. 26)

Dasen (1974, p. 408) claims that

> Aboriginal children do not, apparently, go through the period – well known to European parents – of asking 'why'. This is probably due to the cultural norm of accepting the laws of nature, the social customs, and the decisions of elders without question

The idea that Aboriginal children are not familiar with questions as 'games' and that they do not respond well to the iterative, 'pretend' questions in the classroom is widely held. Harris (1980, p. 155) argued that

> Yolngu children have never experienced in their own culture the use of questioning as a teaching technique or the question-and-answer technique of transferring knowledge. It follows that the yolngu [*sic*] cannot understand why a teacher is asking questions when he knows the answers.

Christie (1985, p. 19) also reported that Yolngu children 'find it confusing to answer classroom questions when it is clear that the teachers already know the answers'. Bavin (1992, p. 322) makes the same point about Warlpiri children:

> The question–answer routine familiar in western societies is not found in Warlpiri society. The adult has knowledge, not the child, and questioning is not used as a teaching device.

The Aboriginal Section of the Education Department of South Australia warned its teachers to reconsider their question and answer routines because Aboriginal children 'find the language of enquiry confusing' and the routine 'incomprehensible' (South Australian Education Consultative Committee – Aboriginal Education Section, 1987). Such advice is still being given to pre-service and neophyte teachers.

Language at Yakanarra

Yakanarra community was established in 1989 on a small excision of land from what was then Cherrabun cattle station, in the Kimberley region of Western Australia. The township of Fitzroy Crossing, about 80 km away, is the service centre for Yakanarra and another thirty or so communities in the Fitzroy Valley. During the wet season, when the Fitzroy River is in flood and the creeks are flowing, Yakanarra is cut off and accessible only by air.

Yakanarra residents are predominantly Walmajarri, a people who, within living memory, left their traditional lands in the northern Great Sandy Desert for the cattle and sheep stations, missions and towns scattered across the Kimberley. The official population of Yakanarra is around 180 but there are usually no more than 130 people in the community at any one time. Most of these residents are under 35; children under 15 make up almost 27 per cent of the population, while persons over 55 are less than half of one per cent.

The traditional language of most Yakanarra residents is Walmajarri, but the language most commonly spoken is Kriol, which is English-based but Walmajarri-influenced. Kriol is now the primary language of almost everyone at Yakanarra. It is the language spoken to children by their caregivers and the primary language of all the participants in this study. Only older people – mostly over 55 – are able to speak Walmajarri with any fluency. Children at Yakanarra do sometimes hear adults speaking Walmajarri, and may even be briefly addressed in the language, but these occasions are rare. Children learn some Walmajarri at school, where it is taught for three and a half hours a week, usually by presenting thematically arranged word lists and practising words as separate lexical items in games and puzzles. Inherent in the methodology is the assumption that the children are unable to produce the language, and neither the children nor their teachers expect prolonged use of the language. Standard Australian English (SAE) is used as the language of instruction in the school; and the children hear English on the radio and the television, as well as on the DVDs, videos and CDs that are frequently played in the community. All the caregivers are able to use SAE though not all are equally proficient.

The participants

This chapter focuses on four children who were part of the larger study: Lyell, Beth, Edna and Mira (names have been changed for publication). Lyell is the only boy. He has one older sibling, a sister. Their parents, both aged twenty when the project started, are from different language backgrounds: the mother is a confident speaker of English, Kriol and Walmajarri and is also literate in all three languages; the father is a Nyigina man from Derby, fluent in English and Kriol but not a speaker of his traditional language.

Beth has no siblings but spends much of her time in the home of her grandparents surrounded by her aunts and young cousins. Beth's mother, 28 at the time of the first recording, has a passive knowledge of Walmajarri and is also a confident speaker of near standard English. During the life of the project Beth's father has been absent. He has never lived with his daughter or her mother.

Edna is the second youngest in her family, and an older sister and a younger brother still live at home. Her mother is the second oldest mother in the group, aged 36 when the project began, while her father was 38. Both parents are Walmajarri and are able to speak the language, but do not do so with their children. The mother is a confident speaker of near standard English; the father is far more reluctant to speak in English and is less proficient.

Mira has two brothers, one older, one younger. Her parents were both born in Derby and both were 24 when the project commenced. Neither is able to speak Walmajarri (or any other traditional language). The mother is, however, a confident speaker of near standard English; the father is very reticent in any language but those closest to him report that his English is good. The family has a home of their own and Mira's interaction with older Walmajarri speakers is limited even though her grandfather lives at Yakanarra. According to her mother she is never addressed in Walmajarri.

Data collection

The data were collected over a period of 3 years when the children were between the ages of 2 years; 6 months and 4 years; 7 months (ages are hereafter represented in numerals only, for example, 2;6, 4;7). In all but one of the sessions, the children were recorded with their mothers. Although the children are recorded with a caregiver in every session, they are not exclusively one-on-one situations. Other people wander in and out of the recording sessions at times, and siblings, usually preverbal babies and toddlers, are also included in some of the sessions. Video recordings were made of all the sessions and most were also separately audio recorded. The recordings were transcribed using the conventions of the CHILDES Chat system (MacWhinney, 2000).

The location of each recording was usually determined by the caregiver in response to circumstances, such as the number of people in and around the home, and the heat. In some cases, the time and location were chosen to suit the work schedule of an adult participant. Children and caregivers were recorded on the verandas and inside their homes or other community houses and on the veranda or inside the unoccupied rooms of the kindergarten and school. The band room of the school was the preferred location for a number of the sessions because it was new and located away from the main buildings of the school. It also provided a large space in which children could play, and was judged by all to provide the best refuge from the heat because it was equipped with the best air conditioners in the community.

The sessions were largely based on activities that were prompted by toys and books supplied for the purpose, including: a series of textless picture books produced by Carmel O'Shannessy (see Chapter 12) for Warlpiri children, which feature real and imagined scenes of Aboriginal life; large baby dolls, a baby bottle, baby clothes and pushers; a doctor's kit; shopping toys consisting of a cash register, toy groceries, toy money and a key card; a doll's house and little people dolls; a school bus; crocodile puppets; play-dough with rolling pins, cutters and moulds; plastic animals; and wooden puzzles (an alphabet and a hand puzzle).

The materials were chosen to stimulate talk in general, and not to encourage the use of questions in particular. The choice of material for each session was largely based on the need to engage the child, to provide a variety of activities for each child across the sessions, and to ensure that all children shared the same activities across the sessions. It was the children's interest, however, that was of primary concern in the choice of material. Some toys were more successful at engaging the children than others and what one child embraced with great enthusiasm, another would find of no interest at all. So the toys and books varied from child to child and from session to session, although each child was exposed to each toy or book at least once. Children and their caregivers at times also picked up and used toys and books of their own.

The data: frequency and number of questions in caregiver speech

If Aboriginal adults were reluctant to ask questions or sought to restrain their children from doing so, we would expect to find that there would be few questions in the caregivers' input to children. However, at Yakanarra 21 per cent of caregivers' utterances are questions. Two earlier input studies, in English, which argued that caregivers' speech to children was characterised by frequent use of questions, found similar percentages (Broen, 1972; Snow et al., 1976). The figures, shown in Table 2.1, indicate that in the speech of caregivers to their children questions appear in greater frequency than they reportedly occur in the speech between adults speaking English to each other (Sachs et al., 1976).

Unfortunately percentages can disguise the differences between children's language experiences. Not only can they hide the variation that exists between children, they can also hide the variation that exists in the language input of

Table 2.1 Percentage of utterances that are questions in the three studies

Study	Percentage of utterances that are questions
Broen (1972)	24
Snow et al. (1976)	22
Yakanarra data	21 (1,432 questions)

any one child since the number of questions directed at a child can vary enormously from one recording session to the next. It is true that the variation between the participants in any one study in which there is a shared language and culture can be as great as that which exists between studies in which the language and the culture are very different. In his Bristol study, Wells (1986) found that some children had almost ten times as much language addressed to them as others. Gallaway and Woll (1994, p. 205) warned against generalising from small-scale studies precisely because individual variation could be great; they reported that some of the caregivers in their study 'used as few as six questions and some as many as 60 in the first 100 utterances'. At Yakanarra there is great variation too, as shown in Table 2.2.

Individual children can be asked many more questions in one session than they are asked in another (see Sessions 1 and 3 for Lyell, and Sessions 14 and 15 for Mira), just as they can be exposed to more caregiver talk in one session as opposed to another. The ratio of questions to utterances can also vary

Table 2.2 Numbers of questions and utterances and the percentage of utterances that are questions

Child	Caregiver	Session no.	Age of child (years;months)	Number of questions	Number of utterances	Percentage of utterances that are questions
Lyell	Bella	1	2;8	36	262	14
		2	3;8	99	463	21
		3	3;8	210	728	29
Beth	Sally	4	2;6	78	220	35
		5	2;6	64	220	29
		6	4;6	57	316	18
	Michelle	7	4;6	69	328	21
Edna	Hazel	8	2;7	71	378	19
		9	2;7	89	410	22
		10	3;7	110	480	23
		11	3;7	52	445	12
		12	4;7	102	445	23
		13	4;7	68	613	11
Mira	Lisa	14	3;6	101	330	31
		15	3;6	54	283	19
		16	4;6	83	463	18
		17	4;6	89	318	28
Total				1,432	6,702	

greatly from session to session, though a higher ratio in any one session does not necessarily correlate with a higher number of questions. The 64 questions asked of Sally in Session 5 represent 29 per cent of the total number of utterances addressed to her while the 69 questions asked of her in Session 7 is only 21 per cent. More strikingly, the 210 questions asked of Lyell in Session 3 is 29 per cent of the total utterances addressed to him while the 78 questions to which Beth is exposed in Session 4 is 35 per cent. What is clear from the data is that each child is exposed to more questions in some sessions than in others and that some children are asked more questions by their caregivers than others. This seems hardly surprising. However, such variation is often overlooked in discussions about Aboriginal people and their use of questions. More often one particular discourse style is said to characterise the verbal interaction of all Aboriginal people. When it comes to asking questions, Aboriginal people are said to do so reluctantly. Yet nothing in the conversations between the caregivers and their children at Yakanarra lends support to this assumption; under the circumstances in which this data were collected, in one-to-one conversations with their children, caregivers frequently asked questions.

Question forms

Wh-word questions are common in the data. They make up an average of 59 per cent (848) of all questions in the input while those questions that only allow for limited answers such as *yes/no* and *tag* questions average 41 per cent (584).

This is somewhat unexpected for two reasons. First, *yes/no* questions, whether in Kriol or English, lighten the linguistic burden on the interlocutor; they require a response that is limited to one of two polar opposites, positive and negative. As Huddleston and Pullum (2002, p. 868) put it, 'the propositional content of one answer is expressed in the question itself, and that of the other is obtained by reversing the polarity'. It would be reasonable to expect that this form of question making would predominate in the conversations adults have with young children. Secondly, it has often been observed that Aboriginal people prefer to ask questions in an 'indirect way' using declarative forms that function as *yes/no* questions or using *tag* questions (Berry & Hudson, 1997, pp. 144–146; Eades, 1992, p. 36; Reeders, Chapter 5). While there are numerous examples of these question forms in the data, they are not the most common form of questions addressed to the children. There are few studies that report on the ratio of polar to *wh*-word questions in caregiver input, but one study does suggests a similar pattern. Savic (1975) found that the questions asked of fraternal twins in Serbo-Croatian, between the ages of 14 and 36 months, comprised 229 *yes/no* questions (20 per cent) and 1,446 *wh*-word questions (80 per cent).

Table 2.3 presents the range and number of *wh*-word questions to be found in the caregivers' speech to children. *What, where* and *who* are the most frequently used *wh*-word question forms. Between them they account for 90 per cent of the total number of *wh*-word questions found in the data.

While many researchers have focused on children's production of *wh*-word questions, far fewer have looked at input. Savic (1975) in Serbo-Croatian, Forner (1979) in German and Clancy (1989) in Korean, have all recorded questions addressed to children. Their data, as summarised in Table 2.4, confirms the prevalence of translation equivalents of *what, where* and *who.*

All three studies were longitudinal ones in which the children were at least 12 months younger at the end of the data collection than those at Yakanarra; yet, there is a consistency between the studies that survives their numerous differences. As shown in Table 2.5, each study reports that *what* is by far the most common *wh*-word question found in the caregiver input, followed by

Table 2.3 Numbers of *wh*-word question forms

Total questions	What	Where	Who	Whose	Which	How many	Why	How	When	Total *Wh*-
1,432	400	216	151	34	16	10	16	2	3	848

Table 2.4 Percentage of *what, where* and *who* questions across four studies

Study	Percentage of *what, where* and *who* of total *wh*-**word** questions in caregiver input
Savic (1975)	71
Forner (1979)	90
Clancy (1989)	79
Yakanarra	90

Table 2.5 Distribution of *what, where* and *who* questions across four studies

Study	What (%)	Where (%)	Who (%)	Other *wh*-words (%)
Savic	36	18	17	29
Forner	59	21	10	10
Clancy	58	14	7	21
Yakanarra	47	25	18	10

where and then *who* (Forner, 1979; Savic, 1975) and *where* and *how* (Clancy, 1989).

In all but three sessions in the Yakanarra data, *what* questions predominate; and in those three sessions in which it doesn't the *where* questions, the second most frequently asked *wh*-word questions, predominate. This seems to confirm the point made by Rowland and her associates (2003), that the complexity of a word and the frequency with which it is used are often strongly correlated. They note that the most frequently produced *wh*-words are those that Bloom and her associates (1982) found to be the most syntactically and semantically simple – *what* and *where*.

In Kriol *what* questions cover a variety of semantic and pragmatic functions and their syntax can be both simple and complex. The *what* question can request information about a thing (Example 1) or a quality (Example 2) or a state of mind (Example 3) and the information sought can be the subject, complement or object of a sentence.

Example 1

Beth (child):   wat det?
                   what's that?

Sally: det pamarr de luk.
                   that's the rocky hill there look.

Example 2

Sally (caregiver): wat kala dis?
Beth: *kala red.*

Example 3

Bella (caregiver): oh wat song yu nou?
                   what song do you know?

Bella: wat song yu laikim?
                   what song do you like?

Lyell: am detwan epi bethdei.
                   um that happy birthday.

A *what* question can also refer to actions and can co-occur with lexical verbs that are light and general (Example 4; what Bloom and associates (1982) refer to as pro-verbs), or verbs that are more specific and restricted (Example 5).

Example 4

Lisa (caregiver):	wat yu dumbat?
	what are you doing?
Mira:	ting haus.
	um a house.

Example 5

Hazel (caregiver):	wat i tjeisimbat?
	what's he chasing?
Edna:	burluman.
	cattle.

The single word utterance *what* is also the most common form used by caregivers when something a child has said is not heard or understood. In these cases the question is either requesting the repetition of the entire utterance (Example 6) or just the most salient part (Example 7). In Example 7, Bella tries very hard to understand what Lyell means by *tola*. She asks a number of *what* questions in a number of ways: *wat* is placed in the sentence final, initial and even medial position. Bella even resorts to Standard English and uses the copula *is* – *wat's Tola* – before settling once again for the more standard Kriol form – *wat darran*? This is all to no avail, as Lyell fails to elaborate or explain the word at the centre of the misunderstanding.

Example 6

Lyell (child):	wat krokadail bait?
	what do crocodiles eat?
Bella:	ola wat?
	all what?
Lyell:	wat krokadail wat krokadail bait?

Example 7

Bella (caregiver):	wel wat yu garra meikim?
	well what are you going to make?
Lyell:	am tola.
Bella:	ei?
Lyell:	tola.
Luciele:	a wat?
Lyell:	tola.
Bella:	wat Toni?
Bella:	yu garra meikim Toni?
	are you going to make [something for] Toni [Lyell's cousin]?
Lyell:	na tola tola.
Lyell:	tola.
Bella:	tola wat tola?
Lyell:	na.
Bella:	wat's tola?
Bella:	wat darran?
Lyell:	na nating.
Bella:	ai dono wat darran.

It is difficult to see how *what* questions could be said to be syntactically or semantically 'simpler' than *where* or *who* questions, neither of which allow for either the variety of semantic and pragmatic functions nor the range of possible answers. This shows the importance of not assuming that *wat* in Kriol is identical in behaviour to *what* in Standard Australian English. The frequency of *what* in the Yakanarra data may be due as much to its versatility as it is to its perceived simplicity. There are also contextual and pragmatic factors that may contribute to the relative frequency of *wh*-word questions. English speaking children are said to be more likely to hear, and to have occasion to use, *what* and *where* questions rather than *who* questions because they are far more likely, in a familiar situation, to be asked about objects and places than people (Bloom et al., 1982). Context may even be a factor when arguably more complex *wh*-word questions such as *how*, *why* and *when* are taken into account. These question forms are more cognitively demanding and necessitate a level of understanding beyond that required for most *what* and *where* questions, but they are also dependent upon situational opportunities that are less likely to arise spontaneously. At Yakanarra, the context which gives rise to questions about procedures, causation or time appears far more limited than that which produces the other *wh*-word questions.

The more syntactically and semantically complex *wh*-word questions, *how*, *why* and *when* are not often used by caregivers at Yakanarra, particularly with very young children, but this is not uncommon. These forms occur infrequently in other studies that have recorded questions addressed to children of a similar age (Clancy, 1989; Forner, 1979; Savic, 1975). *How, why* and *when* questions require children to both understand the concepts and be able to encode them linguistically and for this reason caregivers may be reluctant to use the more demanding *wh*-forms until their children are of an age when they can reasonably be expected to answer them. When they do use such questions, they often provide the children with assistance as Bella does in Example 8 where she imbeds a *why* question (*watfo* in Kriol) in a polar question to which Lyell (3;8) responds appropriately though not correctly (he understands that a *yes* or *no* is required and so nods his head even though he does not know why domestic turkeys are called *gabilgabil* in Kriol). In both Examples 8 and 9 Bella suggests or provides the answer for her son.

Example 8

Bella: yuno watfo dei kolim gabilgabil?
                    do you know why they call it a gabilgabil?

[Bella holds a little plastic turkey up to Lyell and he nods his head.]

Bella: i go gabilgabilgabilgabil [Bella makes a turkey sound].

Bella: i go laik det si.
                    he goes like that see.

Lyell: ye.

Example 9

[Lyell has just made some blue play-dough cars]

Bella: haumatj blu ka?
                    how many blue cars?

Lyell: tu.

Bella: oh.

(Continued)

Example 9—Cont'd

Bella: watfo?
why [two]?

Bella: wan fo Titania en Lyell?

Lyell: ye.

Bella: en wodabat mami?
and what about Mummy?

Lyell: ai meikim mami wan.
I'm making Mummy one.

Bella: oh yu meikim mami wan na.

When Mira, at age 3;6, starts to peel off the play-dough 'fingernails' that her mother, Lisa, has painstakingly made for her, her mother tells her that the little dolls who are sitting in front of her are asking *why*:

Example 10

Lisa: dei sei worrong Mira bin bagadimap.
they say why did Mira wreck them.

Lisa: dei luginat yu.
they're watching you.

Mira: ai bagadimap.
I wrecked them.

Lisa: dei luginat yu.
they're watching you.

Lisa: sei watfo Mira bin bagadimap.
[they] say why did Mira wreck them.

By the age of four, each child in this study has been recorded being asked *why* questions, and requires less assistance to answer these questions. When Lisa is called by her daughter Mira on the toy telephone (Example 11), she wants to know the purpose of the call and so asks two *why* (*watfo*) questions: the first receiving a limited answer and the second, reformulated into a *what* question, receiving a more elaborate response. The third *why* question, about the reason for the trip to Djugerari, gets a humorous response without the need for repetition or reformulation.

Example 11

Mira:	[ringring ringring].
Mira:	halo.
Lisa:	halo.
Lisa:	hu dijan? *who is this?*
Mira:	mi Mira.
Lisa:	hu?
Mira:	mi Mira.
Lisa:	Mira wat yu ringinap fo?
Mira:	yu.
Lisa:	watfo?
Lisa:	wat yu garra telim mi? *what do you want to tell me?*
Mira:	gowin la ting. *going to what's-its-name.*
Mira:	gowin la Djugerari. *going to Djugerari.*
Lisa:	ei? *eh?*
Mira:	gowin la Djugerari.
Lisa:	hu? *who?*
Mira:	ai gowin la Djugerari. *I'm going to Djugerari*
Lisa:	oh yu gowin Djugerari?
Mira:	ye.
Lisa:	watfo?
Mira:	gidim biya. *to get beer.*
Lisa:	wel kaj siyu. *well go on see you.*
Mira:	siyu.

In Yakanarra, *why* questions are used, albeit infrequently, by caregivers: 16 questions out of total of 848 *wh*-word questions. The fact that these *why* questions occur infrequently is not surprising given the limited context that gives rise to their use and the age of the children. There is enough evidence in the language corpus, however, to suggest that both adults and children seek to make sense of the world around them by asking about causes and reasons. Their traditional language, Walmajarri, after all, has two words for *why* (*nganajangka* meaning *what from* and *nganapurru, what for*). One of the earliest stories written in Walmajarri about first contact with cattle includes questions from a child who wants to know why he was told that cattle always gore people when the cattle that he encountered were frightened of him and walked away (see Peter Skipper's story *The Talkative Child* in Richards et al., 2002). Before they reach school age the children at Yakanarra have been asked to provide reasons for the cause and purpose of events and phenomena. They have learnt to respond to these questions appropriately (11 of the 16 *why* questions are answered appropriately, though not always correctly). In turn, the children have requested such information. When Edna, at age 3;7, plays doctor and injects her mother's baby (doll) she asks, *watfo ai garra pudum la im?* (*why do you want me to inject her?*), when 4-year-old Beth picks up the toy otoscope she asks: *watfo det ting?* and *wat dijan fo* requesting information about the purpose of an unknown object; her mother Sally replies, *fo irrs yu garra luk leeit la im (for ears you have to look inside, like that)*.

Display questions

The questions asked by the caregivers of their children serve a number of functions. Some request information that the questioner does not have (reference questions) while others appear to seek information already known to the person asking the question (display questions). Some seek confirmation of previous utterances while others ask for clarification.

It was predicted that very few display questions would be found in the caregiver input since Aboriginal children were said to have little or no experience of such questions. Yet, as shown in Table 2.6, display questions made up

Table 2.6 Distribution of question functions

Total number	Reference	Display	Confirmation	Clarification	Other
1,432	335 (23%)	519 (36%)	412 (29%)	59 (4%)	107 (7%)

36 per cent of all the questions asked of the children, while reference questions constituted 23 per cent. The children at Yakanarra are frequently asked questions that request information already known to their adult interlocutor.

Example 12

Hazel (caregiver):	hu dis manga iya?
	who's this girl here?
Edna:	tharran Kinokino.
	that one's Kinokino.
Hazel:	Roxania.

[Edna has volunteered a boy's name, her mother has corrected her with a girl's name]

Example 13

| Sally: | we jina fo beibi? |
| | *where's the baby's foot?* |

[Beth grabs the baby doll's foot]

Example 14

Lisa (caregiver):	haumatj pipul de?
	how many people are there?
Lisa:	tu?
	two?
Mira:	wan tu thri fo.
	one two three four.

Such display questions are not asked by caregivers in order to gain new information from their young charges, but can, like any questions, play a number of roles in caregiver discourse: to facilitate understanding and learning, direct and sustain attention and encourage participation in the conversation. Questions that require children to display their knowledge may appear to be primarily a pedagogic tool; yet, such questions are asked not only to introduce or reinforce knowledge about people, body parts or numbers, as they are in the Examples 12–14, they are also asked to teach children something about the game of conversation, in particular the process of turn-taking. This is at its most obvious when the questions are directed at preverbal babies. In Example 15, Lyell's father Gary is holding his wife's 10-month-old nephew, Snoop in his arms. He cups his hand to his ears and pretends to call the boy up on the phone as both he and Bella role-play the exchange. In Example 16, Milly is holding her 3-week-old baby boy Eason over her shoulder before she hands him over to her husband Jason.

Example 15

Gary:	helo Snoop hau yu tok on de fon ei? *hello Snoop how do you talk on the phone eh?*
Gary:	Snoop hau yu tok on de fon? *how do you talk on the phone?*
Bella:	helo nena. *hello nanna.*
Gary:	helo Snoop. *hello Snoop.*
Gary:	we yu? *where are you?*
Bella:	helo Snoop.
Gary:	ei kaj aim tokin to yu on de fon. *hey go on I'm talking to you on the phone.*

Example 16

Milly:	wel watsaida yu wandim? *well which side do you want?*
Milly:	wel yu wanda go wokinraun? *well do you want to go move about?*
Milly:	wel yu go wokinraunbat. *well you go moving about.*
Milly:	hu garra teikimbat yu? *who is going to take you?*
Milly:	wel yu wanda go wokinraun ei? *well do you want to go and move around eh?*
Milly:	oba iya Adam iya. *[come] over here Adam here.*

In both cases, questions enable the caregivers to construct a conversation with a very unequal partner. By taking the children's turn themselves they model the conversational exchange. At Yakanarra, the question and answer routine is something with which children are made familiar at a very early age. They are led to understand that questions, whether they be reference or display questions, anticipate a response. At times this is done through question and answer games such as that which is played in the backyard of Lyell's grandmother's house in Example 17, with Lyell's aunt Jo-Anne, Lyell (3;8) and two of his cousins Megan (3;6) and Davina (3;7).[1]

Example 17

Jo-Anne:	hufo ded Mack? *whose dad is Mack?*
Davina:	mi mi mi mi mi. *me me me me me.*
Jo-Anne:	hufo ded? *whose dad [is he]?*
Jo-Anne:	Mack?
Davina:	mi.
Jo-Anne:	pa. *yes.*
Jo-Anne:	hufo ded Barney? *whose dad is Barney?*
Davina:	Molly.
Jo-Anne:	hufo ded Barney? *whose dad's Barney?*
Jo-Anne:	na Megan fo ded. *no he's Megan's dad.*
Jo-Anne:	hufo ded Gary? *whose dad's Gary?*
Megan:	main. *mine.*
Jo-Anne:	na yo ded Barney. *no your dad is Barney.*
Davina:	Lyell.
Jo-Anne:	hufo ded Gary? *whose dad is Gary?*
Megan:	Lyell.
Jo-Anne:	ye.

The suggestion that Aboriginal people feel little obligation to answer questions (Harris, 1980, p. 151) and that it is socially acceptable for them to ignore questions (Christie, 1985, p. 12; Eades, 1983, p. 183) is not supported by the Yakanarra data. Sixty-four per cent of questions asked of children are answered by them. More significantly, those questions to which the children do not respond or to which they respond inappropriately (providing a response that has no bearing on the question) are often followed up by the caregivers with another question. Forty-five per cent of all unanswered questions in the data are repeated or reformulated. Hazel's persistence in Example 18 is not unusual. After helping Edna to make a house with some wooden blocks she wants to know whose house it is and she continues to ask Edna the same question in a variety of forms until she gets a response. Children are often pressed for an answer when they do not respond, and they in turn expect their conversational partners to respond to their questions.

Example 18

Hazel:	hufo haus dijan?
	whose house is this?
Hazel:	hufo haus?
	whose house?
Hazel:	Ezekeil payi?
	Ezekeil, is it?
Hazel:	Becky?
Hazel:	Nina?
Hazel:	Nina fo haus?
	is it Nina's house?
Hazel:	iya Edna en sista?
	here [this one's] Edna and sister's?
Edna:	na fo ting.
	no fo what's-his-name.
Hazel:	hu fo?
	whose?
Edna:	dedi.
	daddy.
Edna:	fo dedi dijan?
	this one's daddy's?
Hazel:	ei?

Edna:	fo dedi fo blok?
	[it's] daddy's for his block of land.
Hazel:	a
	oh
Hazel:	en wadabat?
	and what about?
Edna:	en detwan fo dijan.
	and that is for this.
[Edna pretends to give Hazel a house key.]	
Hazel:	ai obinim.
	I'll open it.

Conclusion

Anyone who has come to know Aboriginal children well is aware that they are curious about their world and that they give expression to that curiosity by asking questions. During the last field trip to Yakanarra in 2006, one of the authors, Karin Moses, recorded the questions that were asked of her within minutes of her arrival back in the community. As she walked to the store she was greeted by Lyell's young cousin Nigella (2;6), who clasped her hand and then started to play a question game with her as they walked, asking *hufo det rok?* (*whose rock is that?*), *hufo det dirt?* (*whose dirt is that?*), *hufo det geit?* (*whose gate is that?*), *hufo det haus?* (*whose house is that?*). Once they had reached the store, Edna (5;7) and her two friends Shakira and Zoranah, both six, excitedly ran up to her and this time real questions were asked: *wat yu silip oba deya?* (*are you sleeping over there?*), *weya yu silip?* (*where are you sleeping?*), *wat yu mam neim?* (*what's your mum's name?*), *wat yu kolim?* (*what do you call her?*), *wat yu ded neim? wat yu kolim? hufo det het?* (*whose hat is that?*), *we yu hom? yu flai la plein? yu kam brom Melbourne, yu got a dalingwan Melbourne?* (*do you have a boyfriend in Melbourne?*), *yu got a dauta? hufo det ka? wai yu draibing Mary fo ka?* When she noticed that a bag of dried mangoes had been cut open rather than torn open, Edna asked, *wat yu katim fo dis?* Shantari and Zyllianah, who had never been recorded before and had not seen a mini-disc recorder asked *wat dis? wat is neim? wat yu tok in det fo?* When the girls became aware that the skin on Karin's hands was peeling they wanted to know *wai yu got sam blista?* (*why is your skin blistering?*), *wat brom?* (*what from?*) *wat hepin?* (*what happened?*) *warrong?* (*why?*) and *i pein?* (*does it hurt?*).

It may be that the way in which children talk to non-Aboriginal adults is different from the way in which they talk to Aboriginal community members. Indeed, this is to be expected given that even very young children are able to make a number of adjustments to their speech to accommodate different conversational partners. However, the numerous and varied questions asked by the children are more likely to be prompted by the arrival of a 'new' person, an infrequent visitor about whom relatively little is known and of whom new information can be gleamed, rather than by the fact that that person happens to be non-Aboriginal. At the very least, the children's interrogation displays an ability to use a wide repertoire of questions and to ask them without inhibition in certain circumstances.

All this would appear to prepare the children well for the question and answer routine of the classroom: they are accustomed to being asked a variety of questions by adults, they are familiar with display questions and questions that are part of games; they understand the *why* questions; and they realise that questions expect a reply. Yet, these very same children can be surprisingly reticent once they enter school. Edna, who was one of the most precociously verbal children in the group, who at the age of two-and-a-half could turn a chair into a truck and wooden blocks into rifles, knives, cigarettes and firewood and who would allow her mother to be engaged in the play by answering her questions and asking questions herself, has taken to putting things into her mouth at school. Like the other children, she is reluctant to answer the questions asked by her teacher and very rarely asks any herself. If it appears that the language of enquiry once they reach school is 'confusing' and the questioning routine 'incomprehensible' to the children at Yakanarra, it is not because question and answer routines as a teaching device are unknown to them. It is far more likely that these children often find the Standard English spoken by their teachers incomprehensible and the situation in which they are asked to perform (individually, in front of their peers and uncertain of the correctness of their response) one that is liable to expose them to shame (see also Moses and Wigglesworth, Chapter 6). Anyone acquiring another language requires more time to process the language, to understand what is being asked of her or him and to formulate a response. A teacher unused to such hesitancy may be uncomfortable with the delay and fill the silence with a response of her own or more questions. Like most other Aboriginal children in remote area schools in Australia, the children in this study who have commenced school at Yakanarra have found themselves in the charge of a newly graduated monolingual teacher who has never had sole responsibility for a class, has never had contact with remote Aboriginal children, and has no training in teaching English to speakers of other languages. They have also found themselves in a class of 15 children ranging in age from 4;7 to 7. Under such circumstances, it is possible to suggest a number of reasons for the children's lack of participation in the question and answer routine other than their unfamiliarity with the exchange; it is also possible to conceive of changes that would result in the children becoming more active participants in classroom discourse and their acquisition of Standard Australian English.

Note

1. Small children at Yakanarra are often asked questions about relationships and this is not surprising in a society in which relationships are not only highly valued but also complex. The people at Yakanarra are linked to each other in two fundamental ways, by 'blood' and 'skin'. Each person belongs to a family, or more correctly an extended family, and has a biological connection to the people in that family; these 'blood' relationships are ones with which most of us are familiar. However, each person at Yakanarra also belongs to one of eight subsections, or skin groups to which they have been assigned before birth. This means that each child at Yakanarra has a number of 'mothers' and 'fathers', 'grandmothers' and 'grandfathers', and every other kind of kin too. A question, such as the one that features in the 'whose father is' game, is not as easily answered in Yakanarra as it might be elsewhere.

References

Bavin, E. (1992). The acquisition of Warlpiri. In D. Slobin (ed.), *Crosslinguistic Study of Language Acquisition* (pp. 309–71). Hillsdale, NJ: Lawrence Erlbaum Associates.

Berry, R. and Hudson, J. (1997). *Making the Jump*. Broome, WA: Catholic Education Office, Kimberley Region.

Bloom, L., Merkin, S. and Wootten, J. (1982). Wh-questions: linguistic factors that contribute to the sequence of acquisition. *Child Development, 53*(4), 1084–92.

Broen, P. (1972). The verbal environment of the language-learning child. *Monographs of the American Speech and Hearing Association, No. 17.* Washington DC: American Speech and Hearing Association.

Christie, M. J. (1985). *Aboriginal Perspectives on Experience and Learning: The Role of Language in Aboriginal Education.* Geelong, VIC: Deakin University Press.

Clancy, P. (1989). Form and function in the acquisition of Korean wh-questions. *Journal of Child Language, 16*, 323–47.

Dasen, P. R. (1974). The influence of ecology, culture and European contact on cognitive development in Australian Aborigines. In J. W. Berry and P. R. Dasen (eds), *Culture and Cognition* (pp. 381–408). London: Methuen.

Drinkwater, B. A. (1981). A question of questions. In A. Nesdale, C. Pratt, R. Grieve, J. Field, D. Illingworth and J. Hogben (eds), *Advances in Child Development Theory and Research* (pp. 131–49). Nedlands, WA: University of Western Australia.

Eades, D. (1982). You gotta know how to talk: information-seeking in Southeast Queensland Aboriginal society. *Australian Journal of Linguistics, 2*(1), 61–82.

Eades, D. (1983). 'English as an aboriginal language in southeast queensland'. Unpublished PhD thesis, University of Queensland, Brisbane.

Eades, D. (1985). English as an Aboriginal language. In M. J. Christie (ed.), *Aboriginal Perspectives on Experience and Learning: The Role of Language in Aboriginal Education* (pp. 24–28). Geelong, VIC: Deakin University Press.

Eades, D. (1992). *Aboriginal English and the Law*. Brisbane: Queensland Law Society Inc.

Forner, M. (1979). The mother and LAD: Interaction between order and frequency of parental input and child production. In F. R. Eckman and A. J. Hastings (eds), *Studies in First and Second Language Acquisition* (pp. 17–44). Rowley, MA: Newbury.

Gallaway, C. and Woll, B. (1994). Interaction and childhood deafness. In C. Gallaway and B. J. Richards (eds), *Input and Interaction in Language Acquisition* (pp. 197–218). Cambridge: Cambridge University Press.

Grey, A. (1973). Towards understanding Aboriginal children. In *Aboriginal Children in the Classroom: Proceedings of Seminar for Teachers of Aboriginal Children in the Taree Inspectorate* (pp. 10–58). Taree, NSW: Office of the Inspector of Schools.

Hamilton, A. (1981). *Nature and Nurture: Aboriginal Child-rearing in North-Central Arnhem Land*. Canberra: Australian Institute of Aboriginal Studies.

Harris, S. (1980). *Culture and Learning: Tradition and Education in Northeast Arnhem Land*. Darwin, NT: Northern Territory Department of Education.

Harris, S. (1984). Aboriginal learning styles and formal schooling. *The Aboriginal Child at School, 12*(4), 3–23.

Huddleston, R. and Pullum, G. (2002). *The Cambridge Grammar of the English Language*. Cambridge: Cambridge University Press.

MacWhinney, B. (2000). *The Childes Project: Tools for Analyzing Talk*. Mahwah, NJ: Lawrence Erlbaum Associates.

Malcolm, I. G. (1982). Communication dysfunction in Aboriginal classrooms. In J. Sherwood (ed.), *Aboriginal Education Issues and Innovations*. Perth: Creative Research.

Moses, K. (1995). 'The silence of the frogs'. Unpublished MA thesis, University of Melbourne, Melbourne.

Nichol, R. M. (2005). *Socialization, Land and Citizenship among Aboriginal Australians*. Lewiston, NY: The Edwin Mellen Press.

Philips, S. U. (1972). Participant structures and communicative competence: warm Springs children in community and classroom. In C. P Cazden, V. P. John and D. Hymes (eds), *Functions of Language in the Classroom*. New York: Teachers College Press.

Richards, E., Hudson, J. and Lowe, P. (2002). *Out of the Desert: Stories from the Walmajarri Exodus*. Broome: Magabala Books.

Rowland, C. F., Pine, J. M., Lieven, E. V. M. and Theakston, A. L. (2003). Determinants of acquisition order in wh-questions: re-evaluating the role of caregiver speech. *Journal of Child Language, 30*, 609–35.

Sachs, J., Brown, R. and Salerno, R. (1976). Adults' speech to children. In W. Von Raffler-Engel and Y. Lebrun (eds), *Baby Talk and Infant Speech* (pp. 240–45). Amsterdam: Swets & Zeitlinger.

Savic, S. (1975). Aspects of adult–child communication: the problem of question acquisition. *Journal of Child Language, 2*, 251–60.

Snow, C., Arlman-Rupp, A., Hassing, Y., Jobse, J., Joosten, J. and Vorster, J. (1976). Mothers' speech in three social classes. *Journal of Psycholinguistic Research, 5*, 1–20.

South Australian Education Consultative Committee – Aboriginal Education Section. (1987). *Teaching Aboriginal Children.* Adelaide: Education Department of South Australia.

Watts, B. H. (1973). Teaching strategies to arouse motivation in culturally different children. In *Aboriginal Children in the Classroom: Proceedings of Seminar for Teachers of Aboriginal Children in the Taree Inspectorate* (pp. 160–90). Taree, NSW: Office of the Inspector of Schools.

Wells, C. G. (1986). Variations in child language. In P. Fletcher and M. Garman (eds), *Language Acquisition Studies in First Language Acquisition.* Cambridge: Cambridge University Press.

3
Storytelling styles: a study of adult–child interactions in narrations of a picture book in Tennant Creek

Samantha Disbray

This study examines the way that adults interact with children during storytelling. The analysis of a small set of narrations of a picture book by nine adults to children aged between 1;5 and 4;8 identified two storytelling styles. Some adults chose a collaborative style and co-constructed the story with the child. Others chose an elaborate storytelling style building the story through repetition and rephrasing. Some tendencies relating to the age of the child listener were found. When telling stories to younger children, adults concentrated more on gaining and maintaining attention and collaborated less than with older or more verbal children. All adults used repetition and elaboration and it is argued that this is a feature of Wumpurrarni English storytelling more generally. The study also shows some ways that the traditional language *Warumungu* is used in contemporary speech styles to children.

Introduction

Iya *maanjun*-wan, *julaka*. Ola bois dei gad jangayi. Dei bin goin hanting du faindim dat *julaka* deya na. Dei bin jeisim na, dei bin jeisim dat *julaka,* an dei pudum na nes. I lukinat dadei nes-*kana*, dat *julaka* deya.

[Here's a little one, a bird. All the boys have shanghais. They went hunting to find that bird. And there, they chased it, they chased that bird, and they put it in a nest. He's looking that way into the nest, where the bird is.]

This is how a Tennant Creek mother told a story to her young daughter, based on a wordless picture book (Egan, 1986) about boys hunting birds with shanghais. Notice that the language used contains both words from the traditional language, Warumungu (features from Warumungu are italicised above and throughout the paper), and words such as 'jeisim' for 'chase', which come from Wumpurrarni English. Wumpurrarni English is the English-based contact language spoken in Tennant Creek. Middle-aged Warumungu women, such as the mother here (M6), have grown up in a society where people tell stories to each other and to children as they sit on the ground, accompanying their stories with drawing in the sand (see also Eickelkamp, Chapter 4). However, they have all gone to school, and are familiar with books, and with using them to engage children's attention. While parents generally don't collect books for their children or use the town's library, many do buy books and sometimes look through them or read them out with their children.

In this paper I analyse 13 storytelling sessions, eight with children under 2;7 and five with children over 3;6 years of age. My aim is to understand how adults interact with the children in telling stories; how they are sensitive to the child's level of attention, how they collaborate with children in the storytelling, through questioning and prompting and how, through repetition and elaboration, they 'build' a rich and exciting tale. Repetition in narrative has been identified in other Aboriginal speech communities (Bavin, 2000; Walsh, 2006).

Although only 13 narrations are analysed, these allow some glimpses into the ways that Indigenous parents in Tennant Creek tailor their storytelling style and interaction according to the age of the child. I will first give some background to the study of narrative, before introducing the participants and the data. I then analyse the data for interaction style, and conclude with a discussion of the findings.

Telling stories and storytelling styles

Children develop storytelling skills as they grow up and this development begins at home. The cognitive and linguistic developmental processes required to tell a story have been the focus of most studies, which have examined children's narratives in one language (Bamberg, 1987; McCabe and Peterson, 1992; Peterson and McCabe, 1983) or cross-linguistically (Berman and Slobin, 1994;

Hickmann, 1995). Few studies have considered multilingual environments such as those found in much of Indigenous Australia. From a socialisation perspective, studies have shown that the way people talk to children and tell stories to them model notions of 'a good story' held by their speech community and this influences children's development of this oral genre. Heath (1983) and Watson (2001) discuss this with respect to the kinds of narrative experiences African American children have in their homes, schools and communities. They document children's skilful mastery of the oratory performances valued in their communities. And they consider how this affects the child's performance in mainstream school settings, particularly in relation to learning to read and write.

A few studies have examined more specifically the role of parental input and the differences in style that they might choose to use in narrations with children. These studies have used experimental rather than ethnographic data and have generally considered one of two narrative events: how parents get children to tell stories about themselves, and how parents tell stories to children using books as prompts. They have sought to establish a link between how the parents talk to the child and how, later on, the child talks (Peterson et al., 1999; Peterson and McCabe, 1996). Interactions over book-prompted narrations often involve adults asking the children questions, and giving the children feedback on their contributions. A number of researchers have found correlations between the frequency and type of questions adults ask and their feedback to children's contributions on the one hand, and children's later language performance on the other. Findings have informed home-learning programs aimed at involving parents in developing children's pre-literacy skills (Valdez-Menchaca and Whitehurst, 1992; Whitehurst et al., 1988). Minami (2002) investigated interaction between Japanese mothers and their 4- and 5-year-old children and found that the more questions the mother asked and the richer her feedback, the longer the responses from the child were. Minami also described a scaffolding routine these mothers commonly used in joint book narration. Here mothers asked a direct question about the content of the book, expecting a response from the child. After the child responded, the mothers echoed or evaluated the response. This three-part sequence, Initiation–Response–Evaluation, has also been identified in parent–child interactions of North American families (Cazden, 1988a; McCabe and Peterson, 1992).

Finally, parents change the way they talk to children as the children grow up. Pellegrini et al. (1985) found that English-speaking parents adjusted their interactional styles to the child's level of communicative competence in a book-reading activity. Sénéchal et al. (1995) reported a significantly higher proportion of utterances aimed at gaining and maintaining attention by English-speaking mothers of children aged 9 and 17 months, as compared with mothers of children aged 27 months. The mothers of the 27-month-old children asked more questions of these older children than the mothers of the younger children. Dickinson et al. (1992) found that in joint narrations with children between 3 and 4 years of age, mothers made fewer contributions as children grew older, allowing the child to take on greater responsibility for shared reading. Wigglesworth and Stavans (2001) working with older children (3–7 years) found similar patterns. In a further study, McArthur et al. (2005) found that mothers of 24-month-old children focused on objects, characters and actions more than parents of children aged 30 and 36 months, who devoted greater attention to internal states such as feelings, thoughts and intentions.

Traditional languages, contact languages and child language

In Australia, little work has been done on either children's language or contact languages in Indigenous communities. One area that has been the topic of much discussion is the role of questions in adult–child interactions, in contact varieties and in traditional language settings (see Moses and Yallop, Chapter 2; Reeders, Chapter 5). A small number of studies have investigated child language in Creole- and Aboriginal English-speaking settings (for instance, Harkins, 1994; Kaldor and Malcolm, 1985; Malcolm, 1992; Rhydwen, 1992). Such studies have focused on children's language production and development, and the educational implications for Creole- and Aboriginal English-speaking children in school. There has been almost no investigation of the type of language input children in such settings receive generally, or in specific language events, such as storytelling.

Tennant Creek, the participants, and the data and method

Tennant Creek: language situation

The data for this study are part of a more extensive corpus collected in Tennant Creek for the Aboriginal Child Language Acquisition Project (ACLA) (see Meakins, Chapter 13; Moses and Yallop, Chapter 2; Wigglesworth and Simpson, Chapter 1). Tennant Creek is a small, remote town situated in the Barkly region of the Northern Territory. The population of the town is around 3,500 people and half are non-Indigenous. Warumungu is the traditional language of the country upon which Tennant Creek is located and is the main ancestral language of most of the families involved in the ACLA project. Warumungu people have undergone language shift to Wumpurrarni English (WE) and Standard Australian English (SAE) (Graber, 1988; Rhydwen, 1992), a situation that causes many Warumungu great concern. Full speakers of Warumungu are generally over 50 years of age. These older speakers use Warumungu with other older speakers and also with younger non-fluent speakers, who generally reply in WE, and may 'insert' (Muysken, 2000) Warumungu elements. Speakers between 30 and 50 years of age may be 'partial speakers' (Gal, 1989; Tsitsipis, 1998). They understand Warumungu and may use some words and phrases, although they do not have mastery over all grammatical constructions and the full vocabulary ('hard language'). These speakers, by virtue of their extensive active knowledge are able to 'insert' Warumungu items heavily into the WE they speak. Younger speakers, below 30 years of age, may be 'passive speakers' (Gal, 1989; Tsitsipis, 1998), that is, they understand and use some Warumungu words or structures in their speech, and may insert some lexical items also, though less than partial speakers. Most of the Warumungu that children hear is in insertional code-switches and so this practice is important for language learning and maintenance.

WE is now the primary language of everyday communication among the Indigenous people in Tennant Creek, at home and in work places; and is the primary language of younger generations. WE is an English-based Creole language, with many similarities to Creole languages spoken in other parts of northern Australia, such as Roper River Kriol (Munro, 2004; Sandefur, 1979) and Fitzroy Valley Kriol (Hudson, 1985). The presence of Warumungu features in WE is one aspect that distinguishes WE from other varieties.

SAE also plays an important part in the linguistic ecology. It is spoken by some Indigenous people as well as by non-Indigenous people who live in the town. It is the language of education, the media, commercial interactions between Indigenous and non-Indigenous people. This intense contact is a source of variation in WE, as many speakers switch between 'light' or acrolectal (closer to SAE, the source language of this creolised code) and 'heavy' or basilectal styles (further from SAE) of WE, depending on the context of the interaction.

Table 3.1 Participants, focus child and storyteller at time 1 and time 2

No.	Age time 1 (years;months)	Age time 2 (years;months)	Child	Storyteller	Age of storyteller
1	1;7	–	M	Mother	26–30
2	1;7	–	F	Grandmother	65+
3	2;1	–	M	Mother	26–30
4	1;5	3;6	F	Mother	20–25
5	2;1	4;2	F	Grandmother	40–45
6	2;6	4;6	F	Mother	36–40
7	2;7	4;8	F	Mother	30–35
8	2;7	–	M	Mother	26–30
9	–	4;8	F	Mother	26–30

Participants

The 13 stories used in this analysis are taken from recording sessions with nine children in Tennant Creek. To explore age-related differences in adult story-telling styles, two sets of stories narrated from the same story-book prompt are analysed. There are eight stories in the first set, told to five girls and three boys. The children were aged between 1;5 and 2;7 at the time of the first recording (shown as 'time 1' in Table 3.1). The second set includes five narrations, four of which were recorded approximately 2 years later, told by the same caregivers to the same children as in set one (Children 4–7). One additional narration (Child 9) was recorded at another time. The children were aged between 3;6 and 4;8 in the second set of recordings and all were girls.

The storytellers were all women; seven were mothers of the focus children and two were grandmothers. All but two[1] of the adults participated regularly in the ACLA project and the data set here represents a small sample of the total recordings made with each speaker.

The data and method

The prompt

The book used to elicit the stories was created at a literacy production centre at another Central Australian Indigenous community (Egan, 1986), and is referred to here as the 'Shanghai story'. It contains 11 pages, and consists of a series of line-drawn pictures with no text. It was chosen for the relevance of its content, boys hunting with shanghais, which is a common activity in the community. The story depicts the following scenes:

Page	Story action
1	Three boys holding shanghais.
2–3	The boys follow a bird and find it in its nest.
4–5	The bird jumps out and runs away, the boys take chase.
6–7	One boy trips on a stick and two continue the chase.
8–9	One boy steps on a prickle and one continues the chase.
10–11	The last boy runs into a tree and the bird reaches the safety of its mother.

Data collection

For the first storytelling, the caregivers were given some time to familiarise themselves with the book and then asked to tell the story to the child. Usually the child sat beside or on the storyteller's lap and so both could see the pictures. The narration was recorded on video. The repeat narrations were recorded roughly 2 years later. The caregivers were asked to tell the story once again and this session was also recorded on video. The recordings were transcribed for analysis.[2]

As part of the data collection for the ACLA project, caregivers were regularly asked to tell stories from book prompts, and this activity proved to be very popular for both caregivers and children. Children enjoyed sitting close to their caregivers or in their (grand)mother's laps, sharing time looking at pictures, listening and discussing the story.[3]

Approach to the analysis

Initial investigation of the stories revealed three interesting patterns in the adult–child interaction. These were the ways and extent to which adults

1. gained and maintained a child's attention;
2. used repetition in the narrations;
3. engaged the child's collaboration.

To analyse the interactions and storytelling style, a quantitative approach was taken. Each clause in each narration was coded for its content and its function in the storytelling. A clause was identified as a sequence of speech separated from other speech by a pause, or by a grammatically complete set of words (Sénéchal et al., 1995). Each clause was categorised into one of four general categories based on those devised by Wigglesworth and Stavans (2001), who studied the narratives of Hebrew-speaking Israeli and English-speaking

Australian parents telling a story to their children. The basic coding system was well suited to the WE data. However one category, story clauses, was expanded to examine repetition and elaboration common in the WE interactions. The four general categories were:

1. Story clauses
2. Focusing clauses
3. Story-related conversation
4. Responses to children's contributions.

When an adult described the events in the story or provided comments about the events or characters this was coded as a story clause, for instance, from the example above *dei bin go hanting du faindem julaka* (they went hunting for a bird). Story clauses were then coded to explore repetition, which is discussed below. When an adult tried to gain or keep the child's attention on the activity (i.e. listening to the story) or a detail of the story, with phrases like '*luk iya*' and '*si*', this was coded as a focusing clause. Attempts to involve the child in co-telling the story were coded as story-related conversation. These clauses were generally direct questions about the story, objects, characters and locations, for example, *wat ding i gadim*? (what's he got?). And finally, responses to children's contributions were coded. These included confirmation of the child's utterance, with phrases like '*ye*', statements, which repeated, corrected or added something to what the child had said.

To measure the overall story length the number of clauses in each story was counted. The number of words in the story was also counted.[4] This is important for considering the relationship between interaction style and the amount of adult talk.

Story analyses

Story length

The nine adults told stories of varying lengths, as shown in Tables 3.2 and 3.3. There was no correlation between the age of the child and the number of words or clauses. While the grandmother (GM) and mother (M) of the two very young children (GM2, M4) told the shortest stories, the mother (M1) of one of the youngest children (aged 1;7) told one of the longest stories. A comparison of the individual narrations which were recorded at both time 1 and time 2 (story numbers marked in bold) shows that three of the stories (4, 5 and 7) were longer (in terms of number of words) at time 2 and one story (Story 6) was shorter.

Table 3.2 Length of story, time 1

Story number	Total clauses	Total words	Words per clause
1 (1;7)	72	369	5.12
2 (1;7)	26	94	3.61
3 (2;1)	50	250	5.00
4 (1;5)	29	117	4.03
5 (2;1)	44	189	4.29
6 (2;6)	80	419	5.23
7 (2;7)	31	134	4.32
8 (2;7)	41	229	5.58
Average	**46.62**	**227.75**	**4.71**

Table 3.3 Length of story, time 2

Story number	Total clauses	Total words	Words per clause
4 (3;6)	27	137	5.07
5 (4;2)	66	297	4.50
6 (4;6)	49	309	6.30
7 (4;8)	35	166	4.74
9 (4;8)	41	124	3.02
Average	**43.6**	**186.6**	**4.72**

Interactions

To look at interaction and storytelling styles, a profile of each narration was created, showing the percentage of each clause type in each story. We start with story clauses: those clauses devoted to telling the story. In Figure 3.1, the stories recorded at time 1 (1–8) are shown on the left side of the table, and the second set, the time 2 stories (4–7 and 9) are on the right and separated from time 1 by a space.

Two patterns begin to emerge in Figure 3.1. In most narrations over 65 per cent of the clauses were storytelling clauses (see the bars for M1, GM2, M3, M4, GM5 and M6 at time 1; and M4, M6 and M7 at time 2). In these stories the speaker devoted most of the clauses to telling the story. Narrations with less than 60 per cent of story clauses on the other hand represent a different pattern (M7, M8 at time 1 and GM5, M9 at time 2), which will become clearer in the following figures.

All speakers repeated and rephrased story clauses or parts of clauses to build an episode in the story, as in Extract 1 by M6 (SD006B) in the introduction

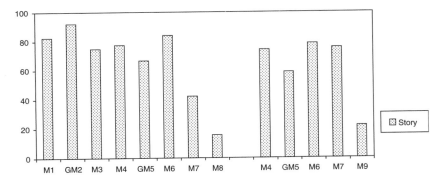

Figure 3.1 Storytelling clauses.

Extract 1: M6 (SD006B)

dei bin jeisim na	they chased it
dei bin jeisim dat *julaka*	they chased that bird

   To investigate repetition in the narrations, the story clauses that described a story detail for the first time (Story) were counted separately to those that in some way repeated this information. There were a couple of ways that speakers used repetition; by repeating the whole clause (Repeat); by rephrasing all or part of a clause (Rephrase); or by repeating one part of the same information and elaborating on it (Elaborate); and finally, some of the information repeated was by code-switching, that is, repeating a Warumungu word or phase in WE or a WE word or phrase in Warumungu (Code-switch). The most common types of repetition were rephrasing and elaboration, and this is shown in Extract 2 from M3's narration of pages 7–10 of the story, to her son aged 2;1.

Extract 2: M3 (SD018)

Page 7

Story	dubala bin jeisin na	two were chasing it
Elaborate	dubala na jeisim im *nununu* *julaka* iya na *pawumpawu*	the two of them were chasing this little bird, poor thing
Story	*pawumpawu* i bin ran da *julaka* beibiwan	the poor thing, it ran, that little bird
(Focus)	luk iya	look at this
Rephrase	i bin ran	it ran

Page 8

(Focus)	yu luk iya	you look at this
Story	ah i bin pokim im	oh, it poked him

Elaborate	deya si, *nyili* bin pokim im in da fut	there see, a prickle poked him in the foot
Rephrase	si *nyili* bin pokim im	see, the prickle poked him

Page 9

Story	deya wanbala *yungkurnu* na ranin,	And one monster is running
Story	jeisim im na lilwan *julaka* beibiwan	(it's) chasing the little baby bird
Rephrase	wanbala ranin na	one is running
Rephrase	ye jeisimbat im *pawumpawu*	ye still chasing it, poor thing

Page 10

Story	*wartarra*! i bin purldan na tri na	oh no! he fell down by the tree
Story	ye mangki im nakim im	ye, the monster knocked into it
Rephrase	mangki im purldan na *pawumpawu*	the monster fell down, poor thing
Repeat	mangki i bin nakim im	the monster, he knocked into it

This investigation showed that the adults who used a high proportion of story clauses, like M3, were rephrasing and elaborating extensively. Between 35 and 50 per cent of the story clauses in these narrations were repetitions of some type. These are described as 'elaborate narrations'. These speakers 'built' the story up, describing a detail of the story, rephrasing it and elaborating, lingering on the picture, and often recapping it before moving on. They also often used changes in rhythm, drawing out syllables to stress the actions that happened for a long time. They used high pitch for tension and excitement at unexpected developments, and falling tones to express completion or a shift to the next event. These crafted narrations were very entertaining to listen to. Six of the seven elaborate narrations were told at time 1 when the children were younger (M1, GM2, M3, M4, GM5 and M6). One elaborate narration was told at time 2 to an older child, by M6.

Repetition was found in all stories, though not to the same extent as in the 'elaborate narrations'. These speakers (M7, M8 at time 1; and GM5, M4, M7 and M9 at time 2) repeated or rephrased in approximately 15–20 per cent of the story clauses.

Another form of repetition, in the narrations, involved code-switching that may be described as 'instructional code-switching'. Speakers repeated a WE word or phrase from a previous clause in the other language; that is, from

Warumungu into WE as in Extract 3 by M6, or from WE into Warumungu, as in Extract 4, from GM2:

Extract 3: (SD006B)

M6: iya luk *kujjara*.	Here look, two
M6: *yarnti, kujjarra*	One, two
M6: wan, tu.	One, two

Extract 4: (SD015)

GM2: jeisim dei jeisim	they kept chasing after it
GM2: *jina kuranayina*	running after it

Four adults used this type of repetition and their stories featured relatively high proportions of different Warumungu words or forms.[5] These narrations were by the three eldest speakers (GM2, GM4 and M6) and one younger speaker (M1).

Focusing clauses

Figure 3.2 shows the proportion of story clauses (shown in Figure 3.1), in proportion to focusing clauses. Focusing clauses are used to draw the child's attention to the shared activity, or to a detail in the story, usually *luk* (look) clauses, for example, *yu luk iya* ('you look here') – often repeated a number of times, particularly with younger children. All of the caregivers used focusing clauses, although the proportion of these varied, as Figure 3.2 reveals.

Overall the proportion of focus clauses tended to be slightly lower with the older children. For the most part, these findings match with those of

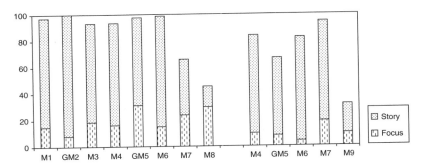

Figure 3.2 Focusing clauses.

Wigglesworth and Stavans (2001) and Sénéchal et al. (1995) who found that adults used less 'attention recruiting comments' with older children.

Figure 3.2 highlights another feature of the elaborate narrations. All are made up completely or almost completely of storytelling and focusing clauses (see the bar charts for stories by M1, GM2, M3, M4, GM5, M6 at time 1; and at time 2 for M6 and M7). All of these adults used a particular interaction routine in their storytellings. This involved the adult drawing the child's attention to the picture on a page (Focus), and then describing the events depicted (Story), and possibly drawing their attention to a particular detail they wished to emphasise or elaborate, then repeating, rephrasing or elaborating on a clause. The mothers monitored the child's attention, keeping them on task or drawing them back when necessary. Extracts 2 and 5 from M1 show this pattern. The boys in the story are given the nicknames of the child and his brothers.

Extract 5: SD079

Focus	ah luk fes	have a look first
Story	deya tribala man	there are three men
Elaborate	shangayi-*jangu*	they have shanghais
Elaborate	tribala man, Pappa, Limlim an Jarti	three men, Pappa, Limlim an Jarti
Rephrase	lil Mappa, Limlim, Jarti	little Mappa Limlim an Jarti
Story	dei bin go	they went off
Story	oh jukjuk!	oh a bird!
Elaborate	an dei bin go faindim jukjuk *nunu*-wan	and they went and found a little baby bird.
Story	dei bin lukim jukjuk	they saw the bird
Focus	iya luk	here look
Story	dei bin go	they went
Focus	yu luk	*you have a look*
Story	*nunu* jukjuk raning iya, jukjuk	the little baby bird is running away

To fill in the profile for the four 'collaborative' narrations (M7 and M8 at time 1; and GM5 and M9 at time 2) and the narrations by M4 and M6 (at time 2) we now turn to look at story-related conversation.

Story-related conversation

In story-related clauses adults collaborated with the child in telling the story. They generally did this by posing direct questions; asking the child to label

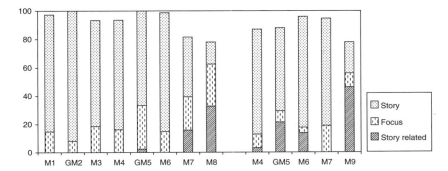

Figure 3.3 Story-related conversation.

objects or their locations, or to describe actions and events, and sometimes the location of these. As discussed above, the elaborate narrations were made up of largely story and focus clauses. These adults used few or no story-related clauses, as can be seen in Figure 3.3. The story-related clauses appear at the bottom of the bar chart of the narration, with focus clauses, then story clauses on top.

The profile of the four collaborative stories (M7 and M8 at time 1; and GM5 and M9 at time 2) is now becoming clear. These speakers used a high proportion of story-related clauses, particularly in relation to the proportion of story clauses. Three other narrators also used some story-related clauses: GM5 at time 1 and M4 at time 2 used very few while M6 at time 2 used somewhat more, although this last mother told a long story using a great proportion of the story clauses. Though she invited some interaction, it was less than in the stories described as collaborative.

Adults engaged in a number of strategies to get their children to join in telling the story such as question and answer routines, prompting and giving feedback on, and recasting children's utterances. Most questions were *wh*-questions, requiring the child to label an object, character or location. The adults were rarely seeking information outside of the pictures and so knew the answer. Such questions are display questions, which Moses and Yallop (Chapter 2) propose play a number of roles in caregiver discourse, such as facilitating understanding and learning, directing and maintaining attention and, as the current data shows, encouraging participation in the conversation. The pattern in these interactions tended to consist of a focusing clause, a *wh*-question, prompting where necessary the child's response and generally some type of feedback, similar to the Initiate–Response–Evaluation routine described in other studies (Cazden, 1988b; McCabe and Peterson, 1992; Minami, 2002). While this sort of routine has been unsuccessful in school settings (Moses and Wigglesworth, Chapter 6), Moses and Yallop (Chapter 2) show that it is common in adult–child interactions at Yakanarra, although Reeders has observed very different routines in her study (Chapter 5).

Extract 6 from M8 is a good example of a mother focusing, questioning, prompting and giving feedback.

Extract 6: (SD012)

M8: luk arm.	M8: look at his arm.
M8: wat i gatim? wat ding gatim?	M8: what's he got? what thing has he got?
M8: jangayi (whispers)	M8: shanghai (whispers)
C8: olat jangayi	C8: all of them (have) shanghais
M8: ye, olat gadim.	M8: ye, they've all got them.
C8: jangayi deya, jangayi deya, jangayi deya.	C8: shanghai there, shanghai there, shanghai there.

M6 and M9, who collaborated with older children used some additional strategies. M6, for instance, asked her 4;6 daughter if she remembered the story, and then asked her questions which required her to predict what would happen next ('*wat I garra du na*?' What is he going to do now). In the narration by M9, an older child, the 8-year-old daughter who was also present, took over the co-construction, contributing long stretches to the narration. This mother didn't just prompt her daughter and acknowledge the response, she prompted elaborations from this older child (line 5). When necessary, the mother steered her back to the story depicted, as line 11 in Extract 7 shows

Extract 7: (SD008)

1. C9: an afta dat *kartti* bin foldan	1. C9: and after that the man fell down
2. M9: *wanppan pawumpawu*	2. M9: fell down, poor thing
3. M9: weya i bin foldan?	3. M9: where did he fall?
4. C9: i bin foldan	4. C9: he fell down
5. M9: weya -*kana*?	5. M9: where?
6. C9: langa tri, next to da tri	6. C9: at the tree, next to the tree
7. C9: an da *julaka* i bin kam itim im	7. C9: and the bird, it hit him
8. C9: na nat itim im, um, um	8. C9: no, it didn't hit him, um, um
9. C9: i bin go, um	9. C9: it went, um
10. C9: *julaka* bin puffed out! na, na!	10. C9: the bird got puffed out! no, not really!
11. M9: im-*kayi* mami bin gitim.	11. M9: its mother got it

12. C9: im-*kayi* mami bin/im/im-*kayi* mami *julaka* bin kam	12. C9: its mother/it/the mother bird came
13. C9: an im nakulim na	13. C9: and she cuddled it
14. M9: oh nakulwan	14. M9: oh, cuddling

In her time 2 narration, GM5 used some novel prompting strategies. This grandmother used a high proportion of Warumungu items in both narrations, but at time 2 she prompted her granddaughter (aged 4;8) to repeat some of the Warumungu words and phrases she inserted into the story. Lines 1–8 of Extract 8, show how the grandmother looked at the first page of the book and assigned the two of the characters kin relations. She pointed to each character, named the kin term and looked at the child, who picked up on this visual cue and repeated the terms. Lines 9–14 (narrating page 6 of the book) show that the grandmother instructed the child to repeat a clause.

Extract 8: (SD103)

1. GM5: *kampaju*	GM5: father
2. C5: *kampaju*	C5: father
3. GM5: *ngamirni*	GM5: mother's brother
4. C5: *ngamirni*	C5: mother's brother
5. GM5: *kaarnu*	GM5: boy
6. C5: *kaarnu*	C5: boy
7. GM5: ye	GM5: ye
8. GM5: dei goin	GM5: they went
9. GM5: dei jeisimbat *purtangara junga*	GM5: they really chased after it
10. GM5: *pawumpawu*	GM5: poor thing
11. GM5: *pawumpawu* inti?	GM5: it's a poor thing, isn't it?
12. GM5: yu tok '*pawumpawu* dat *julaka*'	GM5: you say 'that poor bird'
13. C5: '*pawumpawu* dat *julaka*'	C5: 'that poor bird'
14. GM5: dei jeisim gin	GM5: they kept on chasing it

In the collaborative storytellings the caregivers were more likely to spur child contributions and in turn, respond to these contributions. We turn now to response clauses, completing the profile of all narrations,[6] in Figure 3.4.

Responses to child utterances

In most cases adults acknowledged children's comments (Extract 8, line 7) or recast (Extract 6, line 5) or corrected them (Extract 7, line 11). The response clauses are shown at the bottom of the bar graph, then story-related conversation, focus and story clauses.

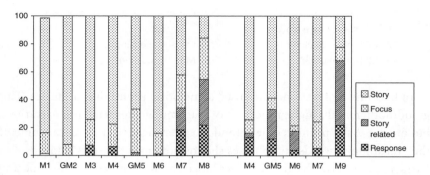

Figure 3.4 All clauses.

The narrators who adopted a collaborative style tended to give a high proportion of responses (M7, M8 at time 1; and GM5 and M9 at time 2). In the other narrations, children made verbal or non-verbal contributions, which were acknowledged by the caregiver, as the presence of response clauses indicates (M3, M4 at time 1; and M4 and M7 at time 2). Extract 9 shows how M4 (at time 1) responds to the non-verbal contribution of her daughter aged 1;5.

Extract 9: (SD010)

M4: NAME yu luk iya	M4: NAME you look at this
C4: (points to the bird in the nest)	C4: (points to the bird in the nest)
M4: ye	M4: ye
M4: damob gadim luk	M4: they've got it
M4: dei bin gidim ina nest	M4: they've got it in the nest

At time 2, the same mother (M4) responded to a number of contributions by her daughter, then aged 3;6. This mother's strategy was not strongly elaborate or collaborative, but the telling was interactive, as the young girl made many contributions, as Extract 10 shows. These were often acknowledged (lines 3,8) and recast (line 8) by her mother.

Extract 10: (SD093)

1. M4: ola men jeisim jukujuk	M4: all of the men chase the bird
2. C4: jeisim im jukjuk	C4: chasing the bird
3. M4: ye	M4: ye
4. M4: ah i foldan na!	M4: oh he falls down
5. M4: foldan reken	M4: falls down
6. C4: deya i foldan na	C4: there he falls down
7. C4: iya im raning, gidim na	C4: here he's running, getting it now
8. M4: ye, tubala raning jeisimbat	M4: ye, two are running, chasing it

M7 (time 1) and to a greater extent M8 collaborated with their children, both aged 2;7, older than most of the children in the time 1 set (aged between 1;5 and 2;7, see Table 3.1). Both of these children were very keen talkers, confident and eager to take part in the storytelling. At time 2 M7 did not use a collaborative style with her daughter then aged 4;8, but encouraged her to listen. When the story was finished, the daughter told her own version of the story. The other two collaborative narrations were told to older children. In the collaborative story by GM5 the child was 4;8 and M9 encouraged her 8-year-old daughter take over the storytelling. Co-construction of stories with capable and older children has been found in previous studies (Dickinson et al., 1992; Wigglesworth and Stavans, 2001).

Discussion

This study has identified two interactional styles in adult–child narrations on the basis of the proportion of clauses devoted to joint-narration and the proportion of story clauses, which included repetition and elaboration. Those with a high proportion devoted to joint narration were termed 'collaborative narrations', and those with a high proportion of story clauses, in which repetition was frequent, as 'elaborate narrations'. Some age-related tendencies emerged. First, elaborate narrations tended to occur with younger children; six of the seven elaborate narrations were told to the youngest children.

It is likely that the mothers of younger children told elaborate stories to young children to keep them interested in the activity, with repetitions to provide them with the information that they required to understand the story. Certainly the mothers of these young children ensured that they maintained the child's interest by telling lively, entertaining stories. In this they were sensitive to the attention span and cognitive level of their children. They 'built up' the story, drawing attention to details in the pictures, describing an event, repeating, rephrasing or elaborating on an element before moving on to the next. However, it is not argued here that elaboration is restricted to stories to young children, as all stories included repetition, including the two that were fairly 'straight' narrations, that is, neither elaborate nor collaborative, by M3 and M6 at time 2, as well as the four stories described as 'collaborative'. In fact, repetition, rephrasing and elaboration have also been found in adult–adult texts recorded for the ACLA project and it is suggested here that this is a feature commonly found in WE narratives and more generally in Aboriginal narrations (Bavin, 2000; Walsh, 2006). Elaboration may occur in the narrations to the young children in this study, partly for the reasons described above, but also as a model for 'good storytelling'.

The 'collaborative' stories, on the other hand, those with a high proportion of clauses in which the child was encouraged to co-construct the narrative, tended to occur more with older children and highly verbal children. Collaborative stories also occurred with younger children (M7 and M8 at time 1). In these cases, it was the children themselves who initiated this collaborative style and their mothers accommodated the children's eagerness to join in the storytelling. They responded to their children's contributions, asking questions, prompting and giving feedback. In the two collaborative stories with the two older children, GM5 and M9 used a wider range of strategies, in addition to those used by M7 and M8.

A further age-related tendency was found in the use of focusing clauses. Though all of the caregivers used these attention gaining and attention maintaining strategies, they occurred more frequently in narrations to young children, in line with previous findings (Sénéchal et al., 1995; Wigglesworth and Stavans, 2001).

The study also provides a glimpse into the rich pool of resources speakers have to tell an exciting and engaging story. In particular it gives some insight into the ways that the traditional language Warumungu is used in contemporary language, and the sort of language knowledge that children are likely to have. This is a larger question within the ACLA project, but the data here are representative of both the use of Warumungu by speakers of different ages and of the kinds of Warumungu insertions found in adult speech. All speakers used at least one Warumungu feature, generally some instances of the Warumungu-derived semantic case-markers,[7] – *kayi*, to express possession and/or the location marking suffix – *kina*.[8] Other semantic case-markers were also used, such as – *jangu* (having) which appears in Extract 5. Many speakers also inserted Warumungu nouns, particularly names of everyday items, such as body parts, which are widely known and inserted in WE generally. Instructional code-switching and also prompting children to use Warumungu (Extract 8) is also found in other interactions in the ACLA data set.

The use of some Warumungu items were important in fostering children's interest in the story. The noun and interjection *pawumpawu* occurred in most of the stories (see Extracts 2,7 and 8), often repeatedly. *Pawumpawu* is often said in reference to a deceased person or their family to evoke empathy and respect grief. It is also used to refer to or address someone one hasn't seen in sometime, and can be translated as 'dear one'. Finally *pawumpawu* can express sympathy at some misfortune, as it was used in the stories here. It was a means for storytellers to evoke sympathy for either the bird or the boys in the face of their various calamities. The use of *pawumpawu* drew children into the story, encouraging an emotional response, as the storytellers went beyond relaying the events at hand, to evaluating events and empathising with characters. This added dramatic affect, making the storytelling more interesting and engaging, was also a means of modelling an appropriate response and associated expression to the children. Another evocative Warumungu nominal is *yungkurnu* (monster-being), which occurred in two of the narrations, referring to the boys. A number of Warumungu terms for monster-like creatures are in wide circulation, known, sometimes seen, and feared by all. They are regularly evoked to harness children's behaviour and movement, especially at night. The use of *yungkurnu* in the narrations contributed to a dramatic and scary, cautionary tale. In one story the grandmother (GM5) gave the human protagonists kin terms, and in two other stories the mothers named them after family members (M1 and M7 at time 1). These were further strategies to engage the child in the story.

This study focuses on adult storytelling style. It has already been mentioned that adults responded to children's willingness to contribute, which shows that the interaction is not one-sided. However, to examine the children's role fully, which as they grew older was clearly a factor in the adult's choice of storytelling style, was beyond the scope of this study. The data presented here provide a glimpse into storytelling styles by caregivers in Tennant Creek. It shows the narrators' sensitivity to the age and interest of the child listener and provides a window into the capacity and enthusiasm among these caregivers for language-rich interaction with young children.

Previous studies on home speech styles and narration by caregivers in particular have sought to explain relationships between children's language development and later performance in school. Narrative plays an important role in the early childhood years, as storytelling from books by teachers (and caregivers in many settings) foster children's transition into their own early reading. The current study offers some insight into this complex process in which many variables are at play. A very clear but general observation that relates to children's transition into formal education is that children in this speech setting are not first-language English speakers. The language they learn at home is structurally different to SAE and these differences go far beyond the use of Warumungu features. Similarities at the level of words are often only superficial. With respect to storytelling styles, the use of repetition is not a notable feature of SAE narration, and further research would be required to consider how this manifests in children's later language production and whether this stylistic difference impacts in classroom settings. Language is one among a number of important variables impacting on education outcomes; there are many others such as child health, in particular ear health (see Galloway, Chapter 10), attendance, and home and teacher expectations of the child's performance, and dynamics of power in classrooms (see Moses and Wigglesworth, Chapter 6).

Notes

1. Two mothers, M7 and M8, participated during the first year of the 3-year study only, which is why no repeat narration at time 2 was possible. However, approximately 7 hours of video recordings were made with these families.
2. The recordings were transcribed and coded in the Child Language Analysis program (CLAN) (MacWhinney, 2000). The WE was transcribed using the Kriol orthography developed by Sandefur (1979) and found in Lee (2002). The *Warumungu* was transcribed using the orthography developed for *Warumungu* as used by Simpson (2002).
3. I made copies of a number of the picture book prompts on the request of a number of caregivers. I also collected second-hand picture books from jumble sales and second-hand shops and gave these to families in Tennant Creek.
4. Counts were also made of the number of different words *Warumungu* and WE (types) and overall number of words in the two languages (tokens).
5. In these stories the percentage of *Warumungu* types and token was between 12 and 35 per cent.
6. The bar graph for M1 is slightly less than 100 per cent as one utterance was not transcribed as it was inaudible.
7. These forms are derived from *Warumungu*. Their distribution and use differ in *Warumungu* when compared with WE, though their functions and meanings remain close. For a more detailed discussion of the expression of possession see Disbray and Simpson, 2005. As these forms are so common in WE, particularly – kayi, they could be seen as borrowings into WE, rather than insertions of *Warumungu*. However, these forms are counted as *Warumungu* as this is the source language of these forms, and speakers themselves recognise them as *Warumungu*.
8. The suffix may occur as *-kina, -kana* or *–kuna*. The vowel in *-kVna* is influenced by the vowel in the last syllable of the word it is suffixed to, for example, *mami-kina* (at/to the mother), *takka-kana* (in/on/into/onto the hand). *Warumungu* and WE express the relationship of location with these and other suffixes, while English relies on prepositions to do so. Prepositions also occur in WE, sometimes with the location suffix, for example, *na tri-kina* (at/to/in/into the tree).

References

Bamberg, M. G. W. (1987). *The Acquisition of Narratives: Learning to Use Language.* Berlin: Mouton de Gruyter.

Bavin, E. (2000). Ellipsis in Warlpiri children's narratives: an analysis of frog stories. *Linguistics, 38*(3), 569–88.

Berman, R. A. and Slobin, D. I. (1994). *Relating Events in Narrative: A Crosslinguistic Developmental Study*. Hillsdale, NJ: Lawrence Erlbaum Associates.

Cazden, C. (1988a). *Classroom Discourse*. Portsmouth, NH: Heineman.

Cazden, C. B. (1988b). *Classroom Discourse: The Language of Teaching and Learning*. Portsmouth, NH: Heinemann.

Dickinson, D. K., De Temple, J. M., Hirschler, J. A. and Smith, M. W. (1992). Book reading with pre-schoolers: co-construction of text at home and at school. *Early Childhood Research Quarterly, 7*(3), 323–46.

Disbray, S. and Simpson, J. (2005). The expression of possesion in Wampurrani English, Tennant Creek. In S. Musgrave (ed.) *Monash University Linguistics Papers Vol.5, Nos 1 and 2 (Special issue) Language Contact, Hybrids and New Varieties: Emergent Possesive Constructions* (pp. 65–85). Victoria: Monash University.

Egan, A. (1986). *Pintaru-kurlu (The Quail)*. Yuendumu, NT: Bilingual Resources Development Unit, Northern Territory Department of Education.

Gal, S. (1989). Lexical innovation and loss: the use and value of restricted Hungarian. In N. C. Dorian (ed.), *Investigating Obsolescence: Studies in Language Contraction and Death* (pp. 313–34). Cambridge: Cambridge University Press.

Graber, P. L. (1988). Kriol in the Barkly tableland. In M. J. Ray (ed.), *Aboriginal Language Use in the Northern Territory: 5 Reports. Work Papers of SIL-AAIB, Series B, Volume 13.* (pp. 19–32). Darwin, NT: Australian Aborigines Branch, Summer Institute of Linguistics.

Harkins, J. (1994). *Bridging Two Worlds: Aboriginal English and Cross-Cultural Understanding*. Brisbane: University of Queensland Press.

Heath, S. B. (1983). *Ways with Words: Language, Life, and Work in Communities and Classrooms*. New York: Cambridge University Press.

Hickmann, M. (1995). Discourse, organisation and the development of reference to person, time and space. In P. Fletcher and B. MacWhinney (eds), *The Handbook of Child Language* (pp. 194–218). Cambridge, MA: Blackwell Publishers.

Hudson, J. (1985). Grammatical and Semantic Aspects of Fitzroy Valley Kriol. *Work Papers of SIL-AAB, Series A, Volume 8*. Darwin, NT: Australian Aborigines Branch, Summer Institute of Linguistics.

Kaldor, S. and Malcolm, I. G. (1985). Aboriginal children's English – educational implications. In M. Clyne (ed.), *Australia, Meeting Place of Languages*. Canberra: Pacific Linguistics.

Lee, Jason (2002). October Kriol Dikshenri (draft) Katherine Language Centre.

MacWhinney, Brian (2000). *The CHILDES Project: Tools for Analyzing Talk*. Mahwah, NJ: Lawrence Erlbaum.

Malcolm, I. G. (1992). English in the education of speakers of Aboriginal English. In J. Siegel (ed.), *Pidgins, Creoles and Nonstandard Dialects in Education*. (Occasional Papers No. 12, pp. 14–41). Melbourne: Applied Linguistics Association of Australia.

McArthur, D., Adamson, L. B. and Deckner, D. F. (2005). As stories become familiar: mother–child conversations during shared reading. *Merrill-Palmer Quarterly, 51*(4), 389–411.

McCabe, A. and Peterson, C. (1992). Parental styles of narrative elicitation: effect on children's narrative structure and content. *First Language, 12*(3), 299–321.

Minami, M. (2002). *Culture-Specific Language Styles: The Development of Oral Narrative and Literacy.* Clevedon: Multilingual Matters.

Munro, J. (2004). 'Substrate language influence in kriol: the application of transfer constraints to language contact in Northern Australia'. Unpublished PhD thesis, University of New England, Armidale, NSW.

Muysken, P. (2000). *Bilingual Speech: A Typology of Code-Mixing.* Cambridge: Cambridge University Press.

Pellegrini, A. D., Brody, G. H. and Sigel, I. E. (1985). Parents' book-reading habits with their children. *Journal of Educational Psychology, 77*(3), 332–40.

Peterson, C. and McCabe, A. (1983). *Developmental Psycholinguistics: Three Ways of Looking at a Child's Narrative.* New York: Plenum Press.

Peterson, C. and McCabe, A. (1996). Parental scaffolding of context in children's narratives. In C. E. Johnson and J. H. V. Gilbert (eds), *Children's Language, Volume 9* (pp. 183–96). Mahwah, NJ: Lawrence Erlbaum Associates.

Peterson, C., Jesso, B. and McCabe, A. (1999). Encouraging narratives in preschoolers: an intervention study. *Journal of Child Language, 26*, 49–67.

Rhydwen, M. (1992). *The Extent of the Use of Kriol, Other Creole Varieties and Varieties of Aboriginal English by Schoolchildren in the Northern Territory and Its Implications for Access to English Literacy.* Canberra: Department of Employment, Education and Training.

Sandefur, J. R. (1979). An Australian Creole in the Northern Territory: a description of Ngukurr-Bamyili dialects (Part 1), *Work Papers of SIL-AAB, Series B, Volume 3.* Darwin, NT: Australian Aborigines Branch, Summer Institute of Linguistics.

Sénéchal, M., Cornell, E. H. and Broda, L. S. (1995). Age-related differences in the organization of parent–infant interactions during picture-book reading. *Early Childhood Research Quarterly, 10*(3), 317–37.

Tsitsipis, L. D. (1998). *A Linguistic Anthropology of Praxis and Language Shift: Arvanítika (Albanian) and Greek in Contact.* Oxford: Oxford University Press.

Valdez-Menchaca, M. C. and Whitehurst, G. J. (1992). Accelerating language development through picture book reading: a systematic extension to Mexican day care. *Developmental Psychology, 28*(6), 1106–14.

Walsh, M. (2006, March). *Ten Postulates Concerning Narrative in Aboriginal Australia.* Paper presented at the Australian Languages Workshop, Pearl Beach, NSW.

Watson, R. (2001). Literacy and oral language: implications for early literacy acquisition. In S. B. Neuman and D. K. Dickinson (eds), *Handbook of Early Literacy Research.* New York: Guildford Press.

Whitehurst, G. J., Falco, F. L., Lonigan, C. J., Fischel, J. E., DeBaryshe, B. D., Valdez-Menchaca, M. C., and Caulfield, M. (1988). Accelerating language development through picture book reading. *Developmental Psychology, 24*(4), 552–59.

Wigglesworth, G. and Stavans, A. (2001). A cross-cultural investigation of parental interaction in narrative with children at a range of ages. In K. Nelson, A. Aksu-Koc and C. Johnson (eds), *Children's Language, Volume 10: Narrative and Discourse Development.* Mahwah, NJ: Lawrence Erlbaum Associates.

'I don't talk story like that': on the social meaning of children's sand stories at Ernabella

4

Ute Eickelkamp

Chapter Outline

Focusing on the social meaning of storytelling by children in Central Australia, I show that the traditional practice of sand storytelling (*milpatjunanyi*) is at once of contemporary significance and a link to the Dreaming. The Anangu[1] think about stories in certain ways and ascribe psychological functions to sand storytelling that relate to the issues of authorship, communication with Ancestors, 'strengthening the mind', containment and control of emotions, 'free' expression, and knowledge creation and transmission. I point out that the nature of stories by children has changed historically from a predominantly canonical style towards the self-referential reporting of concrete events and describe certain age-related features of sand storytelling, namely the early acquisition of practical skills (posture, movements, beating of wire), the mixture of fantasy and reality in the stories by young girls, and the socially oriented narratives by older girls. The discussion reveals that storytelling, and specifically sand storytelling, is socially effective. Children who create stories are active agents who participate in, rework and integrate themselves into the larger context of their lives and cultural traditions, according to their own needs, capacities and desires.

Introduction

At Ernabella on Anangu Pitjantjatjara Yankunytjatjara (APY) Lands in north-west South Australia, the creation of stories drawn in the sand is a favourite medium for girls to present their thoughts.[2] Since I first began research in this remote community of around 500 people in 1995, I cannot recall a day there which passed without seeing sand stories being performed. The telling of sand stories, like the activity of dreaming (Poirier, 2003), is part and parcel of the daily 'flow of events'. Girls begin to practice the bodily posture and movements of the distinctive technique at about 2 years of age before their narrative skills begin to emerge. Sand storytelling is a life-long practice, but most prolific during childhood and adolescence. It is a very particular form of communication that, through its rhythmic and even musical quality, engages all senses and layers of experience, including those beginning in early infancy (Eickelkamp, Forthcoming).

My starting point for the discussion of the social meaning of sand stories is that children create meaning through play talk.[3] Such a perspective brings forth the well-established observation that, for children, playing constitutes a particular dimension of reality; it can be fun and funny but it is also a serious matter. Through storytelling, children foster reasoning, imagination and memory as they work through difficult issues, re-live and interpret particular events, invent personas that reflect their inner world, or project themselves imaginatively into the future. Furthermore, an understanding of stories by children as a vehicle of meaning-making can contribute to understanding the nature and status of stories in the Anangu society (Klapproth, 2004), and perhaps in Aboriginal societies at large (Duelke, 2005; Hiatt, 1975; Sansom, 1980, 2001).[4] Understanding Aboriginal narrative practices is essential for teachers in their efforts to build on children's storytelling skills as part of teaching them to read and write. As I seek to show, telling stories is a social activity that also involves the narrator's recognition of the role of listeners. In sharp contrast to the short, plain and seemingly non-judgemental utterance with which the Aboriginal children I know impart painful facts – 'My Dad is in gaol', 'My little brother, he's dead' – stories are what John von Sturmer (2005) calls 'socially productive'. A story allows narrator and listener to leave things open to interpretation, to conceal and reveal, to contest and then arrive at a shared version, to include others both in the plot and in the telling (by allowing side comments), and to take turns as narrators. In short, storytelling creates social spaces.

This chapter considers some types of stories, themes, and contexts for performing these – all with a view to understand how the Aṉangu children at different ages produce social meaning through sand stories. The focus here forms only one dimension of a larger, 3-year-long study that seeks to create an understanding of how the children's inner world relates to the social field. The study examines – mostly outside the institutional settings of school and childcare – the symbolic and social development of three girls whose activities I have documented through participant-observation and note-taking, photographs and film, and children's drawings on paper. Fieldwork at Ernabella stretches over 7 months and is distributed over several trips across the 3 years.[5] The girls were 3, 5 and 8 years old when I began focused observations with them at the end of Year 2004. It is their play and their sand stories in particular that I have captured on film. I estimated that, on average, the two older girls, now 7 and 10, would tell sand stories for 2 hours per day, in sessions ranging between 1 minute and 1 hour. Occasionally, a girl would take over the filming and offer a 'guided tour' through the community. At the end of each day, I transcribed and translated the play dialogues from Pitjantjatjara into English with the child's mother (in case of the youngest), or a professional Aṉangu interpreter, or a teenage girl. Good rapport with families prior to working with their children provided the basis of trust that has allowed for my relatively free movement through the community with the observing 'eye' of the camera. The focused observation of and engagement with the three girls is supported by cross-sectional observations of children in peer groups and in the context of family life.

Milpatjunanyi: technique, contexts and language

In sand storytelling, the girl at play sits on the ground alone or with others. She is speaking towards a small cleared patch in front of her where she illustrates her account by drawing in the sand, often tapping a bent piece of wire into the story field as she is speaking. At the end of the session, the marks are wiped out, leaving a smooth fan-shaped patch of sand.[6] The local Pitjantjatjara term for sand storytelling is *milpatjunanyi*, which literally means 'putting [*tjunanyi*] the story-stick [*milpa*]', or *walkatjunanyi* ('making marks'). Sometimes, the practice is simply called 'storytelling' (*tjukurpa wangkanyi*).

The word *milpa* refers to a twig, now a piece of bent wire about 50 cm long, 'story-wire' as the children call it, that is used to beat a rhythm, draw lines, poke and swipe clear the ground, or, less frequently, to point to something outside the representational story field. Unless the storyteller is left-handed, the wire at play is held in the right hand and often employed in alternation with one or several fingers and other parts of the left hand to draw graphs. Before metal wire became available and until about 40 years ago, women used flexible sticks as their story-stick, as well as eucalypt leaves (*nyalpi*) to represent play characters. The wire is a personal possession that, borrowed for too long or stolen by another girl, may quickly become a source for serious argument. Carried slung around the neck throughout the day, it signals being 'street smart', that is, readiness at any moment to demonstrate local knowledge, current relations to peers, and state of mind. 'Putting the story-stick' in a variety of ways also expresses emotions: the wire can be tapped gently on the ground, hammered restlessly, beaten steadily or held in suspension; it is flexed affectionately by stroking it with the hand, or bent and stretched vigorously.

By 'graphs' I refer to simple shapes (see Figure 4.1) – circle or semi circle, square, straight or meandering line, or dots – that are drawn, scratched or poked into the sand. Individual shapes have a range of meanings that are not pre-established, yet personal and group conventions play a role. Moreover, the objects referred to are morphologically related (see also Munn, 1966). For instance, whether in a single story or in separate accounts, a circle usually refers

Figure 4.1 Illustration by a young woman of how she used to play sand storytelling with other girls in a cubby house. Ernabella 2005.
Author's sketch.

to round things such as the wheel of a car, a waterhole, or a bucket. A single line most frequently represents a person. Placed in relation to other graphs and drawn longer or shorter, variations of the simple line illustrate posture (e.g. sitting when strongly bent), location, activity and perhaps relatedness to other people.[7] To illustrate: Remembering her own childhood sand stories, a young woman, mother of the youngest girl I worked with, depicted (Figure 4.1) how she and other girls used to play '*wiltja-wiltjangka*' ('in the playhouse').

In this case there is a double reference to *milpatjunanyi*: She depicted a cubby house by way of illustration in a sand story, and then showed how the girls would play sand storytelling inside the cubby house. The scene traced in Figure 4.1 depicts a number of girls (the small semi-circles whose equal size may indicate that all are of similar age) sitting around a fire (central circle) inside a playhouse in the shape of a traditional shelter called *wiltja* (large circle with opening). A blanket is spread out on the ground (larger rectangle) and there are lunchboxes with hot chips and soft drinks (small squares) from the store that the girls have brought along. The drawing illustrates a generic yet highly realistic situation; the young woman did not say what stories were being shared or who was present, yet other women would readily verify the account as a correct 'template' from their own specific memories of playing 'cubby house'.

Combined with one another and verbally linked to objects, places, people and events in time, the graphs take on specific meanings. They cannot be read like an alphabetical script – but note that the girls occasionally include this into a sand drawing, especially initials of personal names – as they are an integral part of live conversations. In other words, the graphic depictions can only be understood through participation in context-specific communications.[8] Importantly, it is mostly the children themselves who create the contexts for such communications, by finding the time and a reason to play sand stories, by choosing a location, and by identifying what is to be told.

Contexts for engaging in sand stories vary within and across ages. A little toddler girl might be scratching lines into the sand at her grandmother's encouragement, or a group of three, five and even up to fifteen girls between the ages 5 and 12 may be immersed in cheerful and rather noisy exchanges of stories by the side of the road or at school during breaks. A lonely teenager might be absorbed in what looks like the performance of an internal dialogue, as she sits by herself in the yard of her home. Senior women often extend our conversation into visual comments in the sand, thereby transforming the ground on which we sit, and indeed the entire sphere of the group, into a demarcated communicative space. In preparation of a genealogy recording session, a woman might sketch silently her family tree with tallying lines in the sand (see also Dousset, 2003) only to wipe it out and clear the ground when the interview begins.

From around the age of 5, the most frequently drawn motif is the house. Rather than round bush shelters, as in Figure 4.1, girls today depict the floor plan of rectangular houses in the community (Figure 4.2). Such floor plans often set the scene in which a family story is re-enacted, and there is also a guessing game about whose house has been drawn in the sand. Stories by children that relate concrete events from everyday life seem to outnumber children's performances of folk and fairy tales, and, when they do enact such canonical stories, the girls tend to transform the fictional characters into real family members.

Milpatjunanyi is nearly always performed in the children's first language – Pitjantjatjara or Yankunytjatjara. Lesser known dialects and languages spoken by a few children are sometimes mocked. For example, girls mimicked sand

Figure 4.2 Floor plan of a house with two people (U-shapes) sitting outside to the right, drawn by a c.20-year-old woman at Ernabella, 2005.
Author's photograph.

stories performed by a young Luritja speaker, by producing an unintelligible staccato that was meant to imitate the sound of that language.

Tjukurpa: the place of story in the Anangu children's life

O'Shannessy (Forthcoming) has offered pertinent observations about the social functions of stories in the life of Warlpiri children in northern Central Australia. These also hold true for Ernabella: Storytelling in the family context is a highly valued practice and an important vehicle of knowledge transmission. Children recognise that 'talking story' is a designated social technique. Furthermore, adults may encourage children to 'talk story' or they engage in children's play talk in order to manipulate the child's behaviour; for example, to prevent a fight between children.

In the mind of Anangu (meaning 'person' and 'body', but used to collectively refer to Aboriginal people with ties to the APY Lands), sand storytelling is especially important at another level; it is one of many practices of everyday life that adults say originates in the Dreaming. The term for Dreaming, *Tjukurpa*, which refers to all Ancestral manifestations (place, song, design, birthmark, name, oral account of Ancestral action), is also used for stories of any kind. Another term for 'story', but less used by the children, is *ara*. According to Goddard (1992), *ara* can refer to 'story, yarn, history'; 'thing said'; 'occasion, time'; and 'way, custom'. I take the particular meaning range of the two terms as an indication that the sanctioning of action through narrativisation presents an important link between Ancestors and humans, across time and generations. Children not only sanction certain versions of events in their lives through repeated storytelling, they are also regarded to be especially close to the Ancestral realm. And although unaware of the link between their play stories and Ancestral practice, it is precisely the performance of Ancestral activities unbeknownst to the children which demonstrates this link. For the Anangu this link is the foundation for other forms of knowing the Dreaming later in life. It is proper Ancestral Law and custom for children to play in general, and although young women and girls do not tell Dreaming stories in *milpatjunanyi*, it is nevertheless the sanctioned playful practice for girls to tell stories. Like the typical childhood occupations of boys, such as killing birds for eating by throwing rocks at them in the context of make-believe play at being grown up, the gender restriction of *milpatjunanyi* as a female activity is

tjukuritja, meaning something they do in unconscious continuity with Ancestral women's practice. In this sense, children are thought of as following the
'law' of the Dreaming.[9] If *milpatjunanyi* is from the Dreaming, it is a 'small'
Law, not a 'big' one like the man-making ceremonies or determination of
marriage partners (Peter Nyaningu, personal communication). Nevertheless,
the status of sand storytelling as a lawful and ordering activity is important –
not as a ritual performance in the strict sense, but as a ritualised expression in
everyday life. In the *modus operandi* of 'law as story', social efficacy is achieved
by 'witnessing' (Sansom, 1980; von Sturmer, 2002), and in *milpatjunanyi* too
the presence of onlookers and listeners is important. Establishing relatedness
by sharing news and memories is complemented by the personal autonomy
and authorship of the owner of the story-wire who rarely allows her audience
to make a mark in the patch of ground cleared in front of her. Girls often sit
together but simultaneously each performs a different story.

Stories convey a socially significant message, yet not necessarily in narrative
form. Often, the story is only alluded to by personalised signs – marks on canvas, or initials of a personal name written on the wall. These instances make
clear that the message may not be 'in' the story or hidden 'behind' the sign, but
in the fact of the appearance of that sign; already 'telling' that somebody has
made it, at a certain time and place. As von Sturmer (2002) poignantly
observed, making marks is more than linking people, places and time – somebody has created a moment and a place in the first instance by making a mark
then and there. After all, this is how 'story places', that is, Ancestral sites, came
into being, and therefore may be regarded as representations of Ancestral
activity. Here then may lie the primary social meaning of making marks and
of 'talking story' in the realm of Ancestors and living humans alike: to mark
the presence of people, that is, to assert the 'pure and utter beingness of the
person' (von Sturmer, 2002), which is the point of departure for any form of
engagement and communication. Moreover, the 'now' of the mark, and especially the repeated instantiations in sand stories, present an ongoing engagement with memory. Like those senior artists whose paintings flow from a
reverie in Ancestral country, sand storytelling by girls produce a 'stratification
of the memory of events in places' (Dolk, 2006, p. 40). Dolk's view of the visual
poetry of Gija painter, Paddy Bedford, is true for *milpatjunanyi*: an 'imaginary
space' is filled between place, story and gesture made tangible in images.

The filling of an imaginary space with symbols is a complex process in which
thought, image, speech and mark-making gesture are closely intertwined. This
intertwining is also embodied in the story-wire, which is both symbol and

symbol-making tool. As such the story-wire shares with ritual objects their dual meaning-structure (Moisseeff, 2002). Indeed, '*milpa*' is not just any twig (called *punu*), but that which '[has] got story' acquired through use.[10] *Milpa* is not only the storytelling instrument but is also the idea of story and it too can be referred to as *Tjukurpa*.[11]

'Proper stories', different truths

Older women say that, in the past, *milpatjunanyi* was a more formal affair. They remember the cherished custom of boys and girls sitting around an adult narrator before going to sleep, in order to listen to 'bedtime stories', meaning folktales and family stories that have been transmitted for generations and could be labelled 'canonical'. The girls would then enact these canonical narratives that the Anangu sometimes refer to as 'proper stories'. Characteristically, they feature birds (*tjulpu*), butterflies (*pinta-pinta*) and other 'natural' phenomena that represent people and human experience, for example, through such personas as Wati Walawuru (Wedgetail Eagle Man) and Minyma Kaanka (Black Crow Woman), and there is the beautiful story of Kupi-kupi, the Whirlwind that took away a little girl.[12] Undoubtedly, these play stories are anchored in and reflect the transformative power of the Dreaming, and some stories are 'public' or 'open' (*ala*) versions of mythic episodes. However, other stories are not seen to have originated in the Dreaming and instead are said to have been made up by a particular person for the purpose of entertaining the children in the family, or to have existed as 'anyway' stories for a long time.

For children today sand stories are highly realistic and a sign of mental strength, including those that an adult or outsider would regard as fantasy. They most commonly depict events – remembered, as they are being observed, and sometimes in anticipation – that preoccupy the child at the time, consciously or unconsciously, and hence reflect as to how children perceive their everyday life. To relate an experience in the form of a story is called '*kulira wangkanyi*' ('recount'), whereas to make up a story in one's mind that does not relate to an experience or shared knowledge is referred to as '*katangku kulira wangkanyi*' (literally 'the head is thinking a story', meaning 'fantasy'). However, unlike O'Shannessy (Forthcoming) who reports that Warlpiri children only rarely produce fantasy stories, I have observed that young girls in particular are adept at mixing the two types of narrative. Interlacing perceptions with personal associations (and hence subjective experiencing), their story sessions can be fragmentary and replete with transitions from one topic to another, similar to free play in general. Some common early childhood fantasies become collectively instituted (mostly as a kind of monster) and are reported as 'real' even among teenagers.

A distinctive form of narrative is a name guessing game that encourages inferential thinking. The player begins by describing a distinctive feature of the person in mind, for example, 'long curly hair'. She will add further information about family status, place of residence, etc. until another child has identified who is meant. A variation of this game is to write the initials of a person's name in the sand, which may also be used to silently name a particular person in a conversation. The primary function of this form of playful encoding is to test social knowledge and to thereby identify the insider status of the children present.

To be able to identify people on the basis of concealed or 'encoded' messages is indeed of critical importance. A secret language used by Pitjantjatjara teenage girls has been described by Langlois (2006) and one could similarly interpret as in-group markers the prolific graffiti on the indoor and outdoor walls of houses (Kral and Ellis, Chapter 7; Nicholls, 2000), and children's cutting of letters into the bark of trees. I was taken on a graffiti-site-seeing tour by two 7-year-old girls who unravelled the layers of family histories in each room of a residential house, where individuals had left their initials and other 'tags' in an effort to leave their mark – meaning presence – for those who can decipher it.

From middle-childhood onwards, a reportage style of sand stories is prolific and shows commonalities with the narrative traits of traditional Pitjantjatjara folklore.[13] Klapproth (2004, pp. 282 ff.) identified aspects of text-building conventions and story schemata that appear to also characterise at least some contemporary stories by children. These include a 'shifting character focus', the motif of a journey that structures stories into a rhythmic cycle, the 'retracing' of the same event by different characters in a process of slow discovery by way of reconstruction, and an overall non-hierarchical structure. There is an important difference between our approaches – identifying Pitjantjatjara narrative aesthetics in Klapproth's case, and understanding the inner life of individual children in the present study; as also perhaps between the emotional significance that self-created stories have for children on the one hand, and the collectively held stories transmitted by adults on the other. The child who is recounting what happened last night at home, imagines with anticipation the next trip to town, or enacts fantasies of being a mother, is living through a whole gamut of emotions. I also think that children's stories told by adults are emotionally engaging and hierarchical in the sense that they have dramatic peaks that are prosodically emphasised, for example, in the stories mentioned above: when Whirlwind takes the girl away one storyteller launched into a high pitch and then paused looking up into the sky; and the killing of Black Crow Woman was recounted with a tone that evokes heavy blows and sadness.[14]

Interestingly, some girls recognise that their contemporary stories differ from the canonical 'bedtime stories' of their grandmothers. Asked if she liked to tell such kind of stories in *milpatjunanyi*, a very intelligent girl replied, 'I don't talk story like that – only what's in my head.' She meant that, instead of reproducing established narratives, she is used to telling stories about concrete events that she remembers and might want to share with other children.[15] A few weeks later, the same girl revealed another layer of meaning to her explanation. Asked if there was anything at all that she would like to say about being a child at Ernabella, this 12-year-old girl explained, '*Wiya* [no], I can't think. My head's *kura* [bad]. That's what they've told me. I can't do it anymore like before.' She said this as she was busily piling up charcoaled and white rocks collected from a burnt-out house, in concert with several other girls who were getting ready to make floor drawings. Indeed, as one of the oldest, she seemed to be guiding younger girls and her actions appeared entirely co-ordinated. As she had identified it herself, the problem was to create a story out of experiences, even if these are about storytelling and drawing. In this sense, one could say she has difficulty translating action into narrative thinking, rather than thoughts into action.

Perhaps more importantly, the girl's account of her own shortcoming tells us something about the status of the 'story' as a designated social category among children. It is a category of re-enactment or representational performance, and as such different from an event or circumstance *per se*. The girl had come to think of herself as unable to talk in a representative, that is, socially sanctioned, manner (she used to depict with confidence her large family tree just 3 years earlier) because she cannot tell a 'proper story' anymore. The fact that she explained her condition by saying 'they've told me' indicates how strongly self-perceptions are shaped by what others say. This orientation is inculcated in both positive and negative terms from early childhood onwards through socialisation techniques and peer behaviour, possibly more so in the past than now.

Developmental thresholds

Sand stories are an important medium of transmitting oral traditions and family knowledge across and among the generations, including between males (who listen) and females. As in other desert areas, the technique is part of the socialisation process that varies in locally specific ways. Munn described for Warlpiri families at Yuendumu that very young girls do not perform sand stories. Only at the end of late childhood, from around age 9 when the ability to tell stories is consolidated, may girls use the sand story technique to convey personal experiences or invented narratives (Munn, 1973, pp. 63-64). Christine Watson, in her account of Kukatja women's sand drawing at Balgo, explains that children and teenagers are instructed in hunting and gathering, social protocol and behavioural expectations (Watson, 2003, pp. 82-83) through stories performed by women; she does not report storytelling by children.

At Ernabella, sand storytelling begins at a very young age. Children first imbibe the overall movement of *milpatjunanyi* in infancy, namely by watching and listening and by feeling the moving body, while being held in mother's lap. Sometimes other older female relatives may guide the hand of the baby through the sand. From about 2.5 years of age girls create their own story space and try out a variety of speech styles and levels of pretence. If I consider this experimentation with speech styles to be an indication of the emergence of the 'narrated self' (Stern, 1989) in Anangu childhood, then it accords with the developmental stage of symbolic play that psychologists, notably Jean Piaget (1951), have conceptualised for Western children.[16] Make-believe play at being grown up flourishes during the third and fourth years of life, when girls literally create for themselves elaborate love stories and encounters with malignant ogre figures.[17] As mentioned earlier, in sand stories by young children fantasy and memory are closely related and often fuse into a single account. At this stage, graphic depiction and verbalisation appear equally prominent and a story often evolves with the naming of drawn shapes.

From roughly the age of 5, the sand stories begin to cover overtly social events in which the child has participated, such as going on a shopping trip, or a school excursion, or what happened at home. These reportage style accounts are mostly told to other girls and show a marked attention to select details. For example, what an adult would describe as a shopping trip to another community might be pinpointed in the girls' story as 'the trip when the chocolate milk fell off the spare tyre'. These stories are performed with considerable speed, and a high level of action both in the plot and the performance that is characteristic and meaningful in the context of storytelling among peers.

The playing with speech illustrated in the sand affords especial joy because of its acknowledged status as part of an established tradition. Claiming their identity as Aṉangu girls by displaying, with an air of importance, their evolving mastery of the technique, they also discover the following general rule of mindful interaction: you don't just make a statement about something or a person, but you create a story around it. Moreover, I sometimes got the impression that participation in events was cherished because it can then become a story to be owned, even at a point when the event was still taking place (e.g. drawing the story of a football match then and there as the game is in its final quarter). 'Talking story' is a sign of maturity and, rather than a diversion from 'real' social life, an indispensable aspect of it.

A child who shows that she can tell stories has reached a cultural milestone. For example, one girl with notably advanced skills as a performer and imitator of other people's idiosyncrasies of talking, movement of eyes and mouth, and gait, has been called 'Little Woman' (*Minyma Kulunypa*) ever since she was about 2 years old. The term *minyma* is usually reserved for mature women with two children, whereas the term for a girl and a young woman is *kungka*. This playing with life stage terms acknowledges this young girl's capacity to mirror others (through imitation) and 'talk like a woman', which in turn is appreciated as a sign that she is on the best way to becoming a socially productive person. Her mother is proud of her and, in the presence of an outsider like myself, more distant kin suggest that her social skill makes her a proud representative of the Aṉangu culture. Furthermore, the discrepancy between the girl's young age and mature demeanour is amusing and she is often encouraged to perform stories for the entertainment of adults. She willingly does so with pleasure and relishes being watched.

However, it is also possible to unlearn (*ngurparinganyi*) the art of storytelling and this seems to have happened to this most prolific player. At age 5, 'Little Woman' had moved to Alice Springs with her mother. After 7 months of being away from her home community, I asked her to play *milpatjunanyi*. This was on a visit to an Aboriginal community not far from town, which I recount in the present tense.

> She is delighted at my suggestion and we set out to find a piece of wire in the yard of a relative. I set up the video camera, ready to shoot the latest story by my young friend, who smiles at me with anticipation as she sits down on the ground that she wipes clear. She begins to tap the wire, saying, '*Ngayulu, ngayulu* [I, I] . . . *ngayulu*

[I] . . . nyaa [what]?' Again she wipes clear the ground to start all over, yet she is
unable to launch into a story. She seems 'stuck' like a broken record. And indeed,
after yet another unsuccessful attempt, she becomes distressed and runs to her
mother, asking if she could help her tell a story.

At first, I was surprised. I had thought that *milpatjunanyi* was a skill that
would not be forgotten once learnt. However, there is a difference between
technique and story, or form and content, and it is precisely the latter that
requires a meaningful social context in order to function. The little girl was
perfectly able to engage in play dialogues with another toddler and me. What
was missing, I realised, was the continuous prompting and encouragement by
older children and adults, who like taking a child by the hand, thus guide in the
unfolding of the story. Indeed, very young children are frequently prompted
and prodded to repeat what has been said to them, and warmly rewarded when
they do, while creative variations on the part of the child (indicating his or her
personal will) are loudly cheered. This and a high level of repetition are part
and parcel of the socialisation into discursive forms of expression, and it seems
that sand storytelling requires a particularly strong mirroring by others.

Strengthening the mind

Although the official view is that boys do not play *milpatjunanyi*, several young
mothers are allowing and are even encouraging their toddler sons to take up
the story-wire. Possibly reflecting the formal educational input and the new
ideas about child rearing, or having been influenced by the people from
Warlpiri and Arrernte communities where boys and men have been observed
to also perform sand stories (Basedow, 1925, p. 70–71; Munn, 1965, p. 21),
young mothers tell me that it is important for children to play as they like and
to thereby develop their imagination.

Géza Róheim (1945, p. 7; , 1974, pp. 77 ff.) had made a similar point on the
basis of his psychoanalytic research with Pitjantjatjara and Arrernte people in
1929, when he interpreted the game as a form of day-dreaming and fantasy
about the future, especially the girls' future motherhood.[18] I agree that day-
dreaming and the therapeutic effect it affords are important, as Róheim seems
to suggest; this may even have intensified since people began to live perma-
nently in communities where boredom and family conflict pose considerable
stress, especially for young adults. In fact, one mother told me that her daughters play *milpatjunanyi* in order to 'give their mind a rest'. In addition to resting
the mind, the self-absorbed play has another function. Green (personal communication) pointed out that playing sand stories signals 'minding one's own

business', as opposed to being nosy and prying. One can readily see why it is important to have recognised means of distancing oneself from others and especially from trouble in a small community such as Ernabella, where everyone knows everyone else and intersubjective dynamics are intense. Although ill will is often ascribed to strangers, the high level of interpersonal connections is manifested in the strong concern that others want to manipulate one's mind by weakening the will, for example, through dream visitations instigated by 'love magic', bone pointing, or 'modern' magic watched on TV.

Mindfulness and composed thoughtful behaviour are attributes that are highly valued by adults and children alike. Adults expressing their views on socialisation make clear the importance of strengthening the mind through storytelling.[19] Director of the Anangu Education Service, Katrina Tjitayi (Tjitayi and Lewis, Forthcoming), gave an insightful account of her childhood memories of anticipations and the experience of learning; how it felt for her to 'be strong within her mind', and why children's capacity to project themselves imaginatively into the future might have deteriorated. She remembers how children used to be confident about their future, and that storytelling was an integral part of imagining the self with joy as a grown up. Reflective and absorbed play over extensive periods of time appears compromised today because children who spend much time in the communities are distracted by noise and demands and things within their sight, such as commercial toys and entertainment.

At this point, however, children still manage to carve out time for solitary reflection. A 9-year-old girl explained that sand stories are 'for thinking', upon which she made a drawing of just this idea. Spontaneously, she took a piece of white rock and drew the floor plan of a house onto the concrete slab that used to be the veranda of the burnt-out ruin of a home where she was playing with several other girls. Her sketch shows a person in a furnished room sitting on a sofa busy thinking. She did not say what about, because that was not her point. Withdrawal and reflection are especially important in the morning, and children seek to compose body and mind before engaging others.[20] Boys too appreciate the importance of reflection. One early morning, I observed the 8-year-old grandson of a friend sitting on his own in the sun. Still unkempt and before breakfast, he nevertheless looked calm and self-contained. I asked him what he was playing. He replied with a very serious look on his little face, '*Inkantja wiya, kulira*' – 'I'm not playing, I'm thinking'. A 10-year-old girl played *milpatjunanyi* in total silence for about 20 minutes. She had just got out of bed and went straight outside, to sit down on the ground with her back leaning against the brick wall of the house. Looking very sleepy and relaxed, her legs pulled up, she began to draw a silent story into the sand, marking the ground with the wire in between yawns. She would not tell me what it was about, only that she did not depict a dream.

A final illustration

To conclude with a brief example I describe the narrative production of a 6-year-old girl, who performed the European folktale Goldilocks and the Three Bears (see, e.g. Opie and Opie, 1974) in a 25-minute session in front of three other girls who were listening and waiting for their turn. Most notable in this creation is that all characters are named after members of her extended family, including one of the girls in the audience who, at one point, began to protest. A version of the story had been read to the children at school, and the storyteller seemed to use it as a frame to rework family dynamics and at the same time entertain, and thus impress her friends. It is at once 'cheeky' and affectionate. It is 'cheeky' because authority to talk about others and assign roles to them derives in part from the canonical status of the fairytale, which she insists must be told to the end; she dishes out roles to real people like Mother Bear dishes out the porridge. It is also affectionate because her father's sister, who actually cooks porridge for many of the children in the family, is acknowledged, and her three male cousins make for very friendly bears. 'Goldilocks' is the blonde daughter of another aunt, and her closest friend and age-mate. It is she who tried to intervene when the plot depicts her as eating the porridge – an attempt to insert herself as a real person that made her protest look even funnier and the narrator had all sympathies on her side. An intervention on a different level occurred when another girl claimed that she would be the first to see the as yet unborn baby of the pregnant aunt who is cooking the porridge in the story. This reference erupted when the narrator impersonated the youngest boy (little bear) and spoke in a high-pitched baby talk. The intervention provoked the anger of the storyteller. The ending of the story is very conciliatory. Instead of having Goldilocks run away, she changed the plot and makes the youngest boy to ask the aunt if the newcomer could please stay and play with them.

This story illustrates that children move with ease between different social and cultural domains and assimilate material from the classroom into their personal life. It is also a masterful demonstration of how stories can be used to enact, play with and comment on other people without impinging on their personal autonomy; the young narrator has skilfully integrated playing and reality by having inserted real people into a make-believe setting. Her story is in this sense outward oriented and intended to evoke an existing social field. It remains, however, within the family, even though she leaves herself and closest relatives out of the plot – perhaps in an attempt to conceal herself. She does, however, claim her presence in another way, namely by the act of telling a story, which she recounts in full length and great detail, to the point of putting to the test the patience of her friends who are waiting for their turn. Embodied in this example is then what I had earlier referred to as 'social productivity'. Things are left open to interpretation, concealed and revealed, tested and contested, while including others both in the plot and in the telling.

Notes

1. 'Aṉangu', which will be used throughout this book, is the conventional spelling of the name for Aboriginal people from this part of the western desert. The underscored n represents a retroflex nasal sound.

2. The material presented here is from field trips in 2004, 2005, 2006 and 2007 that are part of research-in-progress focusing on children's play and social imagination at Ernabella (Australian Research Council Discovery Project grant DP0556111). Previous research at Ernabella was funded by the Australian Institute of Aboriginal and Torres Strait Islander Studies and Macquarie University. I thank Jenny Green for her critical queries and insightful comparative information. My greatest debt is to the children and families who continue to share their life and knowledge with me, and especially to Margaret Dagg for her excellent transcriptions and translations.

3. Much of the literature on the subject of meaning-making in children's play narratives is in the fields of developmental psychology and play therapy studies (Bretherton, 1984; Emde et al., 2003; Slade & Wolf, 1994), and often inspired by psychoanalytic work with children. Other work includes folklorists (Factor, 1988), anthropologists (Goldman, 1998) and linguists considering meaning-making by children in the context of their play talk (O'Shannessy, Forthcoming). The present discussion does not analyse the content of play stories, which is reserved for another study.

4. Hiatt's (1975) discussion of the challenge to classify Aboriginal narratives is still the most succinct. For engrossing demonstrations of what stories 'do' see Sansom (1980; 2001) and Duelke (2005). None of the authors, however, consider the status of stories in the world of children.

5. In 2007 this totals 369 hours of focused observation with extensive field notes, and c.30 hours of video footage of various play activities, including 159 play talks of various length.

6. A discussion of the symbolic significance of 'clearing the ground' before and after storytelling in the sand is reserved for another occasion.

7. Detailed descriptions and illustrations of Central and Western Desert graphic systems used in the sand and in canvas painting – but not specifically those of the children – have been provided by Munn (1965; 1973) and Watson (2003).

8. For an anthropological discussion of the nature of literacy in Central Australian iconography see Biddle (1996; 2007).

9. For further suggestions about cosmological underpinnings of the gendered practice in a Western Australian community see Watson (2003). As indicated in footnote 10 below, *milpatjunanyi* is also part of the greater symbolic system that binds men, women and children to *Tjukurpa*. Although boys occasionally play sand stories, as a named practice it is considered to belong to the realm of girls and women.

10. Green (personal communication) observes that, in the Arandic region, 'narrators of sand stories are careful with the disposal of the storytelling apparatus, such as leaves. They will say of them that they are '*ayeye-akerte*', literally 'having story'. I assume care is taken because the imbued narrative power represents a kind of agency of the object.

11. There exist symbolic associations between the 'talking' stick and other paraphernalia that forge further links to the Dreaming and other 'mundane' practices. Among the objects that I understand relate symbolically to *milpa* are: the hitting stick of the men (*tjutinypa*) that they use as a clapping instrument in song; the ordinary walking stick of old people who are the guardians of *Tjukurpa*; the digging stick (*wana*) of women in their reproductive age; their fighting stick (*wana*); the poison stick (bone) of the sorcerer; and the women's ceremonial pole (*kuturu*) which, as ancestral body and penis, emphasises the interlinking of body and soul as a necessary condition for the perpetuation of life. Watson (2003) describes similar symbolic linkages in women's sand drawings at Balgo. Highlighting the equivalence between ground and human body, she observes that some kind of agency and consciousness are ascribed to the ground, which thereby becomes a witness to human mark-making on its surface. The local Kukatja terms *walkala* for public sand drawing and *milpapungin* for sand drawings that are accompanied by the rhythmic beating of the wire, have special potency. For example, the latter is associated with the sound of cracking joints that in turn relates to the practice of massaging children and hence to ideas about growth, maturation and sexuality (Watson, 2003, pp. 76-79). Some icons ('graphs') are gendered: the U-shape commonly represents a shelter (*wuungku*), which is linguistically associated with women, birthing, uterus and placenta, while 'the line is related to concepts of flowing and of water, and is associated with masculinity' (pp. 103-4). The 'poking and penetration aspects of walkala are associated with spears and spear-throwers which are symbols of men' (p. 107).

    John von Sturmer (1978, pp. 299–303, 501) made the important observation that humans frighten and swear at the Ancestors in order to manipulate them into performing favourable acts, such as 'increasing' the growth of animals and plants. Among the Wik, people say that they are frightening the Ancestors or spirits by stirring the site up. I am inclined to think that the human manipulation of a story-making (i.e. law-making) instrument is akin to the handling of objects (including places and ritual paraphernalia) with the intention of eliciting Ancestral activity. This has another empirical component: provoking a response and prodding someone into compliance are social techniques that apply to Ancestors and people alike, and especially to young children who are often pinched and poked by others. One could say then that children, when poking the ground in *milpatjunanyi*, are stirring a symbolic place, sometimes with aggression, as if they were prodding another person.

12. Beautiful performances of such folktale are documented in the video *Pitjantjatjara Sand Stories*, 1999, produced by Ernabella Arts and Lucienne Fontannaz.

13. Children are also exposed to a variety of oral texts, including prayers, songs and sermons in frequently held church services; reporting of community issues, naming of problems and planning in the prolific number of community meetings; acted dialogues in movies on television, video and DVD; news and debates on television; and the pedagogical presentations at school. It remains to be examined if and how these differ from the children's stories told in the sand.

14. It is problematic to describe the aesthetic character of stories, when, as Green (personal communication) pointed out, we do not fully understand what constitutes a story in the mind of their creators. Moreover, stories do not exist in a fixed, and in this sense, objective form. The non-hierarchical organisation of content described by Klapproth (2004) could be a surface phenomenon, namely in relation to the performance of stories, especially in the ritual context, which takes into account that some participants know more than others. Furthermore, my impression is that stories for children, such as folktales, are uniquely 'plotted', unusually complete and emotionally engaging.

15. Most such stories that I have recorded contain the self-referential pronoun 'I' and the storyteller appears as one of the protagonists. It is difficult to establish if this presents an innovation. Nevertheless, older women prefer tacit references to the self in canonical accounts and tell me that to speak directly about the self in sand stories is not something they used to do in their childhood.

16. Anthropologists have long challenged Piaget's allegedly 'uncontextualised' model of developmental stages of play (see Schwartzman, 1978, pp. 41–59), which I, however, still find useful.

17. For an extensive psychoanalytical discussion of an ogre figure that features in Central Australian stories for and by children, dreams, play and drawings, see Eickelkamp (2004).

18. A missionary at Hermannsburg, Carl Strehlow (1913; cited by Hersey, 2004, pp. 27–28) described an oracle sand story game played by grown-up Arrernte girls at the turn of the twentieth century. The game is called *ilbamara*, which he translated as 'the fertile one'.

19. Older people especially fear that they might lose their narrative capacities, and a major source of concern is diabetes. A very senior woman told me she was worried her diabetes was going to cloud her mind and diminish her capacity to create narratives for her grandchildren, and to retell old stories or devise coherent accounts of current events.

20. It is regarded as particularly harmful to wake children from their sleep when their soul might still be travelling during nocturnal dreaming.

References

Basedow, H. (1925). *The Australian Aboriginal*. Adelaide: F.W. Preece and Sons.

Biddle, J. L. (1996). When not writing is writing. *Australian Aboriginal Studies, 1*, 21–33.

Biddle, J. L. (2007). Country, skin, canvas: the intercorporeal art of Kathleen Petyarre. *Australian and New Zealand Journal of Art, 4*(1), 61–76.

Bretherton, I. (ed.) (1984). *Symbolic Play: The Development of Social Understanding*. Orlando, FL: Academic Press.

Dolk, M. (2006). Are we strangers in this place? In *Paddy Bedford – Exhibition Catalog* (pp. 17–49). Sydney: Museum of Contemporary Art.

Dousset, L. (2003). Indigenous modes of representing social relationships: a short critique of the 'genealogical concept'. *Australian Aboriginal Studies, 2003*(1), 19–29.

Duelke, B. (2005). Übereine Thematisierung des Möglichen. *Zeitschrift für Ethnologie, 130*, 99–125.

Eickelkamp, U. (2004). Egos and ogres: aspects of psychosexual development and cannibalistic demons in Central Australia. *Oceania, 74*(3), 161–89.

Eickelkamp, U. (Forthcoming). Play, imagination and early experience: sand storytelling and continuity of being among Anangu Pitjantjatjara girls. In G. Robinson, U. Eickelkamp, J. Goodnow and I. Katz (eds), *Contexts of Child Development: Culture, Policy and Intervention*. Darwin and Sydney: Charles Darwin University Press.

Emde, R. N., Wolf, D. P. and Oppenheim, D. (eds) (2003). *Revealing the Inner Worlds of Young Children: The MacArthur Story Stem Battery and Parent–Child Narratives*. New York: Oxford University Press.

Factor, J. (1988). *Captain Cook Chased a Chook: Children's Folklore in Australia*. Melbourne: Penguin.

Goddard, C. (1992). *Pitjantjatjara/Yankunytjatjara to English Dictionary* (second edn). Alice Springs, NT: Institute for Aboriginal Development.

Goldman, L. R. (1998). *Child's Play: Myth, Mimesis and Make-believe*. Oxford: Berg.

Hersey, S. (2004). Aranda games. In *Traditions in the Midst of Change: Communities, Cultures and the Strehlow Legacy*. Proceedings of the Strehlow Conference, 2002 (pp. 26–29). Alice Springs, NT: Strehlow Research Centre and Northern Territory Government.

Hiatt, L. R. (1975). Introduction. In L. R. Hiatt (ed.), *Australian Aboriginal Mythology: Essays in Honour of W.E.H. Stanner* (pp. 1–23). Canberra: Australian Institute of Aboriginal Studies.

Klapproth, D. (2004). *Narrative as Social Practice: Anglo-Western and Australian Aboriginal Oral Traditions*. Berlin: Mouton de Gruyter.

Langlois, A. (2006). Wordplay in teenage Pitjantjatjara. *Australian Journal of Linguistics, 26*(2), 181–92.

Moisseeff, M. (2002). Australian Aboriginal ritual objects. In M. Jeudy-Ballini and B. Juillerat (eds), *People and Things: Social Mediations in Oceania* (pp. 239–63). Durham, NC: Carolina Academic Press.

Munn, N. D. (1965). *A Report of Field Research at Areyonga, 1964–1965*. Canberra: Australian Institute of Aboriginal Studies.

Munn, N. D. (1966). Visual categories: an approach to the study of representational systems. *American Anthropologist, 68*, 939–50.

Munn, N. D. (1973). *Walbiri Iconography: Graphic Representation and Cultural Symbolism in a Central Australian Society*. London: Cornell University Press.

Nicholls, C. (2000). Warlpiri graffiti. In J. Docker and G. Fischer (eds), *Race, Colour and Identity in Australia and New Zealand* (pp. 79–94). Sydney: University of New South Wales Press.

O'Shannessy, C. T. (Forthcoming). Young children's social meaning-making in a new mixed language. In U. Eickelkamp and P. Fietz (eds), *Growing Up in Central Australia: Indigenous Experiences of Childhood, Youth and Transformations*.

Opie, I. and Opie, P. (1974). *The Classic Fairy Tales*. New York: Oxford University Press.

Piaget, J. (1951). *Play, Dreams and Imitation in Childhood* (C. Gattegno and F. M. Hodgson, Trans. 1962 edn). New York: Norton.

Poirier, S. (2003). 'This is good country. We are good dreamers': dreams and dreaming in the Australian Western Desert. In R. I. Lohmann (ed.), *Dream Travelers: Sleep Experiences and Culture in the Western Pacific* (pp. 107–125). New York: Palgrave Macmillan.

Róheim, G. (1945). *The Eternal Ones of the Dream: A Psychoanalytic Interpretation of Australian Myth and Ritual*. New York: International Universities Press.

Róheim, G. (1974). *Children of the Desert: The Western Tribes of Central Australia* (Vol. 1). New York: Harper and Row.

Sansom, B. (1980). *The Camp at Wallaby Cross: Aboriginal Fringe Dwellers in Darwin*. Canberra: Australian Institute of Aboriginal Studies.

Sansom, B. (2001). Irruptions of the dreamings in post-colonial Australia. *Oceania, 72*(1), 1–32.

Schwartzman, H. B. (1978). *Transformations: The Anthropology of Children's Play*. New York: Plenum Press.

Slade, A. and Wolf, D. P. (eds) (1994). *Children at Play: Clinical and Developmental Approaches to Meaning and Representation*. New York: Oxford University Press.

Stern, D. N. (1989). Developmental prerequisites for the sense of a narrated self. In A. M. Cooper, O. F. Kernberg and E. S. Person (eds), *Psychoanalysis: Toward the Second Century* (pp. 168–78). New Haven, CT: Yale University Press.

Tjitayi, K. and Lewis, S. (Forthcoming). Envisioning lives at Ernabella. In U. Eickelkamp and P. Fietz (eds), *Growing Up in Central Australia: Indigenous Experiences of Childhood, Youth and Transformations*.

von Sturmer, J. (1978). 'The Wik region: economy, territoriality and totemism in Western Cape York Peninsula, North Queensland'. Unpublished PhD thesis, University of Queensland, Brisbane.

von Sturmer, J. (2002). Click go the designs: presencing the now in 1,000 easy pieces. *Warburton One and Only: Painted Earthenware by Women from the Milyirrtjarra Ceramics Centre – Exhibition Catalog*. Sydney: Mori Gallery.

von Sturmer, J. (2005). *Prolegomena to a Politics of Announcement*. Darwin, NT: School for Social and Policy Research, Charles Darwin University.

Watson, C. (2003). *Piercing the Ground: Balgo Women's Image Making and Relationship to Country*. Fremantle, WA: Fremantle Arts Centre Press.

Section 2

The collaborative construction of knowledge in a traditional context

5

Elanor Reeders

The relative lack of success of Indigenous students in many societies has caused concern for many years. Studies have shown that parents contribute to school success by modelling appropriate learning strategies. However, appropriateness is determined by educational goals and processes which vary across cultures. It is therefore important to consider how teaching and learning operates in traditional societies. This study draws on natural data from traditional teaching interactions among the Yolngu of Arnhem Land, Australia and examines, turn-by-turn, the form and function of utterances, using a cultural frame to interpret such behaviour. Traditional strategies were found to encourage collaboration but not to force participation thereby upholding an important cultural value of independence and autonomy while still encouraging group unity. These findings have implications for the interaction between Western and Yolngu strategies in the classroom.

Introduction

'What is that? A truck?' 'Then what happened, Tyler?' 'How did you do that?' 'What does a cow say?' 'Do you want to read a story?' Sound familiar? Interacting with our children in this way is natural to most Australian families living in the mainstream society, which I shall call the Australian Dominant Culture (ADC), and we rarely think much more about it. However, disguised in these questions and activities are assumptions about the world and about learning.

It is obvious that a child's learning does not begin at school. Parents begin to teach their children from the start, consciously and unconsciously. The methods of teaching come from the parents' own cultural experience. The strategies they use tend to be guided by the strategies they learned from their own parents and their experiences of learning at school. Hence, many of their forms of talk conform to those used in the classroom, for example, direct questions and display questions, narratives that conform to school expectations, and nominating a child to answer. These linguistic strategies guide a learner's expectations to the sorts of things to pay attention to, how to seek information themselves and how to contribute appropriately. For example, studies suggest that children's experience in the home influence the types of skills they develop (Heath, 1983; Watson, 2001). Watson (2001, p. 43) notes that the 'forms of oral language associated with literacy can be orally transmitted and, once acquired facilitate the acquisition of literacy related skills and success in formal education'.

Children from other cultures in which the type of mainstream education system found in Australia (loosely, a 'Western education system') is relatively new may not be exposed to such types of talk. However, we must assume that there are other linguistic strategies that will facilitate success in the goals and processes of traditional education. In fact, analyses of child language in other oral societies such as those of African Americans (Brice-Heath, 1983; Gee, 1989; Hilliard, 1992; Lamb and Troike, 1972; Lucas and Borders, 1994; Watson, 1997) have noted impressive oratory skills which involve the use of analogy, stylistics and cohesive devices. In traditional settings, children would be exposed to types of talk that guide and model the linguistic strategies that are employed within that culture to assist learning.[1] Such strategies are dependent on the goals of learning and on the culturally appropriate means of information giving and seeking.

Studies of other Aboriginal groups in English-only classrooms have shown that Western classroom discourse strategies such as those described by Coulthard (1992) as an *initiation–response–feedback* structure, are often unsuccessful (Malcolm, 1982; Moses and Wigglesworth, Chapter 6). The fact that the teacher persisted with them regardless is an indication of how unconscious and ingrained they are.[2] There are many factors that might contribute to the failure of such strategies, not the least is the fact that English may be a second (or third or fourth) language. However, both the studies suggest one important factor is the differences in children's and the teacher's expectation of how learning and teaching should proceed and each participants' rights and obligations within the discourse.

What this study aims to contribute is an examination of the linguistic strategies used when teaching in a traditional setting and the rights and expectations of participants within this discourse. I begin by reviewing the setting and the style of the group interactions in which the data were collected. As the goal and context of an utterance has bearing on its interpretation, the analysis is broken down into information-giving and information-seeking exchanges. The first focuses on strategies used when giving children information, for example, how something is explained. Within information-seeking exchanges I examine the strategies used to gain information such as questioning. The analysis focuses on local events and examines the type of linguistic strategy used, how and to what end they function, and considers the cultural constructs that influence them. Finally, I consider consequences for the classroom.

The Data

Djambarrpuyngu: language and people

The Djambarrpuyngu language is one of the Yolngu group of languages spoken in north-eastern Arnhem Land. It has become a lingua franca (common language) in the communities of Galiwin'ku, Gapuwiyak, Ramangining and Milingimbi (Wilkinson, 1991). It is the children's first language and is used in almost all aspects of their home lives. Prior to school, children have very little experience of English; however, much of the instruction in schools, including the bilingual schools, is in English. Yolngu society still maintains its traditional values, ideologies and world view.

Participants

The participants included 6 adults and 15 children. All but one participant speak Djambarrpuyngu. The other language, Liyagawumirr, is a closely related dialect. To protect participants' identity each were given pseudonyms described in Table 5.1.

Table 5.1. Participants

Name	Description
Mia, Ben, Wendy, Acacia, Sarah, Mark, Judy, Bree	Children
Ngunydjuluk, Mary, Rose	Parents' generation (female)
Djapama	Male Elder – Grandparents' generation
Dhiwanti, Djaykung	Female Elder – Grandparents' generation
Elanor	Researcher

The language data

The corpus of language data consists of naturally occurring speech in a traditional setting in which children were being taught successfully.[3] To avoid an ethnocentric conception of where and how teaching might occur, the teaching scenarios were brainstormed and selected by the Yolngu participants themselves. I accompanied family groups (including extended family members) on eight different excursions to the bush or beach. Teaching activities and topics included identifying and gathering various bush foods, dyes and medicinal plants, learning a traditional game, tying knots for fishing and comparing traditional and modern life. Groups consisted between 2 and 4 adults, usually 2–3 of the grandparent generation and one of the parent generation. Numbers of children varied from 2 to 7 but most commonly were around 2–3. One participant was a teaching assistant at the school and eventhough she was not in this role at the time of the study it may have influenced her talk somewhat.

In an effort to reduce the observer effect, I spent at least one day with the participants and spoke only Djambarrpuyngu. I tried to limit the extent of my involvement in the dialogue, however, I did respond when addressed because not doing so would have been interpreted as strange or rude, thereby only increasing their awareness to my presence.

The recordings totalled 7 hours from which nine interactions[4] totalling 31 minutes were transcribed following Du Bois et al. (1993). Here, only silence (ellipses and time in seconds) and overlap (square brackets with numbers sequentially) are represented. Given the small data set, enumeration of data are kept to a minimum. Instead, the focus is on how utterances function within the context. Each transcription was checked by a native speaker and translator, Galathi Dhurrkay.

Interactional style

An interesting feature of the interactions was the group dynamics. On arrival, the entire group did not stay together but people moved off, usually in smaller groups (around 3 people) in the pursuit of their tasks. During the course of the activity, people moved around a lot, joining other groups or wandering off from a group in the middle of conversations. There was no indication that this was considered rude (note Djaykung's departure in Example 1 below). Hence, groups within conversations were fluid.

This said, the Yolngu tended to stay and talk in groups of three or more. The talk was often addressed to the group as a whole. Also, speakers tended not to select a specific individual to take the next turn but rather allowed the hearers to self-select as the next speaker (this is Sacks et al., 1974 turn-taking rule 1a). These tendencies gave the hearers a greater level of control over who took a turn and their own level of participation. Also, in a large group, it distributed the obligation to answer among the group and hence each individual had less responsibility (or obligation) to respond. Both these observations are reminiscent of Walsh's (1991) appealing description of 'broadcast speech' style where participants address everybody present and where the channel of communication is never closed off at the end of interactions. Participants can wander in and out of conversations without a closing comment. Compare this with English speakers, who often think of conversations occurring primarily between two people (Bell, 1984). Of course, talk often occurs in multiparty settings (e.g. in meetings) but it has been suggested that even in these situations there is a cultural predisposition to direct one's talk to another specific individual (Edelsky, 1981). Consider the tenet of public speaking 'Try to look each audience member in the eye'. As such, English speakers may be more likely to direct their speech to a certain person within the group. The speaker selects this person by using various strategies such as eye contact or verbal cues to indicate the select of an addressee (Schegloff, 1996). Doing so exerts a fair amount of control over other participants.

This is not to say that speaker selection never occurs in Djambarrpuyngu.[5] However, its use is dispreferred. I will examine how in certain instances it can be considered rude and the strategies used to avoid it (See section on Obligation to Answer).

Analysis

Information-giving exchanges

Teaching involves the exchange of information, so in this section I will look at some examples of how Yolngu give information and how they explain things to their children. I will show how they do this collaboratively, involving the children, encouraging agreement to be voiced and allowing a consensus to form. Repetitions and lists help this collaboration. I will also examine how the Yolngu, in a multiparty situation, work to ensure that everybody understands and how this leads to recapitulations of what has been said.

Explanations

What is distinctive about Yolngu explanations is that many people – including the children –contribute to an explanation. As members of the ADC, we might conceptualise an explanation as one person telling someone else about something that they know. The Yolngu tend to construct explanations with multiple people adding contributions to what someone else has said. Turn-taking seems to be solely the responsibility of the hearers as there is no obvious speaker selection in words or actions; children are allowed to add what they know or can infer. Their contributions are taken as part of the collaboration.

In Example 1, Rose (an adult) and Mia (a child) collaborate to explain the type of place in which yams grow.

Example 1

Transcript 1 'Duynga ga Riny'tjangu' (yams)

296. Rose:	**dharrwa ga Riny'tjangu.**	
	'Lots of yams.'	
297. Mia:	**dhuwandja dhuwal bala,**	
	'They are in this area over here,'	
298.	**outsidedja ngunhi bala.**	
	'and the outside section over there.'	
299. Djaykung:	**dhuwal rraku XXXX.**	
	'This is my XX.'	
300. Rose:	**balanya nhakun swampy areas.**	
	'Like swampy areas, such as this.'	

301. Mia:	**watergu** 'with water'
302. Elanor:	**hmmm.**
303. Mia:	**nyumukuniny malay,** 'for those small ones'
304.	**[. . . nhawiku]** 'for those um . . . '
305. Ben:	**[yikangu XXXX ngayi] nhuma ga wutthun.** 'xx xxxx you are hitting/digging it'
306. Rose:	**ngunhiyi ngayi manymaktja wänga ngathaw.** 'It's a good place for food.'
307. Mia:	**nhä bili?** 'Which one?'
308. Rose:	**(4.3 seconds) balanya nhakun ngayi nguli raining,** 'Just like when it starts to rain,'

In lines 296–303, both Rose and Mia collaborate to produce quite a unified text. Each turn follows the next with very little overlap (excluding Ben who is much younger). Most utterances are grammatically complete and can stand alone.[6] Pragmatically, however, utterances can rarely stand alone, as they rely heavily on the previous utterance for their interpretation. For the most part this is due to the use of referring expressions that replace things or actions referred to by the last speaker. For example, in Line 297, *dhuwandja* 'this' refers to *Riny'tjangu* 'yam', in line 296 and *balanya* 'one such as that' in Line 300 refers to the areas mentioned in lines 297 and 298. The use of such reference functions to establish that the information is to be considered as an addition to the previous proposition. The referring expressions link each utterance to the previous, thus help in showing that participants are listening to and refer- ring to what the others have said. The collaboration can be described as being like a game of dominos – each contribution is connected and related to the last turn and is brought about by anyone into the open floor, to build the whole. The collaboration ends at line 307, due to Mia's temporary inability to recall the name of the yam which causes her to lose the thread of the conversation and makes it difficult to appropriately manage a turn.

Listing

As part of these information-giving exchanges, participants often start to list sequences. These have a specific rhythm, intonation and rules regarding who can contribute and when. The list, as a whole, has a regular rhythm. The speaker who starts the listing will not immediately add another item but they will wait for another two beats – just enough time for another contribution. A second participant will usually fill this gap, not with a new list item but with a repetition of the original item.[7] If no one repeats, a pause results before the original speaker makes another contribution (Line 40). Several people can repeat an item but each participant does so only once. Thus, there is a primary contributor, the person who is adding new items. This person usually gives three new items (interspersed with repetitions by others) before someone else takes over and starts contributing new items. Sometimes, the final item is removed from the others by a long pause and a conjunction like 'and' or 'or'.

These sequences serve to categorize items and are often bounded by a greater heuristic (Seabirds in Example 2 below). Older speakers actively encourage children to participate in the collaboration. Children can contribute repetitions or they could take over as primary contributors (although no examples exist in the limited data). These sing – song lists are fun, collaborative and contribute to the voicing of consensus.

Example 2

Transcript 5 'Djarrak mapu' (Seabird eggs)

32.	Djapama:	**ngali dhu nhäma dharrwan . . . mapu . . . djarrak.**
		'We will see lots of seagull eggs.'
33.	Ngundjuluk:	**yo.**
		'Yes.'
34.	Djapama:	**yo.**
		'Yes.'
35.	Dhiwanti:	**[bawalamirr] warrakan.**
		'Any animals.'
36.	Djapama:	**[dharrwa]**
		'many'
37.		**bawalamirra**
		'of all types'
38.	Dhiwanti:	**bawala[mirr warrakan]**
		'any animals'
39.	Djapama:	**[djarrak]**
		'seagull'

40.		**. . . (2 beats) getkit**
		'small white seagull'
41.	Ngunydjuluk:	**getkit**
		'small white seagull'
42.	Judy:	**Wo oh**
43.	Mark:	**maypal ngarra guyangar.**
		'I am thinking about oysters.' (dreaming of them)
44.	Djapama:	**gakarrarr**
		'Silver Gulls'
45.	Dhiwanti:	**guthirka**
		'Pied Oyster Catcher'
46.	Djapama:	**guthirka**
		'Pied Oyster Catcher'
47.	Dhiwanti:	**n̲alpa**
		'seabird'
48.	Djapama:	**n̲alpa**
		'seabird'
49.	Judy:	**n̲alpa**
		'seabird'
50.	Djapama:	**nhawi**
		'um, what's it called'
51.	Judy:	**[nhawi]**
		'um, what's it called'
52.	Dhiwanti:	**[gany'tjurr]**
		'seabird'
53.	Djapama:	**gany'tjurr [2 gulwitjpitj 2]**
		'seabird, Oriental plover'
54.	Judy:	**[2 gany'tjurr 2]**
		'seabird'
55.	Djapama:	**dharrwan mapu, ngali dhu malng'maram bili,**
		'We will find lots of eggs, because . . .'
56.	Judy:	**dharrwan mapu gapu.**
		'lots of eggs in the water.'

Grounding sequence

When teaching, and in fact in all conversation, we must constantly try to ensure that our interlocutor has understood what we have said. Even in a two-party system this process is complicated. Clark (1993) proposed a collaborative model to explain the process by which interlocutors negotiate to establish what he terms 'common ground'. The speaker says something but before it is taken up as part of the conversation both speaker and addressee have to establish that the addressee has taken it on board. Only when both think that this has happened can the remark be taken as part of their common ground. The addressee signals that it is part of the common ground either by letting the speaker continue talking or continuing themselves, or else they must signal that there is a problem. If there is a problem, the speaker tries to repair it until the addressee signals that it has become part of the common ground. In Example 3 participants collaborate to establish this common ground.

Example 3

Transcript 1 'Ḏuynga ga Riny'tjangu' (yams)

3.	Mia:	**Nhä dhuwali mala?**
		'What are those?'
4.	Rose:	**Dhuwandja ga nhä Djundumna dhuwandja.**
		'That's . . . is what? Djundum (yams).'
5.	Wendy:	**Wanha Djundumdja mala?**
		'Where are the Djundums?'
6.	Djapama:	**Wanha Djundumdja?**
		'Where is there Djundum?'
7.	Rose:	**Dhuwal nhanngu dharpany.**
		'That is its tree.'
8.	Wendy:	**Wakay!**
		'wow!' (exclamation of counter expectation)
9.	Rose:	**Dhuwal.**
		'Here.'
10.	Mia:	**Balanya mala napurr dhu [ga dharpa] nhäma? Djundumgu?**
		'Like these plants that we can see are the vines of Djundum?'
11.	Wendy:	**[Wakay!]**
		'wow!' (exclamation of counter expectation)
12.	Rose:	**eh**
		'yeah'
13.		**Dhuwali ngayi Djundumdja.**
		'This one is Djundum.'

Mia asks a question about a plant she has seen. Lines 3 and 4 are a simple grounding unit – a section of text that uniquely identifies a referent and becomes part of the 'common ground' (Clark, 1993) – between Mia and Rose. Taking something into the common ground will be called 'grounding' it. Rose demonstrates she has grounded Mia's question by responding. However, in lines 5 and 6, Wendy and Djapama indicate they have heard the word Djundum but have not understood what it refers to. They self-select to take the next turn as speakers to inquire. There is no indication that this self-selection is considered rude as Rose answers them by providing them more specific information. Rose, however, does not take the grounding to be complete until all participants have expressed their understanding, and so, while Wendy expresses understanding in line 8, Djapama has not responded so Rose repeats the reference.[8]

Thus, to help manage the multiparty speech situation, any participant is able to adopt the role of addressee in order to rectify any inadequate under-standing. Hence, this open floor has an important part in ensuring that the entire group establishes mutual understanding.

Recap

An important aspect of Clark's findings was that 'speakers work with their addressees until the addressee has understood them well enough for the cur-rent purposes – and no further' (1993, p. 105). In Example 3, the referent is grounded by the end of line 9. Unexpectedly, Mia then restates the proposition and, by using a questioning intonation, presents it for confirmation. In lines 12 and 13 Rose then confirms her proposition and again restates it. In terms of efficiency, this repetition is not required for the purposes of grounding. This type of recap is common in the data and is also found after much longer discussions.

Far from being redundant, these recaps help to ensure that the whole group understands, including those who overhear and have not contributed. Furthermore, they enable the child to demonstrate the knowledge that she (or he) has acquired and reaffirm the consensus that the group has reached.

Information-seeking

In this environment participation is encouraged; the other side of the coin being a tendency to resist being forced to participate. A common observation of Yolngu speech is the tendency to resist questioning. Observers have suggested that questions are avoided and are often seen to be left unanswered because being inquisitive is considered bad manners (Christie, 1985; Northern Territory Department of Education, 1988). This has been noted in other Aboriginal societies (Eades, 1982; Malcolm, 1980).

The current data does not support such a view. Twenty per cent of all utterances in the information-seeking exchanges were questions. Even in information-giving exchanges nine per cent of the utterances were questions. These figures compare with those found in the study on other Aboriginal parent–child interactions by Moses and Yallop (Chapter 2). While their figures relate to the adults' input, surprisingly, in the current data an overwhelming majority (approximately 90 per cent) of questions were asked by Yolngu children. This is different too from the classroom setting in which the majority of the questions are asked by the teacher (Eagleson et al., 1982). Therefore, Yolngu children are actively involved in their education and have no problems with questions. However, the form of question used often only obliges the addressee to give only a minimal response. When an extended response is desired, the request is implied rather than being directly requested, as will be shown in the discussion following a brief description of the three main forms of question.

Direct questions

Direct questions are usually those that contain a question word such as *nhä* 'what' or *nhakun* 'why'. They are questions by virtue of their form (their grammar).

Example 4

Transcript 1 'Duynga ga Riny'tjangu' (yams)

3. Mia: **Nhä dhuwali mala?**
'What are those?'

Only three forms of question words – *nhä* 'what', *wanha* 'where', and *yol* 'who' – were commonly used, despite Djambarrpuyngu's large range of question words (Wilkinson, 1991). Predominance of these questions has been found in other studies of parent–child interactions (Moses and Yallop, Chapter 2). While these questions are open (have multiple possible answers), they usually refer to something in the immediate context and as such, there is usually only one possible answer.

Only two instances of *nhaku* 'why' which entails an extended response were found in the data. The questions, asked by children, remain unanswered.

The children do not pursue a response. This finding was unexpected given that the children were able to produce such questions, and so there can be no doubt as to their ability to comprehend them. The question must have been heard otherwise the asker would have pursued it. Further evidence is required but it may be that the question was in some way inappropriate in the Yolngu context.

The scarcity with which 'why' and 'how' questions were used may underlie the observation that Yolngu are not oriented to abstract problem solving (Harris, 1990). However, it is not the case that such information is not sought. The next section looks at the strategies used to elicit such substantial information.

Confirmations

The most common form of questions found in the data are the yes/no questions. What is most striking about these question forms is that they present known or inferred information, which the speaker puts forward to others for verification. These questions expect a positive answer. If a negative answer must be given it is hedged. Thus, they are seeking confirmation and agreement.

There are two types in the data. The first is the declarative question, which consists of a statement marked with rising intonation. Such a question requires only a yes/no response.

Example 5

Transcript 1 'Duynga ga Riny'tjangu' (yams)

181. Mia: **nhawi inside ngayi dhu ngathany dhawatthun?**
(lit) 'The food will pop out from inside?'
'Is the actual food itself in the inside?'

The second is the tag question which consists of a statement with an attached tag question marker. This tag expresses some level of doubt as to the truth of the proposition. An example of an English tag question is 'Dinner's ready, isn't it?'. In Djambarrpuyngu, there are four tags: *muka, ngi, ngani* and *eh.*

Example 6

Transcript 1 'Duynga ga Riny'tjangu' (yams)

200. Rose: **yo ngunha Duynga ngi?**
'yes that's Duynga right?'

201. Ben: **eh.**
'yeah.'

All tags in Yolngu expect a positive response. English tag questions can select either a yes or no as the expected response. 'Dinner is ready, isn't it?' expects a 'yes' whereas 'Dinner is ready, is it?' implies the statement is thought to be incorrect and therefore expects a 'no'. Other English yes/no questions such as the second translation given in Example 6 above, imply nothing about the proposition presented – they request new, unknown information.[9]

When asked if there was a form that presented the information in a neutral manner, the interpreter tentatively produced the following direct question:

> **Nhä ḻukanamirr ngayi ?**
> 'Are they edible?'

However, she quickly noted that this form was a little pushy and the original was deemed more appropriate. This suggests that direct question forms are less appropriate.

Since confirmation questions only explicitly request a yes/no answer, it could be argued that they do not seek substantial information. However, these types of questions often receive extended responses. Consider Example 7 below:

Example 7

Transcript 1 'Ḏuynga ga Riny'tjangu' (yams)

243. Wendy:	**Bathan muka ngayi dhuwal ?**
	'These are cooked, right?'
244. Rose:	**Bathan muka ngali bitjan.**
	'Yeah right cooked, that's how we do it.'
245.	**Yaw'yawyun bala,**
	'Dig (them all up),'
246.	**gurthan dhangalkum nhangalkul bala bathanna.**
	'Start a fire for them and then cook (them).'

Rose could have responded with 'yes' but instead provides quite substantial information. This suggests that Rose has taken the question as an implied request for information rather than as just seeking confirmation. This is called an indirect question. In English, we might ask about one's ability – 'Can you close the window?' – but we imply a request for action.

Thus, while these are confirmation-seeking questions in form (i.e. their grammar) they are functioning like direct Wh-questions that seek extended responses. We might consider them then, as a valid alternative to using Wh-questions such as *nhaltjan* 'how' and *nhäthinya* 'what type' as they imply these meanings without using the direct form. For example, the tag question proposed in Example 7 could be paraphrased as 'how are these eaten?'

Triggers

Certain statements, often followed by silence, seem to act as 'triggers' to use Eades' (1982) term. In much the same way as the confirmations seem to imply a request for further information, these statements are intended to initiate discussion on a topic.

Example 8

Transcript 7 'Lämabarr' (Indicator flower)

26. Bree: **Bilawa ngayi ga dhäwunydja, bilawa.**
                'The flower is news, the flower.'

28. Bree: **(2.7 seconds) ngi?**
                'isn't it?'

In line 26, Bree makes a statement about an indicator flower. After a few seconds, she adds a tag question making it explicit that she was in fact requesting information. It can be argued that Bree's original statement was, despite the lack of any overt indication such as questioning intonation, intended as a request for information. Thus, she hoped it would trigger further discussion and therefore information.

Such findings are similar to those of Eades (1982) in her work with Southern Queensland Aboriginal English. However, her work focused on the elicitation of narratives, and she found that triggers were often used to initiate topics whereas direct questions were used to clarify referents within the story. Thus, triggers seem to have a similar function in Djambarrpuyngu but do not follow the same patterns of distribution. It is quite possible that this is due only to the differing contexts investigated.

Both confirmations and triggers present a proposition that is believed or inferred to be true. While they do not oblige the hearer to provide any more than a yes/no answer, they can be taken as a request for information and they provide the opportunity and impetus to provide substantial information.

From a cultural perspective, these strategies allow the teacher to decide when and how much knowledge will be given. This is important in a culture where information is seen to be privileged and given only to the appropriate people at an appropriate time (Sansom, 1980). It also allows the hearer to decide their level of participation (by providing minimal or substantial responses).

Politeness

The use of such indirect requests minimizes or eradicates any obligation to answer. From the perspective of Brown and Levinson's (1987) politeness theory, they attend to the addressee's 'negative face' – they respect the addressee's desire for freedom of action. On the other hand, confirmation requests also provide an opportunity for other members to voice their agreement and show that consensus exists within the group. In fact, given that many confirmation requests are broadcast it allows multiple people to respond in agreement. Thus, these questioning strategies are a powerful means to gain 'positive face' – stressing membership of the same group.

Thus, Yolngu teaching can be characterized by two features. First, it develops children's independence by providing them a measure of control over their level of participation in a conversation. Second, it encourages collaboration and consensus and emphasises the relationship between people in the group. I believe that these strategies employed by Yolngu with their children stress both individual rights and group obligations. The children are made to understand that they have the right to either participate or not to participate, but that the need for consensus among the group governs any verbal contribution they choose to make. Thus, there is both freedom and obligation.

Obligation to answer

A number of observers have noted that in Yolngu and other Aboriginal cultures participants are not obliged to answer questions (Christie, 1985; Eades, 1982; Harris, 1980; Malcolm, 1982; Walsh, 1991). However, such a claim runs counter to the widely accepted linguistic thought that sees questions as projecting or predicting an answer (Christie, 2002; Coulthard, 1992; Heritage, 1995; Sacks, 1995). This means that an answer is required and a failure to give one leaves a very noticeable absence.

Given the propensity for talk to occur in groups, speakers often direct their speech to the group at large (or broadcast speech to use Walsh's (1991) terminology). Also, cultural norms limit the amount of eye contact and so Yolngu may be less likely to select the next speaker using these more tacit techniques (Northern Territory Department of Education, 1988). When a speaker does not select someone to take the next turn any member of the audience may respond. Thus, each member has an equal potential to respond and so the responsibility for answering is dispersed among the group. This weakens the prediction strength of the question. This entails that if a question is broadcast, each individual is less obliged to answer, but in other cases an answer would still be obligatory.

Example 9 confirms this hypothesis and also shows broadcast speech being used as a politeness strategy (see Section on Politeness).

Example 9

Transcript 3 'Nhä nhe mälk?' (What's your subsection)

79.	Sarah:	**manyi.**
		'Grandma.' (child's terminology)
80.		**nhä nhe mälk?**
		'what is your subsection?'
		(*5 lines of task related talk*)
86.	Sarah:	**manyi?**
		'Grandma?'
87.		**nhä nhe mälk?**
		'what's your subsection?'
88.	Dhiwani:	**eh.**
		'Yes.'
89.	Sarah:	**manyi,**
		'Grandma,'
90.	Dhiwanti:	**ngunha bala yindin,**
		'Over there, the big one,'
91.		. . . (1.5 seconds) . . .
92.	Sarah:	**manyi?**
		'Grandma?'
93.		**nhä nheny mälk?**
		'what subsection are you?'
94.		. . . (2.3 seconds) . . .
95.		**yuwalk yuwalk marwat dhakan.**
		'True, true, messy hair' (light-hearted teasing nickname)
96.	Acacia:	**. . . (0.9 second) Dhiwanti . . . wanga nhungu ga?**
		'Dhiwanti someone wants to talk to you?'
		. . . (1.1–5 second) (*smashing shellfish*)

(*Continued*)

Example 9—Cont'd

97. Sarah:	**Dhiwanti!**	
98. Dhiwani:	**. . . (1.2 seconds) dhuwala djäma ngarra ga guyanga.** 'I'm thinking about the work.'	
108. Acacia:	**[nhä nhumalangguny gurruṯumanydjiyu]?** 'What is your relationship between you all?'	
109. Sarah:	**[wakay purple wan] gam!** 'Wow, a purple one see!'	
110. Acacia:	**ya.** 'Look.'	
111.	**dhuwal gam.** 'Here, see.'	
112. Sarah:	**Dhiwantji! Nhämany nhe mälk, Ngunydjuluk lakarama.** 'Dhiwantji! Ngunydjuluk has already told me what subsection it is.'	
113. Dhiwanti:	**Gamanydjan,** 'Subsection' (incorrect subsection)	
114. Ngunydjuluk:	**Bilinydjan.** 'Subsection.' (correct one)	
115. Dhiwanti:	**Gamanydjan.**	
116. Sarah:	**Bilinydjan.**	
117. Dhiwanti:	**Gaminydjan.**	
118. Sarah:	**Bilinydjan!**	

First, note that Sarah's question (Line 80) is not broadcast but specifically selects an addressee. As such we would expect an answer to be obligatory. Sarah's repetition of the question and Acacia's attempt to get Dhiwanti's attention, in line 96, suggest that they both expected an answer. In fact, Sarah's repeated efforts and growing agitation indicates that the lack of response is significant. In line 98, Dhiwanti finally responds with 'I'm thinking about the work' – a pseudo-answer, implying 'I am deliberately ignoring your question'. We might interpret the lack of response as Dhiwanti having felt that the question was inappropriate (Galathi Dhurrkay, personal communication).

This strategy of direct questioning having failed, Acacia revises Sarah's question in line 108 to direct it to all members present. In order to 'broadcast' her question she asks a general question of about the group's relationships of which the specific detail would be part of the answer. It becomes less personal and allows the question to be answered on Dhiwanti's behalf. This strategy allows Dhiwanti to decline answering without being rude and also increases the likelihood that someone will reply. By allowing participants this freedom, this speech style makes the question more appropriate. Unfortunately, an answer is not forthcoming probably due to the enthusiastic interjection by Sarah in line 109. Next Sarah also revises her strategy by suggesting that she already knows the answer. Dhiwanti tests this claim by giving her an incorrect answer.

Most questions, even very indirect ones, do receive an answer. Direct questions and confirmations do oblige an answer and a refusal to answer is imbued with social meaning. However, to be polite, speakers often modify their questions and talk to allow for minimal or non-answers (using confirmations, broadcast speech or triggers).

Pedagogical soundness

These questioning strategies are in fact pedagogically sound. To present a proposition for confirmation children are required to infer or guess at a correct statement. Thus, they are encouraged to make their own inferences and in doing so, the adults clearly identify what level the children are currently at and can extend the children's knowledge effectively. This is essential for effective teaching (compare Vygotsky's (1978) well-established notion that effective teaching must be aimed at the 'zone of proximal development').

Consequences for the classroom

Collaboration and consensus

Many of the linguistic strategies we have discussed allow for participants to voice their agreement with each other. Any new topic goes through a process of collaboration and consensus and the goal seems to be to reach a collectively ratified version rather than to merely hand over knowledge.[10] There are many ways in which consensus is built and agreement voiced in both information-giving and -seeking exchanges. Confirmation questions provide an opportunity for group members to voice their agreement and when they are broadcast are often answered by multiple participants. Grounding ensures that a consensus is reached and recaps voice the agreement of the group. In explanatory exchanges collaboration is built on the links between participants' utterances and expresses agreement with what others have said previously. In addition, the transcripts are littered with repetition which, far from being redundant, voice agreement and fellowship very similar to the sort Liberman (1982) found in central Australia. In other cases, statements are followed by affirmative responses as if a confirmation has been elicited. In Example 10, we can see that this is more than feedback as the proposition is restated (although elided) in agreement:

Example 10

Transcript 1 'Duynga ga Riny'tjangu' (yams)

47.	Rose:	**Dhuwalatjan napurru nguli ga marrtji,** 'We have gone through this area,'
48.	Ben:	**Yakurr!** 'I'm tired!'
49.	Rose:	**collecting balanya mala.** 'collecting things such as this.'
50.	Elanor:	**hmm**
51.	Mia:	**Yo. Limurr.** 'Yes. All of us (did that).'

Consensus is a fundamental part of the information exchange. So much so that when participants fail to speak in a unified voice and there is even the appearance of a disagreement, it is very quickly and carefully rectified as seen in Example 11 below.

Example 11

Transcript 7 'Lämabarr' (Indicator flower)

52.	Mary::	**wangany ngayi dhuwali manymaktja [ga nhawi],** 'It tells us that it's good and um,'
53.	Djaykung:	**[djukurrmirrayirra].** '(they) become fatty.'
54.	Mary:	**[2 maypalmirra 2].** 'there are oysters.'
55.	Djapama:	**[2 maypalmirra 2].** 'there are oysters.'
56.	Mary:	**djukurrmirr ngani?** 'fatty right?'

In line 53, Djaykung collaboratively completes Mary's utterance while she is thinking. However, Mary had a different word in mind and she contributes the term *maypalmirr* (as does Djapama). This leaves the impression that Mary has not agreed with Djaykung and a consensus has not been reached. Thus, repetition in line 56 establishes that she does not disagree. However, for consensus both parties must indicate that they agree and both parties must accept that the other agrees. The inclusion of the tag question requests Djaykung to confirm that she accepts Mary's move. Only when she does this can everyone acknowledge that they are in agreement.

The children are quite involved in the collaboration and building of consensus. Since they display their knowledge in this way, they are not as often quizzed on their understanding as ADC children (See the section on Questions). Yolngu children's expectation is that the group should all collaborate, voicing their agreement and understanding until they have formed a consensus. They are a part of the construction of the knowledge. This is hard to re-create in a whole class setting as turn-taking in such a large group is harder to manage and not everybody can participate.

Collaborative strategies such as voicing agreement, repetition and recaps may also lead to many students answering at once, repeating each other and contributing to another child's answer. From an ADC perspective, it is possible to interpret such behaviour as disruptive; children are discouraged from borrowing or prompting answers, and interrupting other students. This is partly because these strategies are quite functional in small groups but can become difficult to manage in larger ones. In this situation it can be difficult to identify what any individual child knows and what is being copied. From the children's perspective, however, they are working together and being co-operative.

Nomination

The selection of the next speaker is less common in Yolngu conversations (and probably in conversations in general) than it is in the classroom where nominating a child to respond occurs regularly (Coulthard, 1992). However, such selection and questioning forces the child to speak individually, rather than as a collaborating partner within the group. It requires an opinion divorced from the group and such behaviour is seen as taking undue authority and is shameful. In my experience, this is something that makes Yolngu children shy, especially if they do not know the questioner well or there are many other people around. However, given the numbers in the classroom, if a teacher addresses the whole class the responsibility for participating is distributed among the group. Obligation to respond therefore reduces as the size of the group increases. It is more likely that no one or only the most outspoken will contribute.

Lists

It has been noted that Yolngu children enthusiastically engage in parroting and listing tasks (Harris, 1980). These tasks would seem familiar to the children as they are similar to repetitions and the listing constructions. Although they are similar, they do not perform the same function of expressing agreement and do not provide children the opportunity to make their own unique contributions. In addition, the system of categorization that form the basis of Yolngu listing is likely to be very different from that of classroom tasks. Such differences, never made explicit, may cause confusion for the children.

Questioning

In the ADC classroom, direct questioning is a commonly used form of information seeking. I have shown that for Yolngu such questions are less appropriate and we might expect children to resist them (compare Eagleson et al.'s (1982) examples in an Aboriginal English classroom). Questions are usually display questions asked by the teacher. Moses and Wigglesworth (Chapter 6) note that 'there is a tacit understanding that the teacher is interrogating from a position of "power"'. In Yolngu conversation, more rights are afforded to the hearer and so children might not share this expectation and find it pushy and rude.

On the other hand, when children use their own strategies of asking confirmations or triggers in an attempt to gain more detailed information, their implications may not be correctly understood. If a teacher failed to respond to such attempts, this lack of response may be taken as an indication that the question is inappropriate or the knowledge is privileged and will not be pursued. It is important, then, for teachers to recognise these types of questions and respond with further information. Children will then do their own problem solving and present a further proposition for confirmation.

Display questions – those where the asker already knows the answer and intends only to check the addressee's knowledge – are common in ADC classrooms and parent–child interactions (Drew, 1981; Edwards and Westgate, 1994; French and MacLure, 1981). In the Yolngu transcripts, of the relatively few questions asked by the adults only a couple were of this variety. Notably, in

Example 12 the display question is misinterpreted as a confirmation suggesting that this type of question is not the norm.

Example 12

Transcript 1 'Duynga ga Riny'tjangu' (yams)

200. Rose:	**yo ngunha Duynga ngi?**	
	'yes that's Duynga yeah?'	
201. Wendy:	**eh**	
	'Yeah'	
202. Rose:	**nhä Riny'tjangu.**	
	'What is it, Riny'tjangu?'	
203. Wendy:	**yo**	
	'yes'	

Thus, strategies that are adaptive in the child's own society may not function within the classroom. Also an ADC teacher's strategies may appear confusing and rude when interpreted from the child's pre-schooling learning experience. More importantly, the questioning strategies outlined in this section serve to construct and support Yolngu identity as an autonomous individual within a highly interdependent group. As such, a change in style can amount to a change in social identity (Gee, 1989).

Conclusion

Drawing on actual traditional teaching interaction, this study has been able to show how Yolngu successfully achieve information exchange in a manner that is guided by cultural constraints and ideologies. In Yolngu education, children are encouraged to be part of the collaborative construction of knowledge. They participate collaboratively in explanations, in listing sequences and repetitions. They voice the consensus of the group and help in the recap of established knowledge for the benefit of all present.

The continuously open floor and broadcast speech style allows all participants to add their contribution to the flow of discourse, collaboratively building a unified whole. It also allows the role of addressee to be self-selected by the audience rather than being speaker selected. This allows everyone to participate while forcing no obligation to do so. Broadcast speech allows multiple responses, and explanations are littered with repetitions which, far from being redundant, express agreement, fellowship and inclusion in the group interaction.

Questions are not avoided and are used to gain information but their use is governed by the social constraints that determine how knowledge is to be obtained in the Yolngu culture. Questioners take into consideration the hearer's right to participate as they choose and they soften or hedge requests for substantial information by using indirect strategies such as triggers and confirmation requests. This maintains the teacher's right to decide how and when to give substantial information and suggests that this might be a product of cultural conceptions of knowledge as privileged. This questioning style also endeavours to respect the audience's autonomy while also providing a means for expressing unity of opinion by requesting confirmations. Thus it was found that questioning strategies are productive and pedagogically sound and in fact, tied up with Yolngu notions of identity and independence.

In conclusion, looking at the turn-by-turn interpretation of the talk and using a cultural and contextual frame for interpretation, the study by this author has been able to describe the motivation for, and the function of, the linguistic patterns found in Yolngu discourse. It provides a basis for further research into the interpretation of Yolngu interactions in the ADC classroom and incorporation of such learning strategies into classroom settings. It also highlights the need for further investigation into strategies used with older children and in a wider range of contexts.

Notes

1. Other works on traditional Yolngu education include ethnographical descriptions (Bunbury et al., 1991; Buschenhofen, 1980; Harris, 1990; Northern Territory Department of Education, 1988; Thies, 1987). Others, notably Harris (1980), described the sociolinguistic rules of interpersonal speech.
2. No criticism of the teacher is intended here. Discourse structures are unconscious patterns and inadequate cross-cultural and English as a Second Language (ESL) training for teachers in remote communities leaves her with little means to revise such patterns.
3. Measured by observance of children having acquired the relevant knowledge later in the session.
4. Interactions were chosen on the basis that successful teaching was occurring.
5. Examples include use of names, kin terms and designing utterances for specific addressee.
6. As such it differs from collaborative constructions described in English (Coates, 1996), in which two participants collaborated to create one sentence (although one exists in the lines 300 and 301).
7. Repetitions are said with similar intonation and volume, and therefore appear to be equally valid contributions (i.e. they are not prompts or support).
8. Further study of video data would contribute greatly to this analysis as turn management often relies on eye gaze and gesture (Beavin Bavelas et al., 2002).

9. The second translation given in Example 5 is a typical English yes/no question and neither a positive nor a negative answer is preferable (both are acceptable).

10. This conceptualisation fits with Sansom's (1980) notion of the 'word'. He suggests the only thing worth knowing is the 'word' of the group and it is this group-ratified version that holds weight and constitutes the 'truth' at any one time.

References

Beavin Bavelas, J., Coates, L. and Johnson, T. (2002). Listener response as a collaborative process: the role of gaze. *Journal of Communication, 52*(3), 566–80.

Bell, A. (1984). Language style as audience design. *Language in Society, 13*(2), 145–204.

Brown, P. and Levinson, S. C. (1987). *Politeness: Some Universals in Language Use.* Cambridge: Cambridge University Press.

Bunbury, R., Hastings, W., Henry, J. and McTaggart, R. (eds) (1991). *Aboriginal Pedagogy: Aboriginal Teachers Speak Out, Blekbala Wei, Deme Nayin, Yolngu Rom, and Ngini Nginingawula Ngawurranungurumagi.* Geelong, VIC: Deakin University Press.

Buschenhofen, P. (1980). *The Teacher-Linguist as Curriculum Developer.* Darwin, NT: Bilingual Education Section, Northern Territory Department of Education.

Christie, F. (2002). *Classroom Discourse Analysis: A Functional Perspective.* London: Continuum.

Christie, M. J. (1985). *Aboriginal Perspectives on Experience and Learning: The Role of Language in Aboriginal Education.* Geelong, VIC: Deakin University Press.

Clark, H. H. (1993). *Arenas of Language Use.* Chicago: University of Chicago Press.

Coates, J. (1996). *Women Talk: Conversation between Women Friends.* Oxford: Blackwell Publishers.

Coulthard, M. (1992). *Advances in Spoken Discourse Analysis.* London: Routledge.

Drew, P. (1981). Adults' corrections of children's mistakes: a response to Wells and Montgomery. In P. French and M. MacLure (eds), *Adult–Child Conversation* (pp. 244–67). New York: St Martin's Press.

Du Bois, J. W., Schuetze-Coburn, S., Cumming, S. and Paolino, D. (1993). Outline of discourse transcription. In J. A. Edwards and M. D. Lampert (eds), *Talking Data: Transcription and Coding in Discourse Research* (pp. 45–90). Hillsdale, NJ: Lawrence Erlbaum Associates.

Eades, D. (1982). You gotta know how to talk: information-seeking in Southeast Queensland Aboriginal society. *Australian Journal of Linguistics, 2*(1), 61–82.

Eagleson, R. D., Kaldor, S. and Malcolm, I. G. (1982). *English and the Aboriginal Child.* Canberra: Curriculum Development Centre.

Edelsky, C. (1981). Who's got the floor? *Language in Society, 10,* 383–421.

Edwards, A. D. and Westgate, D. P. G. (1994). *Investigating Classroom Talk* (second edn). London: Falmer Press.

French, P. and MacLure, M. (1981). *Adult–Child Conversation.* New York: St Martin's Press.

Gee, J. P. (1989). Two styles of narrative construction and their linguistic and educational implications. *Discourse Processes, 12*(3), 287.

Harris, S. (1980). *Culture and Learning: Tradition and Education in Northeast Arnhem Land.* Darwin, NT: Northern Territory Department of Education.

Harris, S. (1990). *Two-way Aboriginal Schooling: Educational and Cultural Survival.* Canberra: Aboriginal Studies Press.

Heath, S. B. (1983). *Ways with Words: Language, Life, and Work in Communities and Classrooms.* New York: Cambridge University Press.

Heritage, J. (1995). Conversation analysis: methodological aspects. In U. M. Quasthoff (ed.), *Aspects of Oral Communication* (pp. 391–418). Berlin: de Gruyter.

Hilliard, A. G., III. (1992). Behavioral style, culture, and teaching and learning. *The Journal of Negro Education, 61*(3), 370–77.

Lamb, R. D. and Troike, R. C. (1972). *Language and Cultural Diversity in American Education.* Englewood Cliffs, NJ: Prentice-Hall.

Liberman, K. (1982). Some linguistic features of congenial fellowship among Pitjantjatjara. *International Journal of the Sociology of Language, 36,* 35–52.

Lucas, C. and Borders, D. G. (1994). *Language Diversity and Classroom Discourse.* Norwood, NJ: Ablex Publishing Corp.

Malcolm, I. G. (1980). Speech use in Aboriginal communities: a preliminary survey. *Anthropological Forum, 5*(1), 54–104.

Malcolm, I. G. (1982). Verbal interaction in the classroom. In R. D. Eagleson, S. Kaldor and I. G. Malcolm (eds), *English and the Aboriginal Child.* Canberra: Curriculum Development Centre.

Northern Territory Department of Education. (1988). *Living and Learning in an Aboriginal Community.* Darwin, NT: Northern Territory Department of Education.

Sacks, H. (1995). *Lectures on Conversation* (Vol. I and II). Oxford: Blackwell.

Sacks, H., Schegloff, E. A. and Jefferson, G. (1974). A simplest systematics for the organization of turn-taking for conversation. *Language, 50*(4), 696–735.

Sansom, B. (1980). *The Camp at Wallaby Cross: Aboriginal Fringe Dwellers in Darwin.* Canberra: Australian Institute of Aboriginal Studies.

Schegloff, E. A. (1996). Issues of relevance for discourse analysis: contingency in action, interaction and co-participant context. In E. H. Hovy and D. R. Scott (eds), *Computational and Conversational Discourse: Burning Issues, an Interdisciplinary Account* (pp. 3–38). Berlin: Springer-Verlag.

Thies, K. (1987). *Aboriginal Viewpoints on Education: A Survey in the East Kimberley Region.* Nedlands, WA: National Centre for Research on Rural Education, University of WA.

Vygotsky, L. S. (1978). *Mind in Society: The Development of Higher Psychological Processes.* Cambridge, MA: Harvard University Press.

Walsh, M. (1991). Conversational styles and intercultural communication: an example from northern Australia. *Australian Journal of Communication, 18*(1), 1–12.

Watson, C. (1997). Re-embodying sand drawing and re-evaluating the status of the camp: the practice and iconography of women's public sand drawing in Balgo, WA. *The Australian Journal of Anthropology, 8*(1), 104–24.

Watson, R. (2001). Literacy and oral language: implications for early literacy acquisition. In S. B. Neuman and D. K. Dickinson (eds), *Handbook of Early Literacy Research* (pp. 43–53). New York: Guildford Press.

Wilkinson, M. (1991). 'Djambarrpuyngu: a Yolngu variety of northern Australia'. Unpublished PhD thesis, University of Sydney, Sydney.

The silence of the frogs: dysfunctional discourse in the 'English-only' Aboriginal classroom

6

Karin Moses and Gillian Wigglesworth

For most schools located predominantly in Aboriginal communities, Standard Australian English is unlikely to be the first language of its students (Rhydwen, 1992a) and is unlikely to be the major language used by the children in the classroom (Hoogenraad, 1992). The 'English-only' approach to Aboriginal education in most Northern Territory schools means that Aboriginal children who are speakers of a vernacular or Aboriginal English are often submerged in Standard Australian English, the target language, well beyond the point at which input is comprehensible to them.[1] This study seeks to look closely at the discourse patterns that are discernible in one 'English-only' Aboriginal classroom. In particular the focus will be on the way in which the whole-class setting of much classroom discourse, a setting which engenders particular behaviour patterns, precludes the successful participation of Aboriginal students and provides them with little opportunity to display their communicative ability. The study is centred on a small 'English-only' one-teacher school south-east of Tennant Creek and focuses on the discourse patterns that emerge from the whole-class interaction. These interactions, it will be shown, are determined and dominated by the non-Aboriginal teacher and do not encourage effective communication or second language learning.

Introduction

In 2007, the then Minister of Aboriginal Affairs, Malcolm Brough, expressed alarm at the fact that people in many Indigenous Australian communities did not speak standard Australian English. To remedy this, he advocated an 'English-only' approach in primary schools in Indigenous communities, ignoring the fact that almost all schools in Indigenous communities have had an English-only approach for many years. This study focuses on the discourse patterns that are discernible in an 'English-only' Aboriginal classroom, and shows how this leads to a lack of participation in the classroom by the children with very limited opportunities for the children to display their linguistic knowledge.

While the 'English-only' approach to Aboriginal education in the Northern Territory makes use of neither an English as a Second Language (ESL) curriculum, nor ESL qualified teachers, it does provide for the appointment of local Aboriginal 'teaching assistants' who are fluent speakers of the vernacular and whose main job it is to make comprehensible to the students the non-Aboriginal teacher's discourse.[2] In this provision there is some recognition that the 'English-only' classroom has more than one language of instruction. However, since many Aboriginal teacher assistants have limited English language skills (some functioning at the same level as that of the students in their classrooms) and few are given any formal training, language learners in the 'English-only' classroom are often submerged in the target language well beyond the point at which input is comprehensible.

This study focuses on the way in which the whole-class setting of much classroom discourse, a setting which engenders particular behaviour patterns, precludes the successful participation of Aboriginal students and provides them with little opportunity to display their communicative ability.

Aboriginal children from traditionally oriented communities who speak a language other than Standard Australian English generally experience little success in school; few have developed academic skills beyond the level of primary year three or four, and the English literacy rates of these children fall well below the national average (Department of Education Science and Training, 2002; Department of Employment Education and Training, 2004–2005). The reasons for this are many and complex. They include poor attendance rates, poverty and the concomitant problems of health and housing, the disparity between the school's culture and that of the home, the employment of inexperienced staff, high staff turnover and an inappropriate curriculum. But central to any analysis of the effectiveness of Aboriginal education is the problem of communication between teacher and pupils in many Aboriginal classrooms.

Although a number of studies have focused on the communication breakdown in Aboriginal classrooms (Christie, 1984; Harris, 1977), most have employed an ethnographic approach that has made little use of linguistic data. Apart from the work of Ian Malcolm (1979a; 1979b) few have been based on the transcripts of actual teacher/pupil interactions. This study focuses on what can be learned from close analysis of the classroom discourse.

The school

The school which is the focus of this study is a multi-age, single teacher school which at the time of the study had 36 names on the attendance roll. Thirteen were transient (having attended for less than a term) and 23 attended regularly, or semi-regularly. The average attendance was 13 and the ages of the students ranged between 5 and 14. The school was an 'English-only' school in a region where the traditional language, Alyawarr, was considered strong by local linguists, and it was generally believed that the traditional language was the language that the children brought with them to school. Alyawarr belongs to the Arrandic language family that includes Eastern, Southern and Central Arrernte, Anmatyerr and Kaytetye. The 'heartland' of Alyawarr country is some 200 km north-east of Alice Springs but it extends as far as the Barkley Highway (near Tennant Creek) to the north, the Plenty Highway to the south and Mt Isa to the east. Within this region there are significant dialect variations, particularly between the Alyawarr spoken in the region around Lake Nash in the west and that spoken by the communities to the east of it such as Antarrengeny and Wetenngerr (see Green, 1992, p. xii). The community that is the focus of this study lies at the western edge of Alyawarr country, close to Tennant Creek, the largest regional town in the area, and Alekarenge, a large multilingual Aboriginal community. It may be the proximity to both that is partly responsible for the language spoken by the children in the classroom. In this study the children's language is referred to as Kriol, though a more detailed linguistic analysis may indeed conclude that the language they are speaking is a mixed language. The issues surrounding Aboriginal English, Kriol and mixed languages are beyond the scope of this study. The main language spoken by the children at school was Kriol.

The school is remote and there is very little opportunity to hear Standard Australian English. Nor is there any need for it to be spoken within the local community since the teacher and the local cattle-station owners, resident near the community, are the only speakers of Standard Australian English and the linguistic interaction that the community has with them is extremely limited.

The teacher in the school was a young non-Aboriginal teacher who had completed her training, together with some 6 months teaching, in country Victoria the previous year. She had no language other than English and had no background in ESL or intercultural teaching. She had had no contact with Aboriginal people prior to this posting. At the start of the year she, along with other new recruits, was given one half-day induction into 'Aboriginal language and culture' by a non-Aboriginal educational officer. Rhydwen (1992b, p. 26) has likened the provision made by the Department for the language training of new recruits to 'showing someone how to hold a scalpel and sending him or her out as a trained surgeon'.

It is important to keep this in mind in order to avoid making critical assessments about the teacher's performance in the school. This teacher was placed in an extraordinarily difficult position and expected to perform complex educational and administrative tasks under harsh physical conditions with minimal support. These conditions contribute to the very high turnover of staff in remote schools, which in turn makes it difficult for students and Aboriginal teacher assistants, usually appointed from the local community, to develop a relationship with a teacher.

The school 'building' provided for the community by the Education Department was a configuration of three caravans: one housed the main classroom, another the teacher's office and a teaching area (usually reserved for the viewing of videos) and the third an ablution block containing showers, toilets and a washing machine. Power was supplied by a generator located a short distance from the school which, together with the air conditioners mounted in the west-facing walls of the classroom, provided constant background noise to the lessons.

Collection and selection of data

Data were collected by video and audio recordings. The video camera was placed in the front corner of the classroom where it remained on its tripod during classes, sometimes switched on, sometimes off, for a three week period. After some initial comment about the camera, the students grew accustomed to both and even came to feel quite proprietorial about the camera, recording themselves during recess (while no adults were present), dancing, then viewing their performance later in the day. If a lesson took place outside the caravan, the camera was taken outside to record the activities. The tape recorder was placed in varying locations in the classroom.

The main focus of the data in this study is a whole-class session which followed an 'excursion' in which the teacher and children went hunting for frogs in an area of land near the river, where the children looked for and dug up a number of large water-carrying frogs. These were collected, roasted on the coals of a fire and eaten. On the Monday following the 'excursion', the teacher used a book about frogs as the basis of a whole-class session in which she sought to extend the theme. This session forms the cornerstone of this analysis (Text 1). Three other texts, a whole-class session on rocks (Text 2), as well as data from the frog-hunting expedition itself (Text 3), and from the children talking among themselves while copying from the blackboard (Text 4) are also used to illuminate the children's involvement in whole-class discourse and the rules which govern their participation. The texts selected for analysis were representative of the many observations and recordings made during the period.

The frog 'discussion' (Text 1) was chosen as the focus of this study because it provided an opportunity to note the difference between the nature of the teacher–student discourse (about a common theme) outside the classroom (Text 3) and that within the classroom. The session on rocks (Text 2) was selected because it offered an example of whole-class discourse in which student participation was at its highest level. It therefore provided some insight into the conditions under which students responded to elicitations in a large group. The example of students talking among themselves (Text 4) was in large part serendipitous. A speaker of the traditional language had chosen to listen to one of the audio tapes at random. She found the conversation entertaining and offered to help translate it.

The whole-class discourse: an exchange gone awry

The theoretical approach adopted in this study sought to identify and account for those features of the discourse which set it apart from that of the non-Aboriginal classroom and which contributed to the breakdown of communication, without, however, codifying individual utterances and imposing a conceptual framework that would risk excessive cultural bias in the interpretation of the data. While referring to the work on exchange structures in the Aboriginal classroom done by Malcolm (1979a; 1979b), because of the light it sheds on the teacher's expectation of the discourse, we have focused on the linguistic and paralinguistic causes of the breakdown in communication: on the syntactic and semantic nature of the miscommunication, on the role of silences and pauses, of whispers and murmurs in the interaction, and on the nature and purpose of questions in the pedagogical process. To place this analysis in context, it is important to explain not only the immediate environment of the linguistic interaction but also the cultural background that informs the language behaviour of the participants.

Extract 1 is an excerpt from the whole-class 'discussion' on frogs. The most striking feature of the verbal interaction is the extent to which the usual classroom discourse structure has broken down. The primary function of the discourse for the teacher appears to be to develop an understanding of the knowledge and skills that her students possess: to gain evidence, through the way they talk, of their cognitive abilities. According to Sinclair and Coulthard's (1975) description of a classroom's exchange structure, this can be conceptualised as an *initiation* by the teacher, followed by a *response* from the students, followed by some *feedback* by the teacher.

Such a framework, however, describes a 'contractual' agreement which binds students and teachers together on the basis of a common set of expectations about how knowledge is passed on, or information is acquired, as well as expectations about the rights and obligations each party has in the exchange of information. The teacher expects her questions (e.g. lines 26, 35, 37) to be answered by the students, even if the answers are provided reluctantly or constitute little more than one-word unanimated utterances. Such questions are virtually always 'display questions' for the children to display their knowledge, rather than questions to which the teacher genuinely wishes to know the answer. Display questions are asked to determine whether the students know the answer and there is a tacit understanding that the teacher is interrogating from a position of 'power'. When the assumptions that underpin this 'contractual' relationship are not shared, the exchange breaks down.

Extract 1: Text 1

25	**T:**	Frogs jump well. They have long back legs. Their long legs help them to jump
26		What do you think that duck's thinking?
27		[5 seconds]
28	**T:**	He's thinking oh I'd like to eat that frog.
29		Ducks eat frogs?
30		Pelicans? Ducks? And other birds eat frogs?
31		[5 seconds]

32	**C?**	[inaudible whisper -- one word]
33	**T:**	You think so do you?
34		The female frog is bigger. Now the female is the woman and the male is the man
35		You know the sand frogs we dug up?
36		They didn't make a big noise at all did they?
37		Do they ever make a big noise?
38		They have a little noise like a little bird.
39		Do they ever make a big noise?
40		[4 seconds]
41	**T:**	Nah you wouldn't hear them under the ground anyway.
42		In Spring the mother frog lays some eggs in a pond.
43		The eggs are in jelly.
44		Who's seen frogs' eggs down in the creek?
45		Sometimes along the edge in the grass you can see them.
46		[2 seconds]
47	**T:**	Have you seen them when you've been down there swimming?
48	**C1:**	[inaudible; possibly a sound rather than a word]
49	**T:**	What? Clear jelly see-through it is. You can see straight through, little
50		tiny black eggs. Have you seen that down there?
51		[2 seconds]
52	**T:**	Birds like to eat it. Ducks love to eat it. Jelly keeps the eggs safe.
53		What do you think it keeps the eggs safe from?
54		[6 seconds]
55	**T:**	What do you think the jelly keeps the eggs safe from?
56		[4 seconds]
57	**T:**	What would happen to these eggs if they live in the water; they sit in the water?
58		[7 seconds]
59	**C:**	[inaudible whisper]
60	**T:**	What do you think it keeps them safe from? [3 seconds]

The most striking feature of this breakdown is the silence of the students. They consistently do not respond to elicitations (interrogative forms followed by a pause of at least a one-second duration) to which one would expect students in a non-Aboriginal classroom to respond. What is remarkable, however, is the teacher's adherence to an exchange pattern that is so clearly unsuccessful, a pattern which she continues for 30 minutes. Rather, she undertakes to fill the students' roles herself.

One interpretation of this behaviour is that the children are simply being uncooperative in their responses, but this is not supported by the observations. They liked their teacher, often demonstrating their affection physically by stroking and hugging her. Whenever she gave them a directive which involved doing something physical, going to get a ruler or a bucket, they complied. She in turn was extremely fond of them. The children walked at least a kilometre to school, and expected to walk home again in the afternoon when the temperature had climbed, as it did everyday during the data collection, to some 45°C. The decision to attend was their own. In many Aboriginal communities, children are given much more freedom than non-Aboriginal children and neither parents nor others coerce them into going to school (Harris, 1980; Kearins, 1985). It seems untenable to suggest that they attended and then actively refrained from participating in verbal interaction with their teacher. What seems far more likely is that for most of the time during the whole-class discourse the students either did not recognise their teacher's elicitations as such or were unable to respond. This is supported by closer scrutiny of the form that the numerous elicitations took and the context in which they occurred, as discussed in the next section.

Syntactic and semantic misunderstanding

The whole-class session on frogs (Text 1) is scattered with interrogative forms of great variety, all ending with rising cadences. As the following examples, all from Text 1, show some are complex, supplying very little in the way of linguistic assistance as in Example 1, while others require a sophisticated understanding of the use of difficult grammatical features such as adverbs of frequency and conditionals as in Example 2.

Example 1

60	T	What do you think it keeps the eggs safe from?

Example 2

37	T	Do they ever make a big noise?
38		They have a little noise like a little bird.
39		Do they ever make a big noise?
66	T	So what could happen to these eggs?

Some are embedded in discourse that gives no contextual assistance:

Example 3

| 11 | T | They can swim in the water and they can swim well. |
| 12 | | You know what sort of plant that is? |

Others are ambiguous:

Example 4

| 160 | T | How many is two thousand? |

Some of the questions are about the content of the lesson (lines 18, 19) and others are metalinguistic (line 20):

Example 5

18	T	Frogs can stay on land too.
19		They stay where it's damp.
20		What's damp?

Others involve a form of ellipsis which removes the very word which would lexically identify it as a question. Only the rising tone indicates that it is a question:

Example 6

| 29 | T | Ducks eat frogs? |
| 30 | | Pelicans? Ducks? and other birds eat frogs? |

To answer these questions successfully, the students need linguistic resources beyond those they possess. Although English is not their first language, the teacher appeared unconscious of the difficulty the students might have in understanding her. While there are a number of modifications which can be made to the structure of conversations which increase the probability of understanding (Long, 1983), the teacher made very little use of these. She repeated utterances but did not often try to rephrase them. She rarely shifts down lexically and never relinquishes control of the topic. She overlooks signals that she is given in the form of unexpected responses or differing use of lexical items, which would alert her to the problems that the children are having with the language as opposed to the content. When questions remain unanswered she tends to ask other questions presumably in the hope this will enable the students to respond to the original question successfully. If this fails, she moves on to question the students about another aspect of the topic.

The teacher may be assuming that because the children can follow directives and basic conversations, they can follow classroom discourse, precisely the problem discussed extensively by Cummins (2000), who shows that the language of the classroom is far more cognitively demanding and 'context reduced' than is the language of everyday conversation. Thus the ability of students to follow simple instructions in English is no indication that they will be able to understand English explanations or hypothetical propositions.

However, even when the children do attempt to engage with the teacher, the distinctiveness of their use of English, and their difficulty in understanding that of their teacher, is clearly a contributing factor to their reticence in the classroom. The most responsive student, Ruby (C1) who seeks to answer more questions than any other student, has difficulty getting her replies acknowledged or accepted due to semantic and syntactic misunderstanding. Her first audible response (line 67), given after the teacher has fired some 14 questions at the class (none of which has received an audible reply) is not acknowledged:

Extract 2: Text 1

53	T	What do you think it keeps the eggs safe from?
54		[6 seconds]
55	T	What do you think the jelly keeps the eggs safe from?
56		[4 seconds]
57	T	What would happen to these eggs if they live in the water, they sit in the water?
58		[7 seconds]

59	C?	[inaudible whisper]
60	T	What do you think it keeps them safe from?
61		[3 seconds]
62	T	Are these, do you think they're hard these eggs?
63		[2 seconds]
64	T	Hard? No they're very soft not like um cocky eggs with a hard shell.
65		They're very very soft.
66		So what could happen to these eggs?
67	C1	Frog come out
68	T	Snake or a fish . . . could eat them all up.
69		I don't know how the jelly stops it, maybe it tastes horrible

Ruby's response indicates that she has not understood the general train of the questioning (what bad things could happen to the eggs) and how this relates to the use of the modal 'could' in the question in line 66. It is predictable that modality and conditionals would prove problematic to these students given that they are difficult grammatical structures for second language learners. Moreover, modality is conceptually complex and most younger children, whether of an ESL background or not, take some time to understand the conditional nature of such constructions. Further, misunderstanding often occurs when Aboriginal children transpose the hypothetical setting of a question to a literal one (Harris, 1990).

In the case of Ruby's 'failed' response, the context, however, has also contributed to her inability to decode the text. What preceded the question was a statement comparing frogs' eggs to 'cocky eggs', which was the teacher's response to her own question about whether or not frogs' eggs were hard. This in turn was preceded by the question 'What do you think it keeps the eggs safe from?' which, for the teacher at any rate, set the context for the question that Ruby failed to answer successfully. Even if Ruby were able to second-guess the teacher's logic and follow the path from jelly and fish eggs through comparisons with cockatoo eggs to safety from predators, it is clearly overambitious to require her to negotiate the linguistic minefield of pronominal references, and follow the connections that the teacher intended, over several speech acts.

A little later in the discourse Ruby ventures another audible response:

Extract 3: Text 1

80	T	When it [the tadpole] just hatches what does it eat?
81		[3 seconds]
82	C1	Seaweed.
83	T	Seaweed? We haven't got any seaweed in the creek just weeds,
84		dead leaves and things like that.

This time the reply is acknowledged but rejected. Ruby has every reason to be totally baffled by the teacher's 'feedback' since the Aboriginal English or Kriol word for the weeds in the creek is 'seaweed'. The teacher has not realised that many words in Kriol, although originating from English, do not have the same meaning (Rhydwen, 1992a).

There are a number of features about the way in which Ruby's responses are dismissed which are particularly disheartening in terms of progress towards positive educational outcomes for the students. In the context of a discourse in which most initiations are not responded to, the non-acceptance or rejection of a response undermines the very goal which the teacher is seeking – the participation of the students. This is particularly so when the respondent has no idea as to why the contribution has been ignored or rejected. In the case of Ruby, the problem is compounded by the fact that she is seen by the other students as being the most proficient and confident player of the 'school game', and at 13 she is one of the oldest students. When Ruby gets it wrong, there is likely to be a strong sense on the part of the others that no one can get it right.

Pauses and silences

Pauses can be seen as part of the normal structure of discourse, the rhythmic hitch that holds an interaction together; or they can be seen as a form of dysfluency, a sign of malfunction in the machinery of talk (Scollon, 1985). For the teacher, the pauses that follow her elicitations are uncomfortable because she expects them to be filled by the talk of her students and she perceives the silences as negative because they represent the omission of something that she expects. As Tannen (1985, p. 107) argues:

> A silence is differentiated from a pause only by the intentions and conventions of the speaker. Silence and pause can be distinguished only by reference to

prior experience: how long does a person typically pause within the stream of speech, and before taking a turn at speech?

In this classroom teacher and students appear to have different expectations of the timing of responses, but outside the classroom there seems to be more room for adjusting conversational styles. When the students and teacher are out 'hunting' for frogs the nature of the exchange between them differs. While there are many factors that contribute to this, one of the most important appears to be the teacher's willingness to wait for the response as exemplified below:

Extract 4: Text 3

29	T	Why do you think it's got that sticky stuff on it?
30		[students continue to dig for a second frog – 10 seconds]
31	C1	So it can climb up trees and hold.
32	T	So it can stick on the trees
33	C1	Yeah
….		
67	T	How do they dig?
68		They're so soft. It's getting in.
69		Is it burrowing?
70		Maybe it's trying to get out.
71		How do they dig down, do you know?
72		[4 seconds]
73	C4	I don't know.
74	T	O.K. put'em back in the bucket.
75		[5 seconds]
76	C1	They go round and round and round and round.
77	T	Till they get down.
78	C1	Yeah.
79	T	Put'em back in the bucket. We'll go and see if we can find some more.
80	T	Is it going down or coming up though?
81		[much laughter and overlapping talk among the students – 7 seconds]
82	C	Going down.

Here the responses to the questions the teacher asks are forthcoming but are offered in a timeframe determined by the students and not the teacher. Outside the classroom, the teacher seemed far more comfortable with the pauses that followed her questions. Having an activity occurring at the same time as the conversation makes the pauses and silences much less 'uncomfortable', with activity – walking, the looking for 'tracks', digging, catching slippery frogs – 'filling' the perceived silences.

Differences in attitudes towards, and the uses of, silences can have an enormous influence on the way in which participants in a cross-cultural discourse view each other. Scollon (1985, pp. 23–24) suggests that Athabaskans (Native of Canada) are stereotyped by non-Indigenous Canadians, as being 'passive', 'sullen', 'withdrawn', 'unresponsive', 'lazy', 'backward', 'destructive', 'hostile', 'uncooperative', 'anti-social', and 'stupid', largely because of their greater use of silence. Similarly, Nakane (2003), who examined the silence of Japanese university students in Australian tertiary classrooms, found different assumptions about classroom communication, and differences in their perceptions of others both by the Japanese students, and the Australian participants – their peers and lecturers.

Eades (1985) and Malcolm (1993) both found that non-Aboriginal teachers attributed negative characteristics to their Aboriginal students due to what they perceived as the slowness or absence of their verbal responses in class and the pervasiveness of their silences. The teacher in this study accounted for the children's lack of response in classroom discussion by recourse to personality features such as their shyness. She did not at any stage relate their verbal performance to the language situation that she had set up, or comment on linguistic or cultural differences in language use. Her assessment of the students' abilities seemed to be largely based on their performance in whole-class discussions. Ruby (C1), for instance, was described as being bright because she responded 'well' in class discussion, while a number of the other students were labelled as slow because of their inability to do so.

This is a cultural difference. Non-Aboriginal people are often described by Aboriginal people as 'talking too much' and, concomitantly, as being 'pushy', 'nosy' and 'rude' (personal communication with final year Aboriginal teacher trainees at Batchelor College; see also Christie and Harris, 1985; Eades, 1991). Aboriginal children as well as adults are not encouraged to behave in a similar manner, and those that are seen to do so – talking a lot, asking and answering lots of questions – often invite derision.

The fact that the teacher was unaware of these differences in conversational styles, and their cultural foundations, meant that she was unable to develop a way of talking to the children which would maximise their participation in classroom discourse and this clearly contributed to the breakdown in communication.

Whispers and murmurs

Although the most striking feature of the classroom interaction was the lack of students' response to teacher elicitations, another aspect of the discourse which sets it apart from the shared talk of the non-Aboriginal classroom is the inaudibility of those responses that are given: the mouthed, mumbled and whispered replies that are found throughout the discourse.

Extract 5: Text 2

3	T	What do you think is in there before I even let you hear what the noise is?
4	C1	[whispered] Lollies.
5	CC	[much laughter]
6	T	What's that?
7	C1	Lollies

Extract 6: Text 1

76	T	What do [sic] the baby frogs called when they hatch?
77	C1	[mouthing inaudibly]
78	T	Tadpoles that's right.

Extract 7: Text 2

222	T	. . . who knows what that one is?
223	C7	[whisper, looking down] Copper.
224	T	What is it?
225	C7	[slightly louder whisper – covering face with hands and looking down] Copper.
226	T	You're right Sam, what did you say?

227	C7	[very softly spoken] Copper.
228	T	Copper. Who's seen a copper pipe that hot water goes through?

Extract 8: Text 3

217	T	Who can they hide from?
218	C1	[inaudible whisper – possibly snakes]
219	T	Snakes.
220		and who else eats frogs?
221		[7 seconds]
222	T	Please tell me Ruby [C1] ?
223	C1	[inaudible whisper – possibly birds]
224	T	Birds and cats, cats eat frogs?

Both the mouthed reply, which is encoded by the child in an exaggerated movement of lips and mouth but without the use of sound, and the whispered reply appear to be common features of teacher–student interactions in classrooms in numerous Aboriginal communities (Malcolm, 1979b).

Malcolm suggests that the reason for 'whispered replies' may sometimes be what 'the mumble strategy, i.e., making an unclear answer on the assumption that even if it's wrong, the teacher will hear what he wants to hear – the right answer' (1979b, p. 42, citing Holt). There is no doubt that uncertainty, and fear of failure, may be factors in students' deliberately producing answers that cannot be heard distinctly.

This tension is nowhere more dramatically displayed than in the behaviour of Ruby, who, more than any other, attempts to conform to the teacher's expectation of her role in the whole-class interaction. While Ruby (C1) was responsible for most of the responses made to the teacher's elicitations, albeit largely inaudible, so uncomfortable was she with her vocal behaviour, that she persistently filled her mouth with tissues during the session. This was a regular occurrence – she often placed tissues or other objects, such as her necklace, in her mouth. Ruby appeared to be in a dilemma, torn between doing what she understood the teacher wanted and what she knew was expected of her as an Aboriginal person – not to talk too much and not to draw attention to herself.

One way in which the children seek to reconcile their concept of correct language behaviour with that of the school is to chorus answers. This seems to be a highly effective strategy for enabling them to avoid the shame that is associated with being singled out and yet still contribute to the whole-class discourse. Unfortunately the cultural and linguistic rules which govern the way in which non-Aboriginal English-speaking interlocutors interact do not allow for much multiple and simultaneous verbal participation. The rules which govern interlocutors' participation in interactions in many traditional Aboriginal communities permit such overlapping.

When the children call out answers in unison, they feel comfortable with the group response but their teacher does not. The children are told to speak 'one at a time' (Text 1, line 267) or to 'put your hand up please' (Text 2, line 146) because the teacher is concerned with monitoring individual performances and group participation is not easily tolerated.

During the whole-class session on frogs, the teacher initially accepts answers from anyone, not nominating individual students to respond to her questions, but as the discussion gets underway, she becomes frustrated by the non-response of most of the students and the lack of individual responses. She tries to bring several students into the discourse by singling them out – calling them by name (lines 293, 294, 297). The nominated children physically shrink into themselves and provide no response. Towards the end of the session, in her desperate attempt to have all the students say something, she has them stand up (line 298) and insists that they tell her something before they are allowed to be seated:

Extract 9: Text 1

290	T	What else didn't you know about frogs that was in there?
		I didn't know that only the male frog, the man frog, croaked.
		I thought they all sat down there of a [child coughs] night time and went grr grr
		Can you hear them Gertrude [C12], down there?
		What was something you didn't know Earnest [C13]?
295	C?	sh sh
		[5 seconds]
	T	Sean [C10] think about something that was in that book that you didn't know about frogs.
		Everybody everybody stand up up up.
300	C5	[just audible] climb
	CC	[some talk, not in English and not clear]

	T	OK. Up Josie [C9].
		Right you told us something you can sit down.
		You told us something.
305	T	You told us something
	C5	Climb
	T	You said something.
		[3 seconds]
	T	Ben [C5].
310	C5	Climb.
	T	That they can climb what?
		Climb doesn't tell me anything.
		Climb what?
	C5	Climb trees.
315	T	Didn't you know that frogs could climb trees
		[with their] suckers?
	T	Who else can think of something
	CC	[inaudible talk and laughter]
	T	they didn't know already?
		Flick through the pages Andrew [C6].
320	C6	Eat flies.
	T	That they eat flies.
		How do they eat them Andrew [C6]?
		How do they catch them?
	C1	With their tongue.
325	C6	Tongue.
	T	So they can [. . .] yes. Thinking, have a look at the
		pages. Think of something that you didn't know.

[8 seconds – much loud whispering from the children sitting down to those standing up]

330	T	Geoff [C7]?
	C7	[reading] Ducks eat frogs.
	T	Didn't you know ducks eat frogs?
		What else eats frogs?

OK keep looking at the pages, see if you can find something, think of something.

The absence of clear directives suggests that this tactic has been used before. Ruby (C1) and Alison (C2) are given permission to remain seated because they have already told the teacher something – they have been good and are rewarded. These two students proceed to 'stage whisper' appropriate responses for the other students, in an attempt to stop the 'shaming' of which they obviously feel as much a part as the students who are left standing. Two more children are allowed to sit down after giving staccato single and two word utterances (line 303; line 306) and another child reads his response, emotionlessly, from the book: 'ducks eat frogs' (line 331). Words are extracted as painfully as teeth without anaesthetic in a process that effectively precludes any genuine communication, with the majority of the class standing silently while the children seated on the floor try to divert attention from them by whispering ever louder.

This strategy not only causes much distress and embarrassment, it virtually forces the children to choose between two seemingly incompatible moral and linguistic codes. This must inevitably leave them with the impression that English can only be learnt at the expense of, and not in addition to, their own cultural identity.

The children's talk

If all that were known of the spoken language skills of the children was that which was revealed by their participation in whole-class discussions with their teacher, we would have no understanding of what the children could do with language. A glimpse of one instance of the 'chatter' of the children in this classroom demonstrates how vital, sophisticated and complex their use of language can be.

When Sam (C8), Alison (C2) and Valda (C3) are copying from the blackboard, the banter that accompanies this rather mindless activity is brighter and wittier than anything else in which they are engaged throughout their entire school day. Alison lets Sam know that she is further ahead in her copying than he is, and Sam takes up the challenge. Using the metaphor of a motorcar race, he constructs an elaborate fantasy that involves sabotage and magical transforma tions, accusing Alison first of slashing his tyres and causing his car to go backwards, then of throwing a box full of nails on the road and finally of setting his petrol tank on fire (line 46). Initially Alison denies the accusation (line 41) but then, as the charges become more and more outrageous, she resorts to mock indignation (line 47). When Sam has the police out looking for Alison she enters fully into the story, telling him she still has the lead since she gave the police the slip by hiding in some bushes (lines 61 and 62):

Extract 10: Text 4

41	Alison	I never cheatim you I bin keep going – *athew*. I didn't sabotage you, I have kept going straight ahead.
42	Sam	Na you bin cheatem me Ilafa. Ilafa you cheat me. No you sabotaged me Alison. You are still sabotaging me. [Sam makes racing-car noises]
43	Alison	'Canteen'*? You la 'Canteen'? Me la 'coming'. 'Canteen'? Are you up to 'Canteen'? I'm up to 'coming'.
44	Vanesa	'Coming'? 'Me la'barbeque'. Are you up to 'coming'? I'm up to 'barbeque'
45	Alison	Me la 'coming'. I'm up to 'coming'
46	Sam	Ilafa bin thing na chuckim matches la mine petrol Alison's threw matches into my petrol tank.
47	Alison	Well what you reckon youself how come? Well why do you think that (what you think)?
48	Sam	Good job ayeng nantew-akert-anem. It's a good thing that I still had a horse to travel with.
....		
61	Alison	I bin bush-itwel turn irreyel-alheyel iltyemweney-rnem passed. I was turning into a bush as the police went past.
62	Alison	Amper-irreyel-antey-alheyel I bin turn-irreyel-ew. After I turned (into a bush) (the police) kept moving in circles.

* 'Canteen' is capitalised because it refers to the place name 'Canteen Creek'.
Note also the code-switching[3] between the creole and Alyawarr (in *italics*).

The co-operative storytelling then begins in earnest as Sam transmogrifies into the 'Terminator' after his car bursts into flames while Alison abandons her mode of transportation and takes to the sky like a bird. In the ensuing race to the finish, there is much discussion about whether or not Sam is still alive. This is commented upon by Valda whose sing–song 'dead live dead live dead' (Text 4, line84) suggests that her head is spinning with all this claim and counterclaim. Valda concludes her commentary with the word 'barbecue' which lets the other two know where she is up to in case either of them are interested. Alison then says, 'Canteen Creek' playing with the word's actual meaning and its graphic representation. She is not suggesting that she is up to that point in her copying (which would see her behind the other two) but rather that she is so far ahead and away from them that she is actually in Canteen Creek (some distance from the school).

This narrative is action-packed and complicated, involving rapid plot turns and twists. The co-operative nature of the storytelling requires the participants to be quick in responding to changes in the action in order to stay in the metaphorical race. The discourse also involves much simultaneous talk which is tolerated by all – no one demands to hold centre stage. There is much laughter from everyone. The interaction is lively and animated, the intonation of the voices varies dramatically and the pace of the talk alters. The discourse displays a sophisticated level of verbal play that is underlined by humour and stands in stark contrast to the children's participation in the whole-class discourse.

The point of including this discourse, however, is not simply to suggest that the talk which children share among themselves is different from that which they share with their teacher in a whole-class session. One would presumably have difficulty finding a school anywhere in Australia where this were not the case, even if the children and the teacher did speak a common language. But while the casual conversation between children in all schools differs from the more formal discourse of the whole-class session, teachers usually have some access to this children-only talk. They are aware of the banter, the jokes, the arguments and the ribaldry; at times the teacher is even able to join in. Children can engage with their teacher in casual conversation, relate something of personal interest, tell a story or even a joke. Here this cannot happen. The teacher is unaware of the children's abilities with language in casual conversation and cannot engage them in such discourse. Not only does this mean that the children's communicative abilities are never accurately assessed, it also means that the social function of discourse in the classroom is severely curtailed.

The importance of these casual conversations in the classroom cannot be overstated. It is only in conversation with each other that the children are able to make full use of their language skills. They can play with words, make-up stories, recount and explain events and tease each other. In short, they can use language in the complex and highly sophisticated way that people anywhere do to fulfil a wide range of functions. A student such as Sam (C8), who contributed not one word to the whole-class discussion on frogs, can extend and develop his storytelling skills, entertaining and engaging his peers. It seems hardly surprising, then, that Aboriginal students have a marked preference for what is described by many of their teachers as 'busy work': ritualised tasks that require little effort or thought. For Christie and Harris (1985), the proclivity of Yolngu children for such tasks as copying from the board, colouring in pictures and filling in simple puzzle sheets, is a reflection of a learning style that arises from their traditional culture. But the popularity of 'busy work' may also be due to the fact that these effortless tasks provide students with the only opportunity they have in the 'English-only' classroom to engage in real talk. They offer a respite from the remaining classroom discourse which requires constant effort, is often only dimly understood, and at times embarrassing and distressing.

Conclusion

The whole-class discourse, as it is realised in the classroom-based 'discussion' on frogs, fails to work for its Aboriginal participants because neither the form of the linguistic code used in the classroom by the teacher, nor the conventions of its use in that situational context, are ever fully understood by them. The teacher, who establishes the parameters of the 'whole-class' sessions, fails to take into account that her students are second language learners who have had little opportunity to listen to, or use, Standard Australian English. Her apparent inability to modify her language to accommodate their needs, together with her inability to negotiate an appropriate interactional model, effectively denies the children the possibility of developing and extending their linguistic skills. She recognises that the interaction is not working, but she does not know how to make it work. Her attempts to repair the interactional model to which she adheres – to restore its exchange structure – only add to the difficulty that the children have in establishing what conventions are intended to apply.

This is not to suggest that the teacher is deliberately avoiding making the sort of pedagogical and linguistic compromises that appear to be needed. It is more likely that she is simply unaware of the complex linguistic and cultural factors involved and has not had the advantage of appropriate training (see also Lowell and Devlin, 1998) to enable her to identify potential pitfalls and solutions, within a consistent analytical framework.

The classroom interaction places many Aboriginal pupils in a situation in which their cultural identity is constantly challenged. In order to successfully participate, the children have to abandon the rules of language behaviour by which they define themselves as Yolngu, or Warumungu or Warlpiri or Alyawarr; they are expected to perform publicly and individually in a manner which conflicts with the moral code by which they live. As Cahill and Collard (2003, p. 217) write about Aboriginal pupils in 14 Western Australian schools, 'Aboriginals and non-Aboriginal people live in largely parallel worlds, and most schools continue to reside mainly on the non-Aboriginal side of that divide'.

Teachers in these contexts need a comprehensive understanding of the languages and cultures of the Aboriginal children to allow them to find alternatives to ways of managing teaching and learning. Teachers need to search out more appropriate models of classroom interaction for the contexts in which they work. Other models are available for consideration. Montessori schools, for instance, do not revolve around teacher-centred whole-class discourse. Instead, children are encouraged to work individually or in small groups on diverse activities, often of their own choosing, and independent of the teacher. Such a model meshes well with Aboriginal perspectives on children and learning, which focus on the child as an autonomous individual capable of developing and learning without constant verbal instruction (Kearins, 1985, p. 75). It also seems a particularly appropriate model for the multi-age classrooms common in Indigenous remote community schools.

Spoken language plays a central role in educational institutions. It is the medium through which most teaching occurs, and through which students demonstrate their learning; it enables teacher and student to negotiate the social rules of language use within the educational context – to provide for a shared understanding of the rules of the interactional game as it is played out in the classroom; and it is an integral part of the identity that each individual brings to the classroom. Classroom discourse can be said to be functioning successfully for its participants only in so far as it is able to meet these requirements. While this was not so in this case study, we cannot lay blame at the feet of the teacher. Her training simply did not equip her for the situation she encountered on her arrival at the school. She was not trained to learn about other cultures and ways of communication nor in second language learning. As Malcolm (2003) argues, non-Aboriginal teachers of Aboriginal students must have realistic attitudes towards the language codes the children bring to school and must respect and utilise their home language knowledge.

They must also be aware that there are wide differences between Aboriginal groups in language, culture and ways of behaving. Aboriginal teaching assistants play a crucial role in the success of Aboriginal classrooms. It is they who provide the bridge between the two worlds and the two language domains. Both teachers and assistants require development and support that is integrated and that enables them to work as a team. In particular, Aboriginal teacher assistants should not be left at the edges of the classroom proffering the occasional whispered explanations to children. They must be encouraged to see themselves as active participants in the delivery of the curriculum. This would be a good foundation for building a better learning and teaching environment in Aboriginal schools.

Notes

1. A limited bilingual education program has now been reintroduced by the Northern Territory Department of Employment, Education and Training (see http://www.deet.nt.gov.au/education/programs_initiatives/bep/index.shtml).
2. The fact that Aboriginal teacher assistants (TA) are employed as cultural and linguistic interpreters is highlighted by the NT Education Department's policy of allocating TA positions to schools on the basis of their non-Aboriginal staff only. Aboriginal teachers are not entitled to be employed as teaching assistants.
3. Code-switching and code-mixing is discussed in McConvell (Chapter 11).

References

Cahill, R. and Collard, G. (2003). Deadly ways to learn . . . a yarn about some learning we did together. *Comparative Education, 39*(2), 211–19.

Christie, M. J. (1984). 'The classroom world of the Aboriginal child'. Unpublished PhD thesis, University of Queensland, Brisbane.

Christie, M. J. and Harris, S. (1985). Communication breakdown in the Aboriginal classroom. In J. B. Pride (ed.), *Cross-Cultural Encounters: Communication and Miscommunication* (pp. 81–90). Melbourne: River Seine.

Cummins, J. (2000). *Language, Power and Pedagogy: Bilingual Children in the Crossfire.* Clevedon: Multilingual Matters.

Department of Education Science and Training. (2002). *National Report to Parliament on Indigenous Education and Training.* Canberra: Commonwealth of Australia.

Department of Employment Education and Training. (2004–2005). *Annual Report.* Darwin, NT: Northern Territory Government.

Eades, D. (1985). You gotta know how to talk . . . information seeking in south-east Queensland Aboriginal Society. In J. B. Pride (ed.), *Cross-Cultural Encounters: Communication and Miscommunication* (pp. 91–109). Melbourne: River Seine Publications.

Eades, D. (1991). Communicative strategies in Aboriginal English. In S. Romaine (ed.), *Language in Australia*. Cambridge: Cambridge University Press.

Green, J. (1992). *Alyawarr to English Dictionary*. Alice Springs, NT: IAD.

Harris, S. (1977). 'Milingimbi Aboriginal learning contexts'. Unpublished PhD thesis, University of New Mexico, New Mexico.

Harris, S. (1980). *Culture and Learning: Tradition and Education in Northeast Arnhem Land*. Darwin, NT: Northern Territory Department of Education.

Harris, S. (1990). *Two-way Aboriginal Schooling: Educational and Cultural Survival*. Canberra: Aboriginal Studies Press.

Hoogenraad, R. (1992). *Barkly Language in Education Survey: Final Report*. Alice Springs, NT: Northern Territory Department of Education.

Kearins, J. (1985). Cross-cultural misunderstandings in education. In J. B. Pride (ed.), *Cross-Cultural Encounters: Communication and Miscommunication* (pp. 65–80). Melbourne: River Seine Publications.

Long, M. (1983). Native speaker/non-native speaker conversation and the negotiation of comprehensible input. *Applied Linguistics 4*,126–161.

Lowell, A. and Devlin, B. (1998). Miscommunication between Aboriginal children and their non-Aboriginal teachers in a bilingual school. *Language, Culture and Curriculum, 11*(3), 367–89.

Malcolm, I. G. (1979a). 'Classroom communication and the Aboriginal child: a sociolinguistic investigation in Western Australia'. Unpublished PhD thesis, University of Western Australia, Perth.

Malcolm, I. G. (1979b). The West Australian Aboriginal child and classroom interaction: a sociolinguistic approach. *Journal of Pragmatics, 3*(3), 305–20.

Malcolm, I. G. (1993, September). *Aboriginal English Inside and Outside the Classroom*. Paper presented at the 18th Annual Congress of the Applied Linguistics Association of Australia, Adelaide.

Malcolm, I. G. (2003). English language and literacy development and home language support: connections and directions in working with Indigenous students. *TESOL in Context, 13*(1), 5–18.

Nakane, I. (2003). 'Silence in Japanese–Australian classroom interaction: perceptions and performance'. Unpublished PhD thesis, University of Sydney, Sydney.

Rhydwen, M. (1992a). *All You Ever Wanted to Know about Kriol*. Darwin, NT: Northern Territory Department of Education.

Rhydwen, M. (1992b). *The Extent of the Use of Kriol, Other Creole Varieties and Varieties of Aboriginal English by Schoolchildren in the Northern Territory and its Implications for Access to English Literacy*. Canberra: Department of Employment, Education and Training.

Scollon, R. (1985). The machine stops: silence in the metaphor of malfunction. In D. Tannen and M. Saville-Troike (eds), *Perspectives on Silence* (pp. 21–30). Norwood, NJ: Ablex Publishing Corp.

Sinclair, J. M. and Coulthard, R. M. (1975). *Towards an Analysis of Discourse*. London: Oxford University Press.

Tannen, D. (1985). Silence anything but. In D. Tannen and M. Saville-Troike (eds), *Perspectives on Silence* (pp. 93–111). Norwood, NJ: Ablex Publishing Corp.

7 Children, language and literacy in the Ngaanyatjarra Lands

Inge Kral and Elizabeth Marrkilyi Ellis

Chapter Outline

In Australia research on literacy in remote Aboriginal communities tends to focus mainly on schools, methodology, curriculum and the failure of students to meet national English literacy and numeracy benchmarks. In general, minimal attention is paid to the Aboriginal language context and to everyday literacy use in social and cultural practice. This study of language and literacy in a remote Aboriginal community in the Western Desert takes an ethnographic approach to consider the impact of language shift and changed language socialisation practices on the development of linguistic and cognitive skills and to view literacy as a cultural, rather than instructional, process. Literacy as social and cultural practice is explored by tracing intergenerational literacy transmission since the introduction of textual practices, in Ngaanyatjarra and English, from the 1930s onwards. The study indicates that literacy is seeping into social and cultural practices in families where literacy has meaning and purpose in everyday life.

Introduction

In remote areas Aboriginal children appear to be growing up in environments where there are few resources to stimulate reading and writing at home. Commentators commonly write about these children in terms of 'deficit'.[1] However, around the world, ethnographers have studied children and families in different communities and highlighted the strengths of diverse language and literacy socialisation contexts (Heath, 1982, 1983; Schieffelin and Gilmore, 1986; Taylor and Dorsey-Gaines, 1988).

In this chapter we draw on the sociolinguistic and anthropological literature that opens the way to seeing beyond deficit theories (Duranti and Ochs, 1986; Kulick, 1992; Ochs, 1988; Schieffelin, 1990; Schieffelin and Ochs, 1986). We consider how children in the Ngaanyatjarra Lands are socialised into oral practices and the impact of language change in this region. Through ethnography we also show the ways in which literate practices have seeped into cultural processes in some Ngaanyatjarra families.

The Ngaanyatjarra Lands

The Ngaanyatjarra Lands in the east of Western Australia comprise some 250,000 sq kms (or approximately 3 per cent of mainland Australia) fanning out from the tri-state border with South Australia and the Northern Territory. Approximately 2000 Aboriginal people live in 12 communities that comprise the 'Ngaanyatjarra Lands'. Residents are predominantly Ngaanyatjarra speakers, but the speech community also comprises speakers of other mutually intelligible Western Desert dialects (predominantly Ngaatjatjarra, Pitjantjatjara and Pintupi) and adults generally have competence in these local dialects and English.[2] The population of the Ngaanyatjarra Lands includes the first wave of people who came out of the Western Desert in the 1930s and the last wave in the 1960s.[3] The Ngaanyatjarra as a group have never left their country, nor has their land been annexed or occupied by outsiders. Remoteness has protected the Ngaanyatjarra from the more profound ravages of the colonial encounter and their post-contact experiences have been relatively benign.

Language socialisation

In this first section we describe the oral language socialisation environment and discuss changed language socialisation patterns and language shift.

All children acquire their first language or mother tongue through social interaction and language behaviour patterns are acquired through language socialisation (Romaine, 1984; Snow and Ferguson, 1977; Wells, 1979). Language plays a critical role in the 'construction of social identity' (Ochs, 1993). It also acts as an 'agent' for the transmission of culture and it is through language socialisation that children acquire 'the ways and world views' of their culture (Romaine, 1994; Schieffelin, 1990).

Baby talk

Ngaanyatjarra language socialisation begins with the arrival of a new baby who is fussed over with much tactile interaction: cuddling, pinching of cheeks and kissing, in conjunction with the undulating prosodic contours of 'baby talk'.

Studies of baby talk suggest that simplified registers or modifications of adult speech assist in scaffolding the language learning process for young children (Ferguson, 1977).[4] Linguistic studies on Aboriginal child language development note the early stages of verbal communication (Hamilton, 1981; Lowell et al., 1996), including 'baby talk' (Bavin, 1993; Hoogenraad, 2005; Laughren, 1984). Observers characteristically describe an incremental scaffolding approach to language acquisition in the use of diminutives, word reduplication and a specific baby talk lexicon, as well as regular phonological modification of standard adult speech: consonant elision and substitution with accompanying gestural interaction.

Ngaanyatjarra has a distinct baby talk register (Table 7.1) that exemplifies similar features.[5] Caregivers are conscious that through baby talk children learn to speak. Adults intentionally scaffold language to assist young learners in acquiring difficult sounds. This process allows the learner to first understand the semantics of the utterances and then learn a mature way of articulating words. After a certain age children will be teased if they have not acquired standard Ngaanyatjarra forms, that is, proper adult talk.

Oral narratives

By participating in social and cultural practice children acquire the linguistic and cognitive orientations of their elders. As in other Aboriginal settings, the Ngaanyatjarra world is highly social, interactive and verbal. Storytelling and language play (including speech arts such as rhyming, metaphor, alliteration and onomatopoeia) are intrinsic to everyday discourse (Douglas, 1979).

Table 7.1 The distinct baby talk register of Ngaanyatjarra

Baby talk form	Standard Ngaanyatjarra	English translation
Akula!	Ngala!	Eat it!
Kikila/kikilawu!	Tjikila!	Drink it!
Tutula!	Tjutjurla!	Cover it!
Ampu!	Yampula!	Hold me!/pick me up!/hug me!
Awulu	Ngayulu	I – first person singular
Utuna	Nyuntunya	You – second person singular
Atjutjaya	Ngarltutjarra	Poor thing
Nyampi	Nyarnpi	Child's version of a traditional women's dance/song
Nyanya akula!	Mirrka ngala!	Eat the food!
Apa kikila!	Kapi tjikila!	Drink the water!
Uupa	Onomatopoeic sound/gesture	'Kiss'
Nyamnyam	Onomatopoeic sound/gesture	'Yummy'
Nyanya	Onomatopoeic sound/gesture	'Food'

Source: E. Marrkilyi Ellis 2006

Children are immersed in this language-rich environment and acquire the speech styles and oral narratives of their culture by listening to and interacting with those who speak *tjaa yuti* ('strong Ngaanyatjarra') and increasingly with those who 'code-switch' or 'code-mix' between Ngaanyatjarra and English.[6] Children also acquire the lexical and gestural vocabularies that denote kinship relations and the rules that govern social organisation.

In many Indigenous cultures oral narrative has been central to instruction and learning (Basso, 1984; Rogoff, 2003). In the Western Desert, oral memory and the transmission of cultural knowledge and learning through the *Tjukurrpa* (Dreaming) have been intrinsic to the maintenance of a regulatory framework that has bound culture over generations. In the socialisation of Ngaanyatjarra children a fear of *mamu* or 'bad spirits' was (and still is) incul-cated to discipline or keep children obedient (*ngurlutjingalku* or *pinangkat-junku)* and to steer them away from sacred objects or locations (*pikangurlu*). *Mamu tjuma* – stories about 'monsters' or scary spirits – were used to teach children the 'right way' to act. Thus stories for children were told as sanitised versions of the *Tjukurrpa*, as moral tales or simply as imaginative tales. Such stories are still told today, but with diminishing potency and fewer adults are able to articulate the traditional oral narrative style. Alongside the dissipation of contexts for oral storytelling, the transformation of oral genres into simplified written versions for children (or English translations) is also reducing the function of oral narrative as a moral or metaphorical cultural guide.

Developmental studies on the acquisition of narrative competence indicate that 'narrative discourse structures are commonly acquired and internalised by age 10 in a child's process of socialisation' (Klapproth, 2004). We see this exemplified in *mirlpa* the typically female storytelling tradition acquired in childhood throughout the Western Desert and across Central Australia.[7] In this storytelling practice oral narratives accompany drawing in the sand, and iconography, symbolic representations, spoken narrative and gesture are integrated into a 'coherent narrative whole' (Wilkins, 1997). Essential communication and cognitive skills are embedded in the symbols utilised to tell stories. Girls acquire the habit of 'writing' in the sand and transfer it to other surfaces with ease. Now we see numerical and textual elements seeping into this traditional practice with mothers and daughters writing initials and names on the ground with bent 'story-wire' (fencing wire has replaced the traditional use of twigs and gum leaves). Through this practice girls are verbalising stories, drawing cognitive links and matching these with symbols drawn in the sand – all essential 'pre-literacy' skills.

Language shift

Language socialisation practices have, however, altered and changing practices are accelerating language shift. While some oral traditions remain strong, language shift is in process in Western Desert as in other Aboriginal language contexts (Langlois, 2004; McConvell, 1991; Rigsby, 1987). The 2005 National Indigenous Language Survey rates Ngaanyatjarra as 'critically endangered' (AIATSIS/FATSIL, 2005). Whether language death will eventuate is, as yet, unclear. What is evident, nevertheless, is that altered child language socialisation practices have impacted on spoken Ngaanyatjarra.

The introduction of Western schooling and changed social practice has impacted on Ngaanyatjarra cultural processes. Schooling has reduced the time spent acquiring and using complex linguistic structures, routines and speech styles in traditional contexts and Western institutionalised practices, values and expectations have been replacing cultural learning.[8] In the past complex oral and gestural forms were learned, and used by children, *in situ*, with knowledgeable elders telling stories, noting signs of seasonal change in the flora and fauna, observing animal and human tracks and navigating using spatial orientation skills on land and in the night sky. In addition, hunting and gathering provided everyday contextualised occasions for discussion around tool preparation, animal behaviour, sign language, etc. when stalking prey, or during the cooking and distribution of meat according to kinship relationships. It has been suggested that an outcome of changed practices and schooling in English, is that some Western Desert youngsters are 'losing some of the insightfulness of their own language' and may not be achieving 'adequate self-expression in any language' (NLLIA, 1996). The vernacular mother tongue remains, nonetheless, a salient symbol of social identity as the following quote from a Ngaanyatjarra mother exemplifies:

> Ngaanyatjarra is important for everyone because it is their birth, number one language and it's important for them not to lose their language, always keep it, it's their point, their own.

Family literacy

In this section we turn the discussion to family literacy and consider whether literacy has been transmitted and acquired in Ngaanyatjarra families through everyday social and cultural practice.

Literacy research emphasises the importance of family literacy practices as antecedent to successful literacy learning at school (Wells, 1985). Some writers emphasise that literacy is a cultural process and that 'everyday practice' is 'a more powerful source of socialization than intentional pedagogy' (Lave, 1988):

> Children who learn to read successfully do so because, for them, learning to read is a cultural and not primarily an instructed process. Furthermore, this cultural process has long roots at home – roots which have grown strong and firm before the child has walked into school. Children who must learn reading primarily as an instructed process in school are at an acute disadvantage (Gee, 2004).

In mainstream Australia successful literacy learning builds on the long culture of literacy in Western society *and* the foundation of formal schooling. Literacy acquisition also incorporates interactive engagement and participation in other processes, practices and contexts that are meaningful and purposeful at an individual and community level and there is a synergy between all these processes. Research has identified that children from literate school-oriented families commence school better prepared than children from non-literate families who are not school-oriented. In Australian, North American and British middle-class homes 'caregiver talk' or 'motherese' often parallels 'teacher-talk' used in classrooms (Cazden, 1988; Snow and Ferguson, 1977). In these contexts interlocutors scaffold language for children in a literacy-oriented manner. Heath (1982) posits that in such homes children are prepared for schooling through modelled or instructed patterns of language socialisation including: dyadic adult–child question and answer routines and ways of talking about books in literacy-oriented activities that correspond with structured periods of child development. In these ways the continuity between home 'caregiver talk' and the kind of adult–child interactions used in schools is reinforced as children learn the ways of 'taking meaning' from written texts by paying attention to text, by learning how to talk about reading and by having the right interactional style for orally displaying their 'literate orientation' (Heath, 1982). Heath (1982) indicates that where children have *not* been participating in specific school-like oral discourses, literate practices and child-focused instructional activities at home, they are less likely to do well in school after the initial few years.

In most remote Aboriginal communities the historical and social circumstances of literacy learning differ from mainstream Anglo-European contexts and the cultural processes (i.e. the habits and attitudes associated with everyday literacy practices that underpin success at school) are still evolving. Unlike many Western homes, houses in remote communities are generally not print-rich environments and people are often not in the habit of accumulating texts in their camps. Further, as Barton and Hamilton (1998) note, opportunities for literacy are provided by 'the range of resources available to people'. Thus the capacity to buy and store literacy artefacts (including story books, educational toys, activity books and pencils) remains a factor that inhibits home literacy practices in many remote communities (Bat, 2005; Kral and Falk, 2004). Moreover, the more visible and competent literates tend to be adults who participate in the institutional arenas of work, church and community governance and the less literate are often those on the periphery of Western institutional domains.

Literacy transmission in Ngaanyatjarra families

The Ngaanyatjarra, and their neighbours the Pitjantjatjara, have had an unusually long exposure to literacy in English, and in the vernacular Ngaanyatjarra, compared with many other remote Aboriginal groups. English literacy was introduced to this preliterate group with the commencement of schooling at the United Aborigines Mission at Warburton Ranges in the 1930s. For the current generation of school-children some of their great-grandparents were among the first to learn literacy in the mission school. Many of their grandparents then experienced compulsory assimilation-era secondary schooling while boarding in hostels in the towns of the Eastern Goldfields of Western Australia during the 1960s. From the late 1970s most of the current parent generation have attended the government schools established in each of the Ngaanyatjarra Lands communities.

Schooling is, however, only one influence on the acquisition and transmission of literacy practices in the Ngaanyatjarra region. As Street (1994) notes 'literacy processes cannot be understood simply in terms of schooling and pedagogy: they are part of more embracing social institutions and conceptions'. This region also has a history of adult vernacular literacy learning. From the late 1950s missionaries have been teaching vernacular literacy and translating the Old and New Testament.[9] In some 'mission families' literate practices have been building up over three or four generations and Christian literacy practices have seeped into the domestic space. Children have observed their elders learning and reading Christian and secular texts and some children have learned from them. Through ethnographic interviews insights have been gained into the nature of family literacy practices in this community.[10]

Family literacy research indicates the importance of 'memories of literate things' in the transmission of a knowingness about literacy from one generation to the next (Taylor, 1983). Examples from Warburton support this. Mary and Jack began learning Ngaanyatjarra literacy in the 1960s and their daughter Jacinta remembers:

> Bibles, that's all, my mum would read it. I can read Ngaanyatjarra language from my mother . . . When she reads I always see her reading and listening and that's how I got learn.

When Jacinta was a teenager she continued learning to read Ngaanyatjarra from a missionary every afternoon. Mary also taught her grandchildren to read: 'I used to teach all the little kids in this house, at the tree . . . teaching the *Mama* God*ku* book, learning'. Now, she says, her grandson can read the Bible: 'I been learning him to do all that . . . I always sit down and read, sit and read'. Mary's grandson describes how he observed his grandfather reading:

> He know it for English, Ngaanyatjarra, Pitjantjatjara language, three language, he can read, before he used to read. He read newspaper, dictionary, that old first one, first language.

Una's interest in reading was stimulated by observing her mother learning Ngaanyatjarra literacy in the 1960s, she then read with her own children during the 1970s and 1980s. Dawn recalls her children *nyakula nintirringkula* – 'watching and learning' from her as she read the Bible at home. Dawn is now repeating the process with the next generation of children. David contributed texts and drawings to a book (Glass and Newberry, 1979) of published Ngaanyatjarra stories during the 1970s and David's son recollects his father teaching him to read from this book. Patricia's mother began acquiring Ngaanyatjarra literacy in the 1950s when still a school girl in the mission. Patricia learnt English literacy at school in the Eastern Goldfields and later acquired Ngaanyatjarra literacy as an adult and she now works as a language worker. Patricia's adult daughter Lucy is also learning Ngaanyatjarra literacy and does home reading in Ngaanyatjarra with her 5-year-old daughter. Lucy says that she has kept her reading and writing strong by observing her mother: 'when she do it, I look at her when she write and read'.

Jennifer recalls her mother receiving a copy of *Jungle Book* from the missionaries:

> My mother always gets some books from the mail . . . Christian book . . . I used to get it and just help my mother read it, read it aloud so she can hear. Used to read it all the way, finish. I always tell her: 'You have to learn us kids reading . . . like giraffe, elephants, lions, monkeys. African stories'.

Molly says her grandson likes reading because 'we used to keep a book for him all the time, Bible stories . . . and *Three Bears*, we used to buy reading books in the shop and read to him'. Silas is a community leader and recalls reading at home as a child in the mission:

> In my after school when I go home my mother used to read a story, like the Christian story, little baby Jesus . . . So you know I was learning like the education side, school, but my mother was learning on the Christian side Jesus and all the stories. But she also learned me all the dreamtime stories too. Dreamtimes, you know, because they never lost the dreamtime stories, like the Seven Sisters.

In addition, literacy transmission is taking place in some families where the encounter with literacy has been more recent and the parent and grandparent generations were unschooled. Louisa was a child when her family came out of the Gibson Desert in the 1960s and she represents the first generation in her family to acquire literacy. Now she says:

> I read lot Bible, I read any Chapter or any Prophet who wrote Bible . . . I don't know the hard word in the Bible . . . I read, trying to read it, but I can't read it

cause I have to spell it, then I read it. But I pray and like read straight out. Read all
the history in the Bible, New Testament, Old Testament.

Louisa's daughter has also acquired the habit of reading from her mother
and describes how her 'favourite thing' is to sometimes 'read Bible with my
mother, she got a two Bibles, and it's one youth Bible . . . young people's,
English . . . because it's got stories in there'.

These memories and reflections illustrate that the habit of reading has
become transmitted social practice in some Ngaanyatjarra families, and
children have been 'apprenticed' in literacy through observation and 'guided
participation' with mature community members (Rogoff et al., 1993). They
also shed light on the significance of iterative social practices such as Bible
reading (in English or Ngaanyatjarra) in church and at home. In these
communal literacy events everybody participates irrespective of literacy competence, either by decoding or by memorisation and oral recitation.[11] These
children may not be acquiring solitary literacy practices, nor the dyadic oral
and literate skills that match the kind of adult–child interactions used in
school, but they are acquiring the shared, communal literacy practices that
match Ngaanyatjarra sociality.

Children reading and writing:
a special situation

In this section we focus on the development of reading and writing with
children in one family group.[12]

Rosie and Harold were children in the mission and now have numerous
grandchildren and great-grandchildren. Rosie and Harold's granddaughter
Nina is in the third generation to pass through schooling and their great-
granddaughter Rosina is in the fourth. Rosina and Nina observe their elders
assuming responsible community leadership roles requiring English literacy.
Furthermore, Ngaanyatjarra literacy has been taught to three generations in
the family. Rosie and Harold's adult daughters (some of whom went away to
secondary boarding schools in the Eastern Goldfields during the 1960s) still
do vernacular literacy lessons and help with Bible translation work. Nina and
Rosina have been observing their kin learning Ngaanyatjarra literacy and reading the Bible and the Christian song book.

In April 2004, Rosina was 4 years and 5 months old (4.5) and Nina was
5 years and 5 months (5.5). The girls had attended the community-run playgroup before starting schools in 2004. The playgroup functions as a bridge
between the home language socialisation environment and social, oral and

literate practices required for 'school readiness'. The girls are bilingual Ngaanyatjarra–English speakers who enjoy going to school and attend regularly.

Girls' 'writing'

As mentioned earlier, social relationships are illustrated and inculcated through oral narratives and *mirlpa* 'sand storytelling'. Nina's mother Pamela has taught Nina to write her name as the initial letters of her first name, mother's surname and father's surname. Adina also says that when her daughter Rosina was about 3 years old she taught her to write her name as a 'tag' using the initials of family names 'so she can get learn for the first letters' that represent her name. In April Rosina and Nina are both able to 'write' their names as 'tags' and self-describe: 'I'm writing my name'.

Pretend writing and 'invented spellings' (i.e. spontaneous early attempts at writing where children begin hypothesising about spoken and written language using a mix of spelling conventions and mimetic symbols) emerge during the year (Read, 1986). In May 2004 Rosina is drawing pictures and Adina is writing sentences underneath which Rosina memorises and copies. Nina is also drawing pictures and 'writing' stories using invented spellings. These stories are then retold: 'I know go to my *warta* (tree). I know go into my *kapi* (water).' By August Adina is guiding Rosina to: 'do your name long way, not initials' and Rosina finger writes it on the table. Adina also guides Nina to the initial sounds of common words by reinforcing sound–symbol correlations and breaking words into segments. By October, Nina knows most of the letters of the alphabet and has an understanding of the English sound system. Her mother Pamela guides her and writes: 'I LOVE Mummy' on a piece of paper and encourages Nina to copy it. By December, Rosina is 'writing' and retelling stories using left-to-right and top-to-bottom 'pretend' cursive writing on hand-drawn lines, illustrating her comprehension of 'writing-like' behaviour.

In these instances we have seen caregivers and children exploring language and writing with children gaining the prerequisite 'metalinguistic awareness' for successful literacy learning at school (Olson, 1984; Romaine, 1984).

Girls' 'reading'

Most homes in the community have few literacy resources. Any children's books there have generally been borrowed or bought second-hand. Pamela borrows children's stories (in Ngaanyatjarra and English) to read to the children as they go to sleep. Adina says she never buys children's books, but takes her readers home from her Ngaanyatjarra literacy classes. In this family, reading with children has become second nature and is being incorporated into social practice.

In September Rosina chooses a maths concept book and snuggles up to her grandmother Carmel who starts reading to her. As she completes the final page Carmel asks her in English: 'How many green cars? How many wheels?' Rosina knows the routine, but counts the wheels randomly. Immediately Carmel guides her: 'No, you got to do it like this' and scaffolds the literacy event by demonstrating counting in a left-to-right and top-to-bottom motion. Another time Rosina (R) and a non-Aboriginal adult (G) read the same book. In this scaffolded interaction Rosina demonstrates her familiarity with asking and answering book-oriented questions in English:

R: How many red ones?

G: How many red ones? 123456789!

R: How many, which one? Red ones!

G: Red ones, 12345678! Oooh 9 10 11 12 13 14 15 16 17 18 19 20 21 22 23! 23 red ones! Yikes! There's a lot of red isn't there?

R: Lotsa red, little one, bigges', bigges', bigges', bigges' bigges', bigges', big!

G: Yeah, look at the stripey one and the spotty one.

R: Big one, big one, big one.

G: Biggest one?

R: Smalles', smalles', smalles', smalles', smalles'.

G: There's the littlest one right at the end.

R: Little right on the end.

G: Yeah, it's the littlest.

Research in emergent literacy tells us that:

> Children with experience of books and literate stories develop a sense of how text should sound (such as how short and long sentences should alternate for variety and what sentences with subordinate clauses sound like). They imitate the narrative framework, at first without coherent content . . . They copy adult intonation and phrasing in pretending to read books, irrespective of sense they sound like stories as they run pages smoothly using appropriate cadence, with repetition, contrast, counting, and exaggeration. (Rogoff, 2003)

In the Ngaanyatjarra case study it was found that Rosina and Nina rapidly memorised and 'read' favourite stories to themselves or other children. Nina often sat alone 'memory reading' by following the picture cues while turning the pages. One evening she arrived with the children's book *Aladdin* that she had received as a 'reward' from her teacher for going to school everyday. The text was too complex to read word-by-word, so I paraphrased a simple story to match the pictures. Nina quickly perceived my strange reading prosody and no engagement with the text and told me that I was 'cheater reading' and looked for another book. She found the *Three Little Pigs* with text in simple, large font and close sentences marked with graphics. We read it together, and she immediately engaged by cross-referencing her textual and real-life experiences. She asked me: 'Who did this book?' as her grandmother has written a published Ngaanyatjarra version of the *Three Little Pigs* and it's a favourite. She then found this Ngaanyatjarra version on my book shelf and read her grandmother's name on the cover and compared it with the English author's name. In these ways Nina demonstrated emergent literacy practices.

Through ethnographic research it has been possible to observe the ways in which these children interact with text and the mediating role that adults play and how these children are beginning to use oral and written discourse in 'school-like' ways.[13] The children exhibited the decoding–encoding conventions associated with learning to read and write: left-to-right and top-to-bottom progression, letter identification and formation (Wells, 1985). They demonstrated reading-like behaviour, distinguished between conversational prosody and oral reading prosody and displayed other behaviours indicative of an emerging 'literate orientation'.

On return trips in April and September 2006 I again informally observed the literacy practices of these two girls. Both girls still exhibited an insatiable interest in story book reading and engaged whenever the chance arose. By April 2006 Nina was decoding unknown words as she 'read' stories out loud using picture cues and predictive story schemata, while Rosina was counting hidden objects embedded in pictures. Both girls were also playing word games: recalling, spelling and writing known sight words or names of relatives. They also avidly copied and traced words from books, labels, stickers, and instructions on packets and brand names on objects. These words were then superimposed onto 'lines' that rendered the page a visual imitation of a cohesive piece of written text. By September, both girls were independently composing and segmenting simple English sentences and playing self-proclaimed 'tricky writing' games.

Conclusion

In remote Aboriginal Australia literacy learning has been experienced by only a few generations during a concomitant period of profound language shift and cultural change. This is a short time for the cultural processes, that is, the social habits, attitudes and practices associated with language and literacy that underpin success at school, to seep into family life and for intergenerational transmission to take hold. The ethnographic study described in this chapter has emphasised that literacy is a cultural process and suggests that everyday practice may be just as powerful as intentional pedagogy, irrespective of instructional methodology.

It can be conjectured that many Ngaanyatjarra children have not been prepared for school through participating in literacy events, specific school-like oral discourses and child-focused instructional activities at home as the teaching of reading and writing is seen as the job of the school. However, in families where literacy has become a taken-for-granted cultural process it is more likely that children will acquire the habits and values of literacy than in other families, as indicated in the 'special situation' described above where emergent literacy practices are exemplified. Although this situation may be atypical in the remote Aboriginal context generally, this case study does indicate that literacy is being acquired and transmitted 'out-of-school' (Hull and Schultz, 2002) in certain remote Aboriginal contexts.

In general, however, many Aboriginal children in remote communities are not acquiring high order literacy skills at school, but are absorbing the values, skills and mannerisms that their kin associate with literacy. If Aboriginal children do not witness their elders in literate roles then the likelihood of literacy being acquired as social practice by the next generation may be diminished and literacy learning at school may be less effective. Hence, Aboriginal children need to be observing and participating in activities where literacy has meaning, not just for non-Aboriginal people in Western institutional contexts, but in the mature practices of their own community and in the home environment. In the remote Aboriginal context home literacy can be enhanced by increasing family access to literacy resources and providing caregivers with mediated guidance in how to effectively scaffold language and literacy events for children to better prepare them for school success.

Notes

1. Some commentators on Aboriginal education express the view that for children from remote communities to 'succeed' at school the behaviour of the parents will have to change. Johns suggests that schooling in the remote context is 'concerned with overcoming elements absent in the home: peace and quiet, food, civility, reading skills, discussion, use of the English language and the work ethic' and the 'new emphasis on preschool education is an explicit acknowledgement of making up for those things that are missing in the culture of the home and the community' (Johns, 2006, p. 21).

2. References to 'Ngaanyatjarra language' in this chapter may also encompass the other Western Desert dialects spoken in the Ngaanyatjarra Lands.

3. Most recently in 1984 a small family group who had never had contact with European society came out of the desert and now reside at Kiwirrkura community in the Ngaanyatjarra Lands.

4. The term 'scaffolding' is drawn from Vygotsky's notion of the 'zone of proximal development' – a way of guiding learners to a higher level of understanding (Vygotsky, 1978). Literacy researchers have also adopted this concept (Ninio and Bruner, 1978; Rose et al., 1999).

5. For a longer discussion on Ngaanyatjarra/Ngaatjatjarra baby talk and language learning (see Ellis, 2006; Jacobs, 1988).

6. The term 'code-mixing' is used to indicate that interlocutors may not be aware of mixing languages and the vernacular has become 'mixed and/or simplified' (AIATSIS/FATSIL, 2005, p. 28). Whereas 'code-switching' typically involves bilinguals who know both languages well, but choose to alternate between them (AIATSIS/FATSIL, 2005, p. 85). See McConvell (1988).

7. Other references to Western Desert sand story practice include Eickelkamp (2005) and Watson (1997). Also see discussions on sand storytelling in Warlpiri (Munn, 1986) and Arrernte (Green, Forthcoming; Wilkins, 1997). A comparable tradition is noted in the Alaskan Eskimo practice of girls telling 'mud knifing stories' (de Marrais et al., 1992).

8. Shirley Brice Heath comment from presentation at *Imagining Childhood Symposium*, Alice Springs NT, September 2005.

9. Wilf Douglas compiled the first grammatical analysis of Ngaanyatjarra by 1957 and developed a Roman alphabet orthography. In 1963 Amee Glass and Dorothy Hackett commenced a lifetime vocation learning Ngaanyatjarra, teaching vernacular literacy, and translating Scriptures from English to Ngaanyatjarra. They have published a number of significant Ngaanyatjarra texts including the New Testament (Ngaanyatjarra Bible Project, 1999) and the Ngaanyatjarra dictionary (Glass and Hackett, 2003). Still today they continue to teach Ngaanyatjarra literacy, translate the Old Testament and publish Ngaanyatjarra texts. They have been assisted by others including Herbert and Lorraine Howell. In 1982 they formed the Ngaanyatjarra Bible Project with the Ngaanyatjarra people. From the 1990s Marie Geytenbeek and Jan Mountney from the Summer Institute of Linguistics (SIL) were also seconded to the Ngaanyatjarra Bible Project.

10. The data presented in this section are drawn from PhD research by Inge Kral in the Ngaanyatjarra region between 2004–2006 (Kral, 2007). All personal names used in the text are pseudonyms.

11. A similar practice is noted among Afro-Americans where non-literate elders assist their grandchildren in learning to read Scripture by activating their memorised oral 'reading' strategies (Dorsey-Gaines and Garnett, 1996).

12. During 2004 and on subsequent visits Kral observed the development of children's literacy in one extended family group. The literacy events described in this section came to light as a consequence of social interactions with families in and around households in the neighbourhood. As acknowledged in other child socialisation studies (Miller, 1996; Scollon and Scollon, 1981), the presence of the researcher and her relationship with the children has influenced the data.

13. Studies have shown that teachers expect children to mark their narratives with particular elements (Heath, 1983; Michaels, 1981).

References

AIATSIS/FATSIL. (2005). *National Indigenous Languages Survey Report 2005*. Canberra: Commonwealth of Australia.

Barton, D. and Hamilton, M. (1998). *Local Literacies: Reading and Writing in One Community*. London: Routledge.

Basso, K. H. (1984). Stalking with stories: names, places and moral narratives. In E. M. Bruner and S. Plattner (eds), *Text, Play and Story: The Construction of Self and Society* (pp. 19–55). Washington, DC: American Ethnological Society.

Bat, M. (2005). When you can't even buy a bedtime story. *Ngoonjook: A Journal of Australian Indigenous Issues, 27*, 43–61.

Bavin, E. (1993). Language and culture: socialisation in a Warlpiri community. In M. Walsh and C. Yallop (eds), *Language and Culture in Aboriginal Australia* (pp. 85–96). Canberra: Aboriginal Studies Press.

Cazden, C. B. (1988). *Classroom Discourse: The Language of Teaching and Learning*. Portsmouth, NH: Heinemann.

de Marrais, K. B., Nelson, P. A. and Baker, J. H. (1992). Meaning in mud: Yup'ik Eskimo girls at play. *Anthropology and Education Quarterly, 23*(2), 120–44.

Dorsey-Gaines, C. and Garnett, C. M. (1996). The role of the Black Church in growing up literate: implications for literacy research. In D. Hicks (ed.), *Discourse, Learning and Schooling* (pp. 247–66). Cambridge: Cambridge University Press.

Douglas, W. H. (1979). Communication: Aboriginal languages – an overview. In R. M. Berndt and C. H. Berndt (eds), *Aborigines of the West: Their Past and Present* (pp. 39–53). Perth, WA: University of Western Australia Press.

Duranti, A. and Ochs, E. (1986). Literacy instruction in a Samoan village. In B. B. Schieffelin and P. Gilmore (eds), *The Acquisition of Literacy: Ethnographic Perspectives* (Vol. 21, pp. 213–32). Norwood, NJ: Ablex.

Eickelkamp, U. (2005). *The Artifice of Play*. Paper presented at the Imagining Childhood Symposium, Alice Springs, NT: Charles Darwin University.

Ellis, E. M. (2006). 'Ngaanyatjarra language acquisition'. Unpublished manuscript, Alice Springs, NT.

Ferguson, C. A. (1977). Baby talk as a simplified register. In C. E. Snow and C. A. Ferguson (eds), *Talking to Children: Language Input and Acquisition* (pp. 209–35). Cambridge: Cambridge University Press.

Gee, J. P. (2004). *Situated Language and Learning: A Critique of Traditional Schooling*. New York and London: Routledge.

Glass, A. and Hackett, D. (2003). *Ngaanyatjarra and Ngaatjatjarra to English Dictionary*. Alice Springs, NT: IAD Press.

Glass, A. and Newberry, D. (eds). (1979). *Tjuma: Stories from the Western Desert*. Sydney: Aboriginal Arts Board.

Green, J. (Forthcoming). 'Drawing lines in the sand: co-speech, graphics, gesture and sign in Arandic sand drawing narratives'. Unpublished PhD thesis, University of Melbourne, Melbourne.

Hamilton, A. (1981). *Nature and Nurture: Aboriginal Child-Rearing in North-Central Arnhem Land*. Canberra: Australian Institute of Aboriginal Studies.

Heath, S. B. (1982). What no bedtime story means: narrative skills at home and school. *Language in Society, 11*(2), 49–76.

Heath, S. B. (1983). *Ways with Words: Language, Life, and Work in Communities and Classrooms*. New York: Cambridge University Press.

Hoogenraad, R. (2005). *Baby Talk and Baby's Talk: How Do Aboriginal People Scaffold Their Babies into Their First Language? Why We Should Take Aboriginal Languages Seriously in Education*. Melbourne: Paper presented at Applied Linguistics Association of Australia 2005 Conference, University of Melbourne, Melbourne.

Hull, G. and Schultz, K. (eds). (2002). *School's Out! Bridging Out-of-School Literacies with Classroom Practice*. Columbia University, NY: Teachers College Press.

Jacobs, A. M. (1988). A descriptive study of the bilingual language development of Aboriginal children in the goldfields of Western Australia. *Australian Journal of Human Communications Disorders, 16*(82), 3–15.

Johns, G. (2006). *Aboriginal Education: Remote Schools and the Real Economy*. Canberra: Menzies Research Centre.

Klapproth, D. (2004). *Narrative as Social Practice: Anglo-Western and Australian Aboriginal Oral Traditions*. Berlin: Mouton de Gruyter.

Kral, I. (2007). 'Writing words – right way! literacy and social practice in the Ngaanyatjarra world'. Unpublished PhD thesis, The Australian National University, Canberra.

Kral, I. and Falk, I. (2004). *What Is All That Learning For? Indigenous Adult English Literacy Practices, Training, Community Capacity and Health*. Adelaide: NCVER.

Kulick, D. (1992). *Language Shift and Cultural Reproduction: Socialization, Self and Syncretism in a Papua New Guinean Village*. Cambridge: Cambridge University Press.

Langlois, A. (2004). *Alive and Kicking: Areyonga Teenage Pitjantjatjara*. Canberra: Pacific Linguistics.

Laughren, M. (1984). Warlpiri baby talk. *Australian Journal of Linguistics, 4*, 73–88.

Lave, J. (1988). *Cognition in Practice*. Cambridge: Cambridge University Press.

Lowell, A., Gurimangu, Nyomba and Ningi. (1996). Communication and learning at home: A preliminary report on Yolngu language socialisation. In M. Cooke (ed.), *Aboriginal Languages in Contemporary Contexts: Yolngu Matha at Galiwin'ku (DEETYA Project Report)* (pp. 109–52). Batchelor, NT: Batchelor College.

McConvell, P. (1988). Mix-im-up: Aboriginal code switching, old and new. In M. Heller (ed.), *Codeswitching: Anthropological and Sociolinguistic Perspectives* (pp. 97–149). Berlin: Mouton de Gruyter.

McConvell, P. (1991). Understanding language shift: a step towards language maintenance. In S. Romaine (ed.), *Language in Australia* (pp. 143–55). Cambridge: Cambridge University Press.

Michaels, S. (1981). 'Sharing time': children's narrative style and differential access to literacy. *Language in Society, 10*(3), 423–42.

Miller, P. J. (1996). Instantiating culture through discourse practices: Some personal reflections on socialization and how to study it. In R. Jessor, A. Colby and R. A. Shweder (eds), *Ethnography and Human Development: Context and Meaning in Human Development* (pp. 183–204). Chicago: The University of Chicago Press.

Munn, N. D. (1986). *Walbri Iconography: Graphic Representation and Cultural Symbolism in a Central Australian Society* (1973 edn). Chicago: The University of Chicago Press.

Ngaanyatjarra Bible Project. (1999). *Mama Kuurrku Wangka Marlangkatjanya: The New Testament in Ngaanyatjarra and English.* Canberra: The Bible Society in Australia.

Ninio, A. and Bruner, J. (1978). The achievement and antecedents of labelling. *Journal of Child Language, 5,* 1–15.

NLLIA. (1996). *Desert Schools: An Investigation of English Language and Literacy Among Young Aboriginal People in Seven Communities.* (Vols 1, 2 and 3). Canberra: DEETYA and NLLIA South Australian Teaching and Curriculum Centre.

Ochs, E. (1988). *Culture and Language Development: Language Acquisition and Language Socialization in a Samoan Villa.* Cambridge: Cambridge University Press.

Ochs, E. (1993). *Constructing Social Identity: A Language Socialization Perspective. Research on Language and Social Interaction.* Hillsdale, NJ: Lawrence Erlbaum Associates.

Olson, D. R. (1984). 'See! Jumping!' Some oral language antecedents of literacy. In H. Goelman, A. A. Oberg and F. Smith (eds), *Awakening to Literacy* (pp. 185–192). Victoria, BC: University of Victoria.

Read, C. (1986). *Children's Creative Spellings.* London: Routledge.

Rigsby, B. (1987). Indigenous language shift and maintenance in Fourth World settings. *Multilingua: A Journal of Cross-cultural and Interlanguage Communication, 6*(4), 359–78.

Rogoff, B. (2003). *The Cultural Nature of Human Development.* Oxford; New York: Oxford University Press.

Rogoff, B., Mistry, J., Goncu, A. and Mosier, C. (1993). Guided participation in cultural activity by toddlers and caregivers. *Monographs of the Society for Research in Child Development, 58*(8), 1–183.

Romaine, S. (1984). *The Language of Children and Adolescents: The Acquisition of Communicative Competence.* Oxford; New York: Basil Blackwell.

Romaine, S. (1994). *Language in Society: An Introduction to Sociolinguistics.* Oxford: Oxford University Press.

Rose, D., Gray, B. and Cowey, W. (1999). Scaffolding reading and writing for indigenous children in school. In *Double Power: English Literacy and Indigenous Education* (pp. 23–60). Melbourne: Languages Australia.

Schieffelin, B. B. (1990). *The Give and Take of Everyday Life: Language Socialization of Kaluli Children.* Cambridge: Cambridge University Press.

Schieffelin, B. B. and Gilmore, P. (eds). (1986). *The Acquisition of Literacy: Ethnographic Perspectives* (Vol. 21). Norwood, NJ: Ablex Publishing Corporation.

Schieffelin, B. B. and Ochs, E. (eds). (1986). *Language Socialization across Cultures.* Cambridge: Cambridge University Press.

Scollon, R. and Scollon, S. (1981). *Narrative, Literacy, and Face in Interethnic Communication.* Norwood, NJ: Ablex.

Snow, C. E. and Ferguson, C. A. (eds). (1977). *Talking to Children: Language Input and Acquisition.* Cambridge: Cambridge University Press.

Street, B. V. (1994). Cross-cultural perspectives on literacy. In J. Maybin (ed.), *Language and Literacy in Social Practice* (pp. 139–50). Clevedon: Multilingual Matters.

Taylor, D. (1983). Family literacy: conservation and change in the transmission of literacy styles and values. In J. Maybin (ed.), *Language and Literacy in Social Practice* (1994 edn, pp. 58–72). Clevedon: Multilingual Matters.

Taylor, D. and Dorsey-Gaines, C. (1988). *Growing Up Literate: Learning from Inner-City Families.* Portsmouth, NH: Heinemann.

Vygotsky, L. S. (1978). *Mind in Society: The Development of Higher Psychological Processes.* Cambridge, MA: Harvard University Press.

Watson, C. (1997). Re-embodying sand drawing and re-evaluating the status of the camp: the practice and iconography of women's public sand drawing in Balgo, WA. *The Australian Journal of Anthropology, 8*(1), 104–24.

Wells, C. G. (1979). Describing children's learning: development at home and at school. *British Educational Research Journal, 5,* 75–89.

Wells, G. (1985). Pre-school literacy related activities and success in school. In D. R. Olson, N. Torrance and A. Hildyard (eds), *Literacy, Language and Learning: The Nature and Consequences of Reading and Writing* (pp. 229–55). Cambridge: Cambridge University Press.

Wilkins, D. P. (1997). Alternative representations of space: Arrernte narratives in sand. In M. Biemans and J. van de Weijer (eds), *Proceedings of the CLS Opening Academic Year '97, '98* (pp. 133–64). Tilburg University: Centre for Language Studies.

Section 3

Issues in the assessment of children's oral skills

Caroline Jones and Joy Campbell Nangari

Chapter Outline

Appropriately designed assessments of children's oral skills in Indigenous languages have the potential to support effective school- and community-based Indigenous language programmes by guiding programme implementation and evaluation. There is little published research, however, on valid and practical assessment strategies in language revival or revitalisation contexts. This chapter presents an overview of selected oral language assessment strategies which are good candidates for use in language revival and revitalisation contexts, explains the rationale for these paradigms, and discusses their use from the perspective of issues that arise in revival and revitalisation contexts and in Australian Aboriginal language contexts in particular. The chapter argues that in particular, assessment of *receptive* language skills can offer a relatively accurate and worthwhile picture of children's current knowledge of a language. The discussion is informed by our experience trialling some receptive language testing in an Aboriginal language revitalisation context in the central Northern Territory, Australia.

Introduction

Listening and speaking are abilities that a child develops naturally in response to the languages they hear around them, whereas reading and writing require instruction. In many Indigenous contexts, a child has varying degrees of proficiency in a range of languages, including one or more traditional Indigenous languages, a creole and/or a mixed language, and the official or mainstream language of the country. In many Indigenous contexts, particularly where children are not fluent everyday speakers of their Indigenous language, children receive much less and often no instruction in literacy skills in their Indigenous language. This is true of many communities in northern Australia, for example. In such contexts, assessing the oral skills that a child has in their Indigenous language brings many benefits. On a practical level, assessing skills in Indigenous languages can improve the focus of programming and teaching (in Indigenous languages if they are taught, and in other curriculum areas), provides data for evaluating and improving Indigenous language programmes, and this can be used as documentation to support funding applications for such programmes. As McGroarty et al. (1995) point out in their discussion of assessment of Indigenous languages in North America, the testing of Indigenous language ability also formalises skills that are often overlooked or regarded as trivial, and potentially raises the respect for Indigenous language skills in the educational system. The research evidence gained through Indigenous language assessment also improves our theoretical understanding of language acquisition in situations of language shift and language revitalisation, and often sharpens the existing description of the grammar and vocabulary of the Indigenous language being tested. This knowledge has many applications. In the area of communication disorders, it potentially improves clinicians' ability to detect language disorder rather than language difference (see Gould, Chapter 9; Baker and Chenery, 1999). In the area of education, assessment data on a child's heritage and/or home language complements data on the child's skills in the school language (e.g. standard English), with implications for literacy instruction, gifted education and special education (cf. Craig and Washington (2006) for similar arguments concerning child speakers of African American English in the United States).

Assessing children's oral language in any context requires a range of expertise: detailed and descriptively accurate knowledge of the language, some knowledge of good test construction and administration, expertise in interaction with children, and knowledge of the normal course of language development. Doing an assessment of oral language in an Indigenous context, however, is even less straightforward than in a non-Indigenous context. For example, Indigenous languages exist in dialect forms and are often less standardised than languages which have been in written form for much longer.

Formal data on the normal course of development in an Indigenous language, today or in the past, are often also lacking. The required expertise for assessment is typically distributed across Indigenous and non-Indigenous people possessing different knowledge and skills, so accurate testing requires a team approach. There are other social, educational and ethical issues which arise specifically or loom larger in testing language in Indigenous contexts, yet relatively little has been written which can act as a guide in this area. This chapter draws together published information on issues in the assessment of children's oral skills in Indigenous languages. We first describe the international experience of Indigenous language assessment and discuss why the inclusion of comprehension testing has been considered important. We then survey the advantages and disadvantages of established methods of assessing language comprehension, and discuss issues that are reported in connection with these methods in the published literature on Indigenous language assessment or which the authors experienced recently in trialling Indigenous language assessments for Ngarinyman, a language of the Northern Territory, Australia.

Assessing children's oral skills in Indigenous languages

The international experience of Indigenous language assessment

In Australia, successful assessment of children's traditional language skill has recently been carried out using production and comprehension data (see O'Shannessy, Chapter 12). Worldwide, there are many similarities in the linguistic and education situation faced by Indigenous communities. The Indigenous language is often endangered and community members have hopes for their children's education and future that often include maintaining traditional language and culture. For Indigenous community members, teachers, speech pathologists, and language planners, the experience of Indigenous language assessment elsewhere is relevant and instructive.

The assessment of North American languages using community-based test instruments is relatively well described in the research literature. Three documented tests of Indigenous language skill which have been developed are the Hualapai Oral Language Test (HOLT), the Window Rock Oral Language Test: Navajo/English Bilingual Proficiency (WROLT), and the Alchini Bizaad ('children's speech' in Navajo) Comprehension Test or ABC Test. The Hualapai Oral Language Test was developed by a team of teachers, a linguist and community members in the early 1980s, for Hualapai, a Yuman language of south-west USA (see Watahomigie and Yamamoto, 1987). At this time, most of the children spoke Hualapai at home and few had English as their primary language of communication although there was community concern about a decline in Hualapai culture and language knowledge. The measurements of proficiency and improvement in Hualapai language skill that the test enabled helped in part to support a successful bilingual education programme in Hualapai and English. The HOLT measures Hualapai language proficiency in oral language comprehension, spoken and listening vocabulary, understanding of grammatical rules, the ability to question and the ability to communicate (Watahomigie and Yamamoto, 1987, p. 92). In the HOLT, only responses in the Indigenous language are recorded, and responses in English are noted for reference (Watahomigie and Yamamoto, 1987, p. 92).

The Window Rock Oral Language Test is a test developed in the late 1970s for Navajo, another North American Indigenous language. The WROLT is discussed by Francis and Reyhner (2002, p. 169–75) and McGroarty et al. (1995, p. 332–37). McGroarty et al. (1995) explain that although the WROLT is approved by the state of Arizona as a measure of language skill in Navajo, testers and educators have been dissatisfied with the WROLT because it mainly tests Indigenous language production, leading many children to be labelled as lacking in ability in Navajo, or ability in any language ('semilingual'), who are nevertheless known by their community to have a good passive grasp of Navajo. The language production emphasis in the WROLT was one of the driving forces behind the development from 1988 of the Alchini Bizaad Comprehension Test as a fairer test of latent skill in the Indigenous language (McGroarty et al., 1995, p. 333).

As described by McGroarty et al. (1995), the Alchini Bizaad Comprehension Test was developed by a group of educators from the Navajo Nation as a test of Navajo comprehension in grades K-2 (ages 5–7 approximately) that could be administered in a school setting. The purpose of the test was to identify children who had good comprehension skills in Navajo and who could therefore benefit from receiving some of their early education through Navajo language rather than all in English. A three-dimensional diorama was created depicting a Navajo sheep camp (complete with hogan, shade house, corrals, livestock, household items, toys and small dolls as Navajo children).

Although the economics of Navajo communities have changed, such that raising livestock is no longer so central, the children being tested were regarded as likely to have been to a sheep camp with grandparents and to know about the things in it and how it operates. The aspects of language which the questions addressed were agreed upon by the educators, in line with the tradition of Navajo language education, to be the 'heart of the language'. The test comprised questions testing object identification (e.g. 'which one is the sheep?'), understanding locational language (e.g. 'put the dog next to the horse'), physical descriptions ('which one is little?'), quantity ('which one has more rocks in it?') and complex directions ('pick up the red balls and hand them to me'). These items were designed so that children could respond non-verbally with an action, so that the test would measure understanding rather than speaking ability.

Advantages of testing comprehension instead of production

The problematic experience using tests of language production skill as a sole measure of children's Indigenous language skill is not confined to the North American context. In Indigenous communities in Australia, community members often report that at least some children can 'hear', that is, understand Indigenous language but the children can't or don't speak the language 'right through', that is, fluently in its traditional form. In response to this situation, McConvell (1994) proposed language assessment tasks for use in language revitalisation contexts in northern Australia including simple instructions and questions which can be answered non-verbally or without requiring a fluent response in the traditional language.

What the ABC test and the proposals of McConvell (1994) have in common is the insight that a test of language production, or a test requiring a fluent spoken response in the Indigenous language will tend to underestimate the children's real knowledge of their Indigenous language. In non-Indigenous contexts, it is well known that perception leads to production: children tune their perceptual system to the ambient language long before they can speak, and throughout childhood are generally capable of understanding much more sophisticated things than they can say (Jusczyk, 1997). In Indigenous contexts of language shift, this developmental lag may persist longer and/or be more pronounced as children receive less frequent input in the Indigenous language and tend to speak most often in a creole or a non-standard form of the non-Indigenous language. For a true picture of what the children know of their Indigenous language, then, it makes sense to test children's language comprehension instead of (or at least in addition to) language production.

Methods of assessing children's comprehension

A variety of methods have been developed for assessing children's comprehension of words and grammar. Many of these methods were originally developed by developmental psychologists and linguists and have since been adopted into fields such as education and speech pathology, sometimes as part of formal assessment batteries. All tests of comprehension are inherently indirect; the child's response is used to infer their level of comprehension (cf. McKay, 2006). Here we survey a selection of commonly used methods which do not require purpose-built equipment or testing facilities. For further details on these and other methods see the useful summaries in McDaniel et al. (1996) and McKay (2006) who also includes listening to comprehension tasks involving written responses which could be appropriate for students with high levels of literacy.

First, we provide a description of each method and then we discuss the advantages and disadvantages of each method. Where there is experience with the method in Indigenous language assessment the lessons of this experience are emphasised. For all the methods we survey, it will be seen that issues which arise from a language-testing viewpoint can generally be characterised as threats to construct validity, either in the form of construct under-representation (i.e. issues relating to the generalisability of the test sample of the relevant abilities) or construct irrelevant variance (where factors other than the abilities of interest contribute to test scores). Construct under-representation tends to occur with more discrete, traditional testing where particular formal domains are selected which may not allow an accurate picture of language use in context. Construct irrelevant variance, however, tends to be more of an issue in naturalistic tests but can also occur in discrete tests, for example, when memory demands are heavy. Another consideration in any assessment is reliability (i.e. how likely it is that the same score will be obtained on another occasion with the same child, or with a different tester). Reliability is affected among other things by the degree of standardisation of procedures, including scoring. The reader is referred to McNamara (2000) and McNamara and Roever (2006) for a broader discussion of these language-testing considerations.

The act-out task

In an act-out task, the child hears a word, phrase or sentence and is asked to demonstrate the meaning of the item using their own body or using props (e.g. dolls, toys). In its simplest form, the item may be a one-word command (e.g. jump!). The act-out task has been widely used in language acquisition research and is particularly appropriate for understanding the interpretation of pronouns in complex sentences or (very) short stories and reflexive pronouns (e.g. herself, himself).

Goodluck (1996) lists four advantages of the act-out task. First and most important, the act-out task allows the child to give her or his own interpretation of the item. The children's understanding of what the item means might be different from the range of responses predicted as possible or those that might be offered by an adult. Second, every test item is different so response biases in picture-based tasks towards a particular picture or screen location, for example, are minimised. Third, the act-out task can be done by children as young as 3 years and, according to Goodluck (1996), little training is required for the tester. Finally the task is inexpensive and fun for both tester and child.

There are also several well-known disadvantages of the act-out task, as reviewed by Goodluck (1996). Some meanings (e.g. mental states like 'thoughtful', or questions) are hard or impossible to act out. Second, the child may have more than one possible interpretation, but the tester may never know this as the child is likely to choose that which is easiest to act out. Third, it can be hard to interpret act-out responses, since they are open ended, and in addition, the level of a chance response is not known. Fourth, act-out is a cognitively demanding task. The child needs to hold the meaning in working memory while designing and carrying out the actions. Goodluck (1996) suggests the tester should try the tasks themselves to determine the demands that may be placed on the child. A further disadvantage is that very young children (e.g. under 3 years) may simply play with props or do an action if one seems required which may have nothing to do with the expected response. There is also an observed response bias called the 'bird in the hand' strategy where a child who has picked up a toy, to illustrate a participant in an event, will tend to hang on to the toy and keep using it even when the toy stops corresponding to the item they have heard.

The act-out task in Indigenous language testing

In Indigenous contexts, the inherent complexities in a task that is apparently simple, for example, an act-out task, become very apparent. The use of props needs to be carefully considered, as has been done by educators in the development of the ABC test. If props need to be used, the ones selected should be those which are likely to be appropriately interpreted by the children; for example, some stylised toys of European farmyard animals and equipment may not be recognised by Indigenous children as intended. Commercially available generic animals and birds (e.g. parrot finger puppets) may not be recognised in the same way as the local variety they resemble for adults.

The act-out task is a visual and spatial task which involves a personal level of interaction. This is part of its appeal for many community people but is also part of its difficulty. We have observed (and it is also true in non-Indigenous contexts) that it is very easy for the tester to provide intentional or unintentional cues, and children will pick up on these. For example, if the tester asks the child to 'walk to the smoke-tree' the tester may, without meaning to, look briefly in the direction of the right tree. The child can also monitor the tester's facial expression and body language as they do the task. If the tester's face reveals judgement on what the child is doing, the child can adjust their action to try to get 'the right answer'. To minimise these issues, it is important that the tester is well trained in the test items (if live voice is being used), in being aware of their own body language, and in how and why it is important to treat all children alike (cf. Shameem and Read (1996), who found that their interviews, conducted by a native speaker tester in Fiji Hindi in teenagers' homes, had a tendency to become informal and were perceived as a social occasion by relatives, affecting the teenagers' responses). Thus act-out tasks are not as easy to administer as might initially appear and these difficulties go beyond just reading or speaking the test items consistently and scoring a range of possible responses.

Where the test items are more complex than simple commands it may be especially difficult in an Indigenous context to interpret a child's response. A pattern of responding may not be recognised as such until many items have passed, especially if the Indigenous language or the children's vernacular language background is not well understood. Making a video recording of the test session is in principle a good idea as scoring can then be redone in the light of later understanding. However, the use of video equipment may tend to inhibit children's responses (or encourage irrelevant responses) if they are not used to being filmed.

The act-out task requires a child who is eager and confident to communicate what they understand. In Indigenous contexts this may well not be the case even if the task is promoted as a game. The result may then be that the task is no longer fun. A child may intentionally or unintentionally give very minimal or ambiguous movements which can be difficult to score as right or wrong or to interpret. A child who feels repeatedly put 'on the spot' and does not know the answer may choose not to respond to an item or may stop responding altogether. A graded item approach can be helpful, starting with some items that all children will be able to do and praising their effort. Another approach which we have used is to deliver each full-sentence test item first in traditional language only, and then, if the child responds incorrectly or does not respond, to rephrase the item in a mixed language form which progressively corresponds to the vernacular language (see Meakins, Chapter 13). This provides more insight into a child's partial knowledge of the traditional language than an initially incorrect response or no response. There would seem to be potential for this approach to be worked into a formalised and more reliable testing approach in language revitalisation contexts.

Three general considerations in language testing in Indigenous contexts

Three considerations which are general to any receptive oral comprehension task are the instructions provided, the use of recorded audio and computers, and prompts and time allowed for a response. In order to ensure that children's success or otherwise on a task reflects their understanding of the language tested, it is crucial that the tester gives the children clear instructions in the language they understand best, that is, their home language. In Australian revitalisation contexts, this is often a form of Kriol, not the Indigenous language, and not standard Australian English. An Indigenous community member therefore needs to give the instructions. The tester should also provide a couple of practice items where any misunderstanding can be identified and the instructions explained again. It is important for the instructions (and any prompts) to be the same for all children. Live voice is practical for instructions especially if a prompt is required.

Recorded audio is a particularly good idea for presentation to a child in Indigenous language testing; it controls the speech rate, intonation, fluency and exact wording of language delivered to all children. If recorded audio can be incorporated into a computer-based test format, then testing and scoring is more efficient and more accurate, and the tester can focus on the children's attention and the environment. Consideration should be given to who records the audio items. A fluent, well-regarded speaker is important, but elderly speakers are not necessarily the best choice if a younger speaker can do the job. A younger speaker often has a stronger voice and clearer articulation (better teeth, and without speech problems resulting from strokes or hearing loss). In addition, if for cultural reasons the audio recording in a test can only be used while the speaker is alive, then a younger speaker may be a more practical option.

The audio needs to be of the highest quality possible and should be of a better quality than the level of audio quality that might be appropriate for adults. Research indicates that background noise is particularly detrimental to speech comprehension for children, language learners, and hearing-impaired listeners (Nelson et al., 2005); Indigenous children in language revitalisation contexts often fall into all three categories (see Galloway, Chapter 10). Recordings should be made using a high-quality microphone (built-in microphones are often inadequate) and modern digital recording equipment at CD quality or better (44.1 kHz sampling rate, 16-bit resolution), in the quietest conditions possible. The testing environment needs to be quiet and free of visual distractions. High-quality closed headphones are advisable. Inbuilt computer speakers are inadequate.

As in non-Indigenous language testing, providing two to three repetitions of an item is worthwhile. This helps minimise non-responses due to working memory limitations or lapses in attention rather than lack of language knowledge. Any non-responses should be counted separately from errors. If a time limit is used, it should be a long one, for example, 10 seconds (cf. the participation that results with a long wait-time in Moses and Wigglesworth, Chapter 6, and in Western contexts in Tobin (1987)). If the task and the response time allowed can be programmed on computer it will ensure that enough time is provided for children to respond. (Free scripting programmes like PsyScope (Cohen et al., 1993) or PsyScript (Slavin, 2007), or commercial multimedia programmes work well.)

Asking questions

Being able to answer simple questions is a basic capacity in any language. If the child can make an appropriate response it is possible to conclude that they understand the combination of words in the question and any pragmatics associated with the request. It is worth noting that the grammar of question formation in a language can be more complex than it appears (e.g. in English, questions with words like 'who', 'what', 'why' differ from simple statements with respect to the order of verbs and agents and the use of auxiliary verbs like 'did' as in 'What did Peter say?').

Conversational questions are often used to assess children's developing comprehension, from age two and upwards (Miller and Paul, 1995). Questions can be asked during free play with toys, during storybook reading, while watching a puppet play, or without props by asking spontaneous and planned questions which make sense in the testing context (e.g. 'What did you eat for breakfast?', 'How did you get to school?'). McKay (2006) argues that motivational factors are important to address; children need to see value in joining a genuinely communicative exchange, their interest is often sparked by an element of surprise; they also need an introductory session to 'tune in' to the topic and language and need in-task support, via help along the way, in a classroom setting or other informal testing contexts.

Asking questions in Indigenous language testing

Questions are often used as part of Indigenous language testing. For example, questions figure in the HOLT, in the discussion of proposals for the design of Indigenous language testing by McConvell (1994), and in the discussion of oral interviews by Francis and Reyhner (2002, pp. 175–176). Asking questions (without supporting story or pictures) shares some advantages with an act-out task that does not require props: it is inexpensive and does not require materials to be developed (which may be misinterpreted). Asking questions also requires relatively less training for an Indigenous tester to carry out or to score.

Asking questions has a further advantage that it shares with some commands: it is a naturalistic interaction which is familiar to the child and so it is not in itself cognitively taxing or requiring special instructions. In Australia, recent research by Moses (Forthcoming) and Moses and Yallop (Chapter 2) indicates that, contrary to what has become received knowledge about Indigenous interaction styles, asking questions is in fact a normal part of adult–child interaction in at least some remote communities. Testers who want to use questions should be aware, however, that some questions may be more naturalistic or pragmatically sensible than others. Display questions may cause confusion (cf. Moses and Wigglesworth, Chapter 6); for example, if an Indigenous tester asks a child their name the child may not respond because the child knows that the tester knows their name. Francis and Reyhner (2002, p. 176) therefore recommend avoiding such 'known information' questions. This problem is also noted in non-Indigenous testing (e.g. Miller and Paul, 1995) but is probably more acute in small communities where the Indigenous tester knows the child well. However, in revitalisation contexts, community members often regard questions such as 'what is your name' or 'what is your skin' as important questions that a child should be able to answer in the Indigenous language. One way of solving this problem is to use a puppet, toy, computer-based picture or animation who is introduced to the child, and who then asks the child the question. This makes more sense socially, and children usually enjoy this activity. Research by Richards (1996) found the use of puppets to be workable and beneficial in teaching the endangered Australian language Mangarrayi in the classroom.

If the purpose of the language assessment is to measure comprehension skill in the Indigenous language, then care should be taken in how the response is scored. To be a valid measure of comprehension skill (rather than production skill) then, as Francis and Reyhner (2002, p. 176) argue, any response should be scored as correct where it provides evidence that the child understood the question. This includes a range of response types which different children may provide: a nod or other gesture, a yes or no response, a one-word or phrase response, or a full-sentence response in any language. Testers should also be aware that full-sentence responses are an artefact of traditional Western school grammar; they are often not normal responses to a question among fluent native speakers and should not be expected in a language testing situation, either.

Questions in language testing are used commonly in interviews, such as the IELTS test of English proficiency. In such non-Indigenous language-testing situations, typically the actual content is not of interest to the tester and it is the form of the language used in response, and its appropriateness to the question that is scored. In Indigenous language testing the opposite may be true. In Australian Indigenous communities, there is a very close and very important connection between language and culture; this general association is not unique to the Australian situation but it does figure prominently in community members' conceptions of what language, and language testing, is about. As a result, community members involved in devising questions often suggest questions which test cultural knowledge, for example, kinship terms. It is important when evaluating the results of such items to be careful to interpret a non-response or an incorrect response appropriately; a child who provides the wrong skin name in response to the question 'What is my skin?' may have understood the question but does not know which skin is correct. A child who does not respond may not understand the question, or any one word within it (e.g. 'skin'), or may understand the question but may decide not to respond because they do not know the correct skin.

The picture-selection task

In a picture-selection task assessing receptive language, the child hears a word, phrase or sentence and is asked to select from a set of pictures (by pointing or key-press) the picture that corresponds to what they hear. The picture-selection task has been widely used to assess knowledge of different aspects of language (sounds, words and grammar) among normally developing children from minority and non-minority backgrounds, and clinical populations. Picture selection is used by researchers and practitioners in Indigenous and non-Indigenous language contexts. It is familiar from standardised language tests such as the Peabody Picture Vocabulary Test (Dunn, 2007), where the tester says a word aloud (e.g. 'duck') and asks the child to point to the correct picture from a choice of four colour sketch pictures on a printed page.

The picture-selection task can be an informative task when designed carefully. It is also versatile; it can be used to test knowledge of any aspect of grammar or vocabulary which can be depicted in a picture. As Goodluck (1996) points out, the picture-selection task is good for children who are too immature or too shy to do an act-out task well. A researcher who wants to use a picture-selection task needs to pay particular attention to the kinds of pictures used, and to try to use pictures which children are most likely to interpret as the adult tester intends.

Gerken and Shady (1996) outline six considerations when using the picture-selection task. First, recorded speech is recommended, to avoid variation from child to child in how the tester reads the item (as noted above). Second, pictures of foils should be similar in style to the correct picture so that no one picture stands out. All pictures should be simple and brightly coloured. Gerken and Shady suggest clip art or scanned images. Third, testers should be aware that children may have (unpredictable) preferences for certain situations depicted by the pictures so it is recommended that this be controlled by making the foil picture for one item the correct answer on another item. Children may, however, recognise a previously presented picture and select it again apparently because they selected it before. Gerken and Shady suggest devising two sets of linguistic items using the same picture sets, to check on this possibility. Fourth, Gerken and Shady note that having more foils boosts the chances of detecting non-chance responding but they also observe that in practice it is not always possible to find more than one equally plausible foil.

In research on grammar comprehension there are often only two main theoretically plausible interpretations. Fifth, a decision will need to be made whether to present the audio before or after the picture set, especially if the task is computer-based. Sixth, researchers need to decide how to handle unusual responses, such as when the child refuses to select any picture, or more rarely, selects both (sequentially or simultaneously). Gerken and Shady suggest that items be repeated rather than have the item time out, to encourage children not to drop out. Gerken and Shady note the importance of not interpreting non-response as lack of knowledge. They suggest that two-picture responses can be handled by scoring the first picture pointed to, or by discounting the item.

The picture-selection task in Indigenous language testing

In Indigenous language testing, the use of picture-selection task raises all the issues mentioned by Gerken and Shady, and more. A first additional consideration is whether the pictures depict scenes which are familiar and interpretable for Indigenous children. Commercial clip art is often not appropriate. It often involves the Western people, cultural and technological objects and social activities or customs. Clip art is also often more detailed than required (which may be distracting or misleading) and also involves artistic conventions such as pairs of curved lines indicating movement (which Indigenous children may or may not interpret as the artist intended). Illustrations for tasks involving comprehension of grammar and/or words for local things (people, community scenes, plants, animals, birds) are better drawn for the purpose or copied with author permission from other Indigenous language picture book sources. Input from all members of the testing team and pilot testing is required to select or design successful pictures. Community expertise is particularly helpful in ensuring that the situations in the picture set will seem equally plausible to children as children tend to select a picture showing a more plausible event over a less plausible event. Using photos of community people and places, however, is probably not a good idea: the children's excitement at seeing familiar people in the pictures may distract them from the task instructions, they may try to interpret the pictures in the light of their knowledge of those people's lives and habits, or they may select pictures foregrounding people they are closely related to or particularly like.

Other methods

Beyond the act-out task, asking questions, and the picture-selection task, there are a variety of other methods for researching children's language comprehension. These methods have not, to our knowledge, been used in assessing children's comprehension of Indigenous languages. In what follows we suggest some possible pitfalls with their use in Indigenous contexts.

Observation and parent report

One way to assess children's comprehension of a language is to observe natural interactions with a caregiver speaking that language and describe how much the child appears to understand. This has the advantage that no manipulation of the situation is required so the situation is pragmatically normal for the child and no special instructions are required. This technique has shortcomings, however. Children's comprehension of language forms will tend to be overestimated as children may respond to the familiar context and routine and any lack of understanding of the language forms themselves may not be evident. A particular problem with this approach in many Indigenous contexts is that there may be relatively very few (or no) natural interactions which are carried out by the caregiver in the Indigenous language. If the caregiver is not a fluent speaker it may be impossible for them to interact with the child using only fluent Indigenous language. To the extent that they do not normally speak the Indigenous language to their children, the advantage of the situation being 'normal' for the child is no longer there. If the caregiver only rarely interacts with the child using Indigenous language, the researcher may have to wait for a long time for an opportunity to observe Indigenous language comprehension. Even then, it is likely that only limited aspects of the Indigenous language will be used with the child.

Parent report is a technique used by child psychologists and speech pathologists to estimate a child's vocabulary and level of language functioning. The McArthur-Bates Communicative Developmental Inventories (Fenson et al., 2006) are an example of a normed language assessment instrument based on parent or caregiver report. In general, parent report data have known limitations: any survey research is limited by what the respondent reports, which may or may not be true. Parent report can be used to ask parents which words their children already know; this can be an overestimate if the parents do not discount the influence of context or an underestimate if they only report the words their child actually uses. Parent report is also used to estimate a child's language level. This faces the problem that parents may not separate language form from language meaning and may report the most semantically complex meaning the child has said (or that they interpreted their child to have said in the context).

In Indigenous language contexts, using parent report is faced with additional challenges. Literacy in an Indigenous language is often not widespread or well practised, so a written survey may not be a reliable instrument. Parents may know the word orally but not recognise it in a written list. In a situation of language loss, parents themselves may not know the words they are being asked about. Researchers should be mindful that if parents are not fluent speakers, asking parents about their children's knowledge may be confronting for the parents.

The imitation task

In an imitation task, a child hears a word, phrase or sentence and is required to repeat it exactly as they heard it. This task is based on the assumption that in order to hear, remember, and then imitate an utterance a learner must categorise what they hear in terms of their mental grammar. Errors on the imitation task can then be interpreted, the argument goes, as reflecting the current state of their mental grammar. The interpretation of imitation tasks, however, is likely not to be as straightforward as that. Language production acts as a filter on the evidence for language comprehension in this case. If a child has articulation difficulties or experiences difficulty remembering all of the sentence, then not all of the performance on the task can be attributed to comprehension (and mental grammar) alone. It has also been observed in some research that children can imitate more than they can comprehend (Fraser et al., 1963). Such considerations should, we suggest, make researchers hesitate before using an imitation task – at least on its own – to measure language comprehension.

The grammaticality judgement task

A grammaticality judgement task is an activity where a child is presented with an auditory sentence and asked to say whether it is grammatical (sounds 'OK') or ungrammatical (sounds 'funny' or odd). When the child's pattern of judgements is compared with the pattern of judgements of an adult native speaker, the logic is that systematic differences revealing a child's development in language should be evident. This task faces two well-known general issues: that adult native speakers can differ in their patterns of grammaticality judgement, and that children's idea of what is 'funny' or odd may relate not to language form but to the semantic event.

We are not aware of any use of the grammaticality judgement task with children in Indigenous language testing. We further suggest that the grammaticality judgement task is ethically inappropriate in Indigenous language testing. In many Indigenous language contexts, children's grasp of their heritage language may be relatively tenuous and unstable, and is likely to receive less and less support as they go through life, as fewer people around them speak the language. Given these conditions, exposing children to ungrammatical forms of their Indigenous language would probably concern adult speakers of the language. It also raises ethical concerns; research suggests that adult native speakers of English can have their own spelling undermined by repeated exposure to incorrect spelling (Brown, 1988). In a similar way, it would seem that any quantity of ungrammatical Indigenous language, however small, will undermine language maintenance to some extent.

Summary and conclusions

Well conducted assessments of children's oral skills in Indigenous languages have much to offer to community members, teachers, speech pathologists, language researchers and language policy planners. This chapter has described what is known from the published literature about the international experience of Indigenous language assessment. This literature points towards the importance of assessing language comprehension in addition to language production to gain a true picture of the extent of children's knowledge, as many Indigenous children appear to have greater passive knowledge than spoken fluency in their heritage language. Based on our own experience, three methods of assessing comprehension which appear especially appropriate for Indigenous contexts include the act-out task, answering questions, and the picture-selection task. In all cases, if these tasks are to gather accurate data in Indigenous contexts, the testing team needs to be aware of issues which arise in non-Indigenous contexts with these tests (which may loom larger in an Indigenous context) as well as local issues relating to the specific Indigenous language and the children's educational and life experience.

References

Baker, R. and Chenery, H. (1999). Assessment in speech-language pathology. *Language Testing, 16*(3), 243–47.

Brown, A. S. (1988). Encountering misspellings and spelling performance: why wrong isn't right. *Journal of Educational Psychology, 80*(4), 488–94.

Cohen, J., Flatt, M., MacWhinney, B. and Provost, J. (1993). *PsyScope* (Version 1.2.5): http://www.psyscope.psy.cmu.edu/

Craig, H. K. and Washington, J. A. (2006). *Malik Goes to School: Examining the Language Skills of African American Students from Preschool-5th Grade*. Mahwah, NJ: Lawrence Erlbaum Associates.

Dunn, L. M. and Dunn, D. M. (2007). *Peabody Picture Vocabulary Test - Fourth Edition (PPVT-IV)*. Bloomington, MN: Pearson Assessments.

Fenson, L., Marchman, V., Thal, D., Dale, P., Reznick, S. and Bates, E. (2006). *MacArthur-Bates Communicative Development Inventories (CDIs)* (Second edn). Baltimore, MD: Brookes Publishing.

Francis, N. and Reyhner, J. A. (2002). *Language and Literacy Teaching for Indigenous Education: A Bilingual Approach*. Clevedon: Multilingual Matters.

Fraser, C., Bellugi, U. and Brown, R. (1963). Control of grammar in imitation, comprehension, and production. *Journal of Verbal Learning and Verbal Behavior, 2*, 121–35.

Gerken, L. and Shady, M. (1996). The picture selection task. In D. McDaniel, C. McKee and H. Smith Cairns (eds), *Methods for Assessing Children's Syntax* (pp. 125–45). Cambridge: The MIT Press.

Goodluck, H. (1996). The act-out task. In D. McDaniel, C. McKee and H. Smith Cairns (eds), *Methods for Assessing Children's Syntax* (pp. 147–62). Cambridge: The MIT Press.

Jusczyk, P. W. (1997). *The Discovery of Spoken Language*. Cambridge: The MIT Press.

McConvell, P. (1994). Oral proficiency assessment for Aboriginal languages. In D. Hartman and J. Henderson (eds), *Aboriginal Languages in Education* (pp. 301–35). Alice Springs, NT: IAD Press.

McDaniel, D., McKee, C. and Smith Cairns, H. (eds). (1996). *Methods for Assessing Children's Syntax*. Cambridge: The MIT Press.

McGroarty, M., Beck, A. and Butler, F. (1995). Policy issues in assessing indigenous languages: a Navajo case. *Applied Linguistics, 16*(3), 323–43.

McKay, P. (2006). *Assessing Young Language Learners*. Cambridge: Cambridge University Press.

McNamara, T. (2000). *Language Testing*. Oxford: Oxford University Press.

McNamara, T. and Roever, C. (2006). *Language Testing: The Social Dimension*. Malden, MA: Blackwell Publishing.

Miller, J. F. and Paul, R. (1995). *The Clinical Assessment of Language Comprehension*. Baltimore, MD: Paul H Brookes Publishing Co.

Moses, K. (Forthcoming). *Do Dinosaurs Hug in the Kimberley? – The Use of Questions by Aboriginal Caregivers and Children at Yakanarra*. Unpublished PhD thesis, University of Melbourne, Melbourne.

Nelson, P., Kohnert, K., Sabur, S. and Shaw, D. (2005). Classroom noise and children learning through a second language: double jeopardy? *Language, Speech & Hearing Services in Schools, 36*(3), 219–29.

Richards, M. (1996). *Developing Language Teaching Materials for Mangarrayi.* Unpublished MPhil thesis, University of Sydney, Sydney.

Shameem, N. and Read, J. (1996). Administering a performance test in Fiji Hindi. *Australian Review of Applied Linguistics, Series S, 13,* 80–104.

Slavin, S. (2007). *PsyScript* (Version 2.1.0). Lancaster: Lancaster University, http://www.psych.lancs.ac.uk/software/psyScript.html

Tobin, K. (1987). The role of wait time in higher cognitive level learning. *Review of Educational Research, 57*(1), 69–95.

Watahomigie, L. and Yamamoto, A. (1987). Linguistics in action: the Hualapai bilingual/bicultural education program. In D. D. Stull and J. J. Schensul (eds), *Collaborative Research and Social Change: Applied Anthropology in Action* (pp. 77–98). Boulder, CO: Westview Press.

Language difference or language disorder: discourse sampling in speech pathology assessments for Indigenous children[1]

Judy Gould

Speech pathologists provide communication assessment and therapy services for people with communication disorders. When working with culturally and linguistically diverse populations, this requires the speech pathologist to be able to accurately distinguish between communication difference and communication delay or disorder. The body of research investigating how to more accurately assess the language abilities of bilingual and bidialectal populations has increased significantly in recent years. Much of this information is available for Australian speech pathologists to apply in their work with Indigenous children. Given the diversity of cultural and linguistic communities around the world, these recommendations and findings can only act as general assessment guidelines, however. It is certainly the case that there are a number of factors which make Australian Indigenous populations unique and in need of language assessment methodologies which are specifically designed to meet their needs. This importance is further highlighted when one considers that the vast majority of Australian Indigenous children are likely to be assessed by a non-Indigenous speech pathologist whose cultural and linguistic background is typically very different from their own. This chapter discusses how the application of an assessment methodology specifically designed for use with Australian Aboriginal children who speak Standard Australian English as a second variety has been successfully used to obtain connected speech samples during a 5-year longitudinal research project. This chapter also discusses how the method used to obtain the language samples has influenced both the quality and quantity of data obtained and, hence, had the potential to be instrumental in determining whether a child's language abilities were subsequently described as typical or impaired.

Introduction

Jodie[2] lives in an Aboriginal community in rural Queensland and, like other people in her community, she speaks a variety of Aboriginal English as her home language. In 2005, at age 4 years and 11 months, Jodie was assessed by a non-Aboriginal early special education advisory teacher using the 'DABERON Screening Device for School Readiness – Second Edition: DABERON-2' (Danzer et al., 1991). This claims to assess a number of developmental abilities that relate to early academic success such as general knowledge, following directions, colour and number concepts, and knowledge of body parts (Danzer et al., 1991).

Jodie's performance on the DABERON-2 was recorded by the examiner as equating with an Age Equivalent Score of 'less than three years', a Percentile Ranking of 'less than one' and an Overall Rating of 'very poor'. The examiner also incorrectly recorded Jodie's primary language as 'English' on the test form. Analysis of the DABERON-2 test results led the examiner to conclude that Jodie was 'at risk' of experiencing school failure not due to a linguistic and cultural mismatch between home and school, but because Jodie's skill development was overall 'very poor' and her age equivalent score was 'less than three years'.

But Jodie had also received culturally and linguistically appropriate non-standardised language assessments at ages three, four and five. As a speech pathologist experienced in the assessment of Australian Aboriginal children, I conducted these assessments myself. The assessments investigated Jodie's speech production skills, phonological awareness development, receptive and expressive language development, rapid confrontation naming and working memory skills, all of which are important skills for school readiness. Each year of assessment, Jodie's language abilities were found to be appropriate for her age.

So what explains this significant discrepancy between the DABERON-2 standardised test result and the non-standardised assessment results? The DABERON-2 test is a standardised assessment designed for speakers of Standard English. The normative sample has been drawn from 1,647 children living within the United States (Danzer et al., 1991). Spoken language features strongly in the administration of the test. Thus, the examiner's interpretation of the DABERON-2 test result indicated that the problem was language deficit whereas in fact it was language difference. Given the cultural and linguistic differences between Jodie and the normative sample, a test like the DABERON-2 is unable to provide valid assessment data. It is important to note that the examiner's interpretation of these data failed to consider the importance of these linguistic and cultural differences also.

Australian Indigenous populations require language assessment methodologies which are specifically designed to meet their needs. The vast majority of Australian Indigenous children are likely to be assessed by a non-Indigenous speech pathologist whose cultural and linguistic background is typically very different from their own (Speech Pathology Australia, 2001). When conducting assessments of communicative functioning with children, speech pathologists need to focus on the cultural nature of language development. Speech pathologists need to work with and understand the relationship between culture and language in Indigenous communities, and design assessment methodologies which better reflect this. Such assessments will provide more holistic and naturalistic data and ultimately allow a more effective way of understanding and describing communication.

This chapter will discuss how the application of an assessment methodology specifically designed for use with Australian Aboriginal children who speak Standard Australian English (SAE) as a second variety has been successfully used to obtain connected speech samples during a 5-year longitudinal research project. This chapter will also discuss how the method used for obtaining the language samples has influenced both the quality and quantity of data obtained and, hence, had the potential to be instrumental in determining whether a child's language abilities were subsequently described as typical or impaired. The information presented here provides a framework for language specialists working with Indigenous populations to adapt and apply, as necessary, to suit their own particular language assessment situations.

Issues associated with assessing the language abilities of minority and Indigenous children

Language difference or language disorder?

In Australia, the dominant language is SAE. Australian Aboriginal children like Jodie speak a different variety. Her language abilities are what would be expected for a child of similar age living within her speech community. Thus her language abilities are considered to be different but not deficient when compared to speakers of the dominant language. She shows 'language difference' – that is, as Oetting (2004b, p. 297) describes it, 'language variation that is caused by normal linguistic processes (i.e. dialects)'. In contrast, children who are described as exhibiting aspects of language delay or disorder are those children whose language abilities are considered atypical for children of a similar age living within the same speech community. That is, their underlying language learning system is impaired.

Standardised tests are designed to provide information regarding how a particular child performs on a set of specific test items in comparison with other children of that age and language background. Typically, a large normative sample which has a broad representation by gender, race, ethnicity, geographical distribution and family income is provided to allow such comparisons to reliably occur. When standardised tests designed for use with Standard English speakers are used to assess the language abilities of Australian Indigenous children, the chance of these children achieving test scores below those of normative sample is significantly increased (Gould, 1999) and so the use of these tests tend to result in an over-diagnosis of communication disorders among Australian Indigenous children. That is, Australian Indigenous children who are exhibiting language differences are more likely to appear to be presenting with language delays or disorders.

The risk of misdiagnosis for Australian Indigenous children

Children like Jodie who speak a non-standard dialect of English as their first language risk having their language skills inaccurately described by Standard

English speakers for a number of reasons. These reasons include the linguistic and cultural mismatch between the child, the assessor and the language assessments used; the reduced understanding of Aboriginal English (AE) and Aboriginal communication styles by non-Aboriginal language assessors; the influence of 'shame'[3] within an assessment setting; and the vastly differing world views between Aboriginal and non-Aboriginal Australians which are reflected in the way language is used and interpreted by the different speech communities.

For a range of linguistic, cultural and socio-political reasons, non-Indigenous language professionals, with limited or no experience in communicating with Indigenous children, may not identify the extent and nature of communication differences between themselves and AE speaking Aboriginal children. Sharifian (2005) describes how many of the educators teaching in metropolitan Western Australian schools believed that Aboriginal and Anglo Australian students spoke the same dialect. This failure to recognise communication differences may be especially true for those AE speaking Aboriginal children whose AE is very close to SAE in terms of syntax and phonology, but whose ways of understanding and using language may be very different. In an earlier study (Gould 1999), I found that teachers in a rural NSW town demonstrated a limited level of awareness or understanding of the AE spoken by the Aboriginal children in their classrooms. In addition, Aboriginal students who were identified as speaking SAE by their families continued to have their listening and attention skills judged negatively and labelled as 'deficit' by their non-Aboriginal teachers. In fact, the children's pragmatic and listening skills reflected Aboriginal ways of interacting in SAE classrooms such as adopting an eye gaze and body orientation which faced away from the teacher or displaying a reluctance to answer quickly and decisively questions specifically posed to the Aboriginal child within the whole-class setting. The teachers consistently described these as listening or attention deficits or as difficulties interacting in group settings rather than identifying them as valid communication differences. This demonstrated a poor understanding of the pragmatic and social differences evident in Aboriginal ways of communicating. It may also indicate the failure of non-Aboriginal professionals to recognise that difficulties may still occur for Aboriginal children in SAE classrooms even when Aboriginal children have been identified as SAE speakers.

Non-Aboriginal educators and speech pathologists have been described as using deficit terminology when describing the language skills of normally developing AE speaking Aboriginal children (Gould, 2000; Gould and Chatfield, 2000; Harkins, 1994). This inappropriate way of describing the AE speaker's communication system can be interpreted as demonstrating a limited understanding of AE. Describing AE in deficit terms may mean that the language professionals think of AE as an ungrammatical form of Standard English and not as a valid communication system in its own right. Oetting (2004a, p. 294) describes non-standard dialects as including 'socially stigmatised linguistic structures'. Winsa (2000, p. 431) also discusses the lower status given to dialects and states that 'much language planning is directed at the reduction of dialect diversity'. Language assessors sharing one or both of these viewpoints are highly unlikely to be able to conduct accurate assessments of the language abilities of Indigenous children speaking Standard English as a second variety.

A further factor which threatens the validity of language assessments for Indigenous children speaking Standard English as a second variety is the lack of normative data available for the non-standard dialects of English spoken by Indigenous people across Australia. Developmental data for any of the Indigenous languages spoken in Australia is also limited to only a few published studies (Bavin, 1991; Hamilton, 1981; Jacobs, 1988; Lowell et al., 1996). More recently, a number of researchers associated with the Aboriginal Child Language Acquisition Project have been investigating a number of important areas related to language acquisition among Indigenous Australian children living in three different communities (Disbray, Chapter 3; Meakins, Chapter 13; Moses and Yallop, Chapter 2; Simpson and Wigglesworth, Chapter 1). This limited amount of research, however, represents a significant gap in knowledge regarding speech and language development for Australian Indigenous children. Such gaps in knowledge seriously compromise any attempts to conduct accurate assessments of the language abilities of Indigenous children using traditional assessment methods.

Reducing test bias in the language assessment of Indigenous children

The international experience regarding the appropriate provision of language and educational services for bilingual and bidialectal Indigenous children suggests that Australia's situation in relation to the assessment of Indigenous children is similar to that of other countries. The majority of the literature relating to cross-cultural language assessments refers to non-Indigenous, non-English speaking populations within English speaking countries. But the relevant Indigenous-focused literature emphasises the difficulties inherent in Standard English speaking non-Indigenous speech pathologists conducting assessments with their Indigenous children. In relation to the language situation in Canada, Ball et al. (2005, p. 2) state that 'First Nations leaders suggest that First Nations children may be disproportionately misdiagnosed with language impairments,' and that 'this problem may be due in part to dialect differences rather than a speech–language deficit or delay'. Marshall (2000) discusses how Western values and beliefs about how language competency is defined can influence diagnoses of impairment when assessing Indigenous children from non-Western countries. Curran et al. (1996, p. 6) state that, 'American Indian children as a group score lower on the standard norm-referenced measures' because 'they are not as familiar with the language used by the dominant culture'. These findings reflect much of the data emerging from the current study being discussed in this chapter.

A number of different approaches have been proposed as possible solutions for reducing the bias inherent in testing children from linguistic minority or Indigenous populations. Some of these include creating tests which are translated into the language of the child being assessed; working with an interpreter to administer a real-time-translated version of the test (Speech Pathology Australia, 2001); replacing biased items within a test with more culturally appropriate items (Carter et al., 2005); and creating tests which are dialect neutral (Seymour et al., 2003). Apart from the many difficulties surrounding the translatability of texts and the issues surrounding working with interpreters in the language assessment context, none of these approaches is particularly suited to the assessment of Australian Aboriginal children. This is because the context of a testing situation is in itself not reflective of the ways Aboriginal people in many communities typically exchange information and is likely to elicit a 'shame' response in children from such communities. This has the effect of reducing both the quality and quantity of the verbal communication offered and seemingly understood by the child. Attempting to 'Aboriginalise' a test by changing the language of the test or replacing 'white' images with Aboriginal ones does not address this fundamental problem with testing for many Aboriginal children.

An alternative approach is to abandon the attempt to conduct standardised tests which compare performance against a large group, following Mattes and Omark (1984) and Moore-Brown et al. (2006) who argue for the need to conduct non-standardised language assessments with linguistic minority groups. Some of the approaches suggested include the analysis of natural communication samples (Mattes and Omark, 1984); criterion referenced assessment (Mattes and Omark, 1984); an increased emphasis on processing-dependent rather than knowledge-dependent measures (Campbell et al., 1997); dynamic assessment (Gutierrez-Clellen and Pena, 2001; Gutierrez-Clellen and Quinn, 1993); dynamic testing (Chaffey et al., 2003); and activity-based assessment (Gould, 1999). Such approaches would appear to provide a valid alternative, or at least supplement, to standardised testing.

Several Australian speech pathologists have also created non-standardised language assessments for use and in collaboration with specific Indigenous client groups (Bochenek, 1987; Cunningham, Undated; DETE, 2000; Diplock and Wommatakimmi, 2003; Marriot, 2003; Philpott, 2003; Ramage, 2004). The creation of these tools represents an acknowledgement that standardised tests currently administered to non-Indigenous Australian children are often not suitable for use with their Indigenous clients. The authors have expressed varying levels of confidence in the validity and reliability of the assessment tools they have created and all authors describe them as a 'work in progress'.

It is evident that some challenges and weaknesses are inherent in non-standardised forms of assessment. Since the assessment is non-standardised, it can be more difficult to achieve good reliability and validity both of the instrument being used to obtain the data and of the method being applied to analyse the data. More time may be required to complete an assessment. Unless the assessor is a skilled cross-cultural communicator or is working with an interpreter, the potential for cross-cultural miscommunication remains. Conducting non-standardised forms of language assessment also requires the assessor to have access to information regarding normal language development for the child's home language, an understanding of and ability to apply normal bilingual and bidialectal language development processes to the data obtained, an understanding of linguistic theory as it applies to linguistic universals related to the development of language, and possible profiles of language disorder. They will also need access to suitable non-standardised assessment activities or an ability to create their own, as well as access to a bilingual or bidialectal co-worker or translator. All of these potential barriers can deter speech pathologists from contemplating the use of non-standardised assessment methods.

An alternative assessment methodology

Language sampling as an assessment tool

The importance of language sampling as a means of assessing a child's expressive language abilities has been well documented in the literature (Botting,

2002; James, 2001; Nippold, 2004; Westerveld et al., 2004). Language sampling is able to provide information regarding the complexity of a child's discourse skills that a standardised test of morphology or syntax can not. This equally applies where assessments of the expressive language abilities of Indigenous children speaking AE as a home language are concerned. Language sampling with AE speaking Aboriginal children has specific relevance for a number of other important reasons as well. Some of these reasons include the poor reliability and validity of using standardised language tests with AE speaking children; the ability to include AE speaking Aboriginal adults in the assessment situation which has a number of positive benefits in terms of the quality and quantity of language produced by the child; and the chance that AE 'shame' will influence the assessment outcomes is reduced (Gould, 1999).

The influence of 'shame' in communication assessment situations is highly significant. AE 'shame' is not the same as SAE 'shame' or 'being ashamed' (Harkins, 1990). Sharifian (2005) also found significantly different cultural schemas associated with the word 'shame' as it is understood and used by many Australian Aboriginal children. 'Shame' can be a difficult concept for non-Aboriginal Australians to understand. Consequently, identifying and interpreting 'shame' and responding appropriately during a situation where 'shame' is apparent can be very difficult for a non-Aboriginal person (Gould, 2001). Harkins (1990, p. 297) describes 'shame' in certain contexts as seeming to be 'more of a positive moral concept than a negative emotion'. Harkins (1990, p. 301) identifies 'feeling something bad' as a feature of 'shame' and that this feeling 'seems to arise in situations where one does not (perhaps cannot) know the rules for doing the right thing'. Sharifian (2005) also specifically cites novelty of experience as leading to shame. The result of 'shame' is that people may remain silent; 'reluctance to speak is mentioned in most descriptions of "shame"' (Harkins, 1990, p. 302).

Speech pathologists need to realise that formal test situations, by their very nature, are very likely to act as a trigger for 'shame' among Australian Aboriginal children. A speech pathologist who is not competent cross-culturally and who is working in isolation with a child, that is, without an Aboriginal co-worker, may not consider the influence upon the child of not knowing the rules for participating in a speech pathology assessment session, especially when it is conducted in SAE. This speech pathologist may subsequently misinterpret the child's reluctance to speak as a possible indicator of communication impairment instead of recognising it as a culturally valid communication strategy or response in the given situation. Perhaps, most obviously, if a child is reluctant to speak during a communication assessment situation, then the assessor is unable to fully assess a child's speech and language skills. So, situations which are likely to trigger a 'shame' response with Australian Aboriginal children, such as formal testing, need to be avoided and replaced with assessment strategies which encourage active spoken participation, such as natural language sampling.

Throughout the current research project, natural language sampling combined with appropriately designed, administered and interpreted activity-based assessments has been able to

- provide sufficient and comprehensive data to enable the diagnosis of language difference versus language disorder;
- provide analysis of severity of difficulty when present including mild degrees of difficulty or difficulties in a few areas only;
- provide information regarding communication abilities in AE as well as SAE;
- be simple and efficient to administer; and
- be sensitive enough to yield developmental data which could be easily compared over time.

While issues surrounding the collection of natural language samples are being discussed in this chapter, many of the factors being discussed are relevant to the use of activity-based assessment methods also.

The creation or use of naturalistic communication settings is especially relevant in bidialectal language assessments where the speech pathologist wants to examine the child's use of their home language. This is most easily achieved when using natural language sampling assessment methods. Naturalistic communication settings allow the child to talk more freely than within the constraints of a test or an assessment activity designed by and for SAE speakers. This reduces problems causes by differences in world-view (Harris, 1990), as conversations are, as Dooly (2005, p. 97) says 'the speakers' constructed versions of how they make sense of the world'. It is important, therefore, for a language assessor to construct a communication setting where the child can choose the topics of conversation and a way of structuring the narrative which matches with a reality of their own.

Understanding how context influences a child's spoken communication is especially relevant when assessing the language abilities of AE speaking children. For Aboriginal speakers of English, communication is strongly embedded in context in a way that may not be recognised or understood by a non-Aboriginal person (Gould, 2005; Malcolm, 1992, 1994). The Aboriginal children and adults participating in this research tended to primarily include information in their descriptive and directive language that was not implied from the context. The amount of meaning apparent from the context of the utterance is considered in terms of how much information was then encoded linguistically. Information is less likely to be encoded linguistically if the meaning of the utterance is apparent from the context. A child may say, 'In my ting miss', in response to a teacher's question regarding the location of her book. 'Ting' in this case referring to her schoolbag. Another child may say, 'over dere la' accompanied by a wave of a hand in the direction of a table, in response to a question regarding the location of a pair of scissors. While non-Aboriginal children will use this strategy also, during the course of this research project, non-Aboriginal teachers clearly identified the way these Aboriginal children used this context-dependent language as problematic. The identification of this as problematic and indicating a possible language deficit or being viewed as a language skill which needed to be changed was related to the high frequency of usage of this strategy by the Aboriginal children. It has been my experience that other non-Aboriginal language professionals such as speech pathologists draw the same conclusions as the non-Aboriginal teachers in this instance and will also label such language use as problematic possibly indicating a vocabulary deficit or word finding difficulty. It is also common to hear comments such as, 'Someone ting stickin up' in reference to a stick in the sandpit or to hear a direction such as, 'Tie fing up' suggesting to someone to tie up their hair. In all of these examples, the communicative intent remains intact and no communication breakdown occurs. The reason that no communication breakdown occurs is because the use of non-specific terms suggests that, in context, the referent is recoverable and known and that the recipients respond to it as recoverable and known. The language use is treated by both the speaker and listener as appropriate to the context of its usage. It is only possible, therefore, to examine the way an Aboriginal child communicates by examining their spoken language abilities in relation to the wider communication context. As language assessors, speech pathologists need to either create or work within communication assessment contexts that reflect who the children are as AE speakers, something which is only achieved through obtaining samples of their speech in naturalistic contexts.

Language assessment and the cultural nature of language development

Traditionally, speech pathology assessments tend to be impairment-based and involve segmenting the language being assessed into a set of skills and sub-skills until reasons for an apparent deficit in one or more communication areas are determined. This closely equates with a medical model of assessment and intervention. However, language is not a purely biological phenomenon. Also, a medical model of language development does not fit with the integrated view that many Indigenous people have of the world and their place in it (Anderson, 1988; Eckermann et al., 1992; Trudgen, 2000). In order for speech pathology assessments to have credibility in the eyes of Indigenous people they need to more closely reflect this holistic way of thinking. Such assessments of a child's language skills cannot be obtained through administering tests but through examining how the child uses language naturally within these wider communication contexts. It is important to present a view of an Indigenous child which describes their communication abilities in terms of their social needs as well as identifying their specific language strengths and weaknesses. This involves the speech pathologist actively engaging with the child's language community to determine where the child's communication development fits within the wider aspects of that child's family and community life. Such assessments can only occur within the context of the child's language community, not within the confines of a speech pathologist's office or therapy room.

Using language sampling with Aboriginal children to obtain connected speech samples

The language sampling techniques being discussed here reflect those typically used by speech pathologists to elicit connected speech samples with children both in clinical practice and for the purposes of research. The language sampling techniques are: 'Minimally Structured Storytelling' where natural conversation and play within a range of settings and covering a range of topics are videotaped; 'Elicited Story Generation' involving eliciting of first person narratives using picture cues and discussions about photos of people and events from within their community; and 'Story Retelling' of both familiar Western SAE stories and traditional AE stories.

It is useful for a speech pathologist to examine discourse produced in these three different conditions to analyse the influence of cueing and story scaffolding upon the length and complexity of the connected speech sample produced by the child. It was important that I included assessment techniques commonly utilised by speech pathologists. It was also important to compare the different methods commonly used by speech pathologists with some more specifically relevant approaches for use with Australian Aboriginal children to determine whether differences in data collection methods impacted upon the length and complexity of connected speech samples obtained.

The influence of specific sampling techniques upon connected speech

Not all of the sampling techniques being used in this longitudinal study were effective. The language samples obtained during this study have varied according to the situational and linguistic context of the communication setting. Primarily, the sampling techniques varied in effectiveness depending upon the interaction between three main conversational features. The three features were the topic of conversation, the setting of the conversation, and the participants involved in the conversation. All three features were very important in influencing the outcomes of the assessment session.

The most effective sampling techniques, where all three of these features combined to produce lengthy and complex connected speech samples from the children, were the conversations with AE speaking adults from the child's community regarding movies and local Ghost Stories, and videotaping samples of free play. The term Ghost Stories was the label used by the Aboriginal adult involved in the discussions with the children and refers to the local Aboriginal stories belonging to their community. The methods most often employed by speech pathologists such as story retells, elicitation of first person narratives using picture or photo cues, and general conversation about interesting topics or objects elicited the least useful data for analysis. The following speech samples collected from Eddie, aged 4 years and 10 months, are typical of the differences in language produced by the children during a first person narrative elicitation task and during discussions about Ghost Stories with other Aboriginal children and adults from the community.

Setting One:	Elicited First Person Narrative. This task involved the use of a photo of an Aboriginal boy having fallen off his bike as a cue to elicit a narrative from the children.
Eddie:	'He fell off. He got cut. He got cut eh.'
Setting Two:	Ghost story Conversation.
Eddie:	'When I was walkin, when we was going to Uncle X's place (unin), up the emu farm, they was walkin, big one, the ghost.' 'Aunty X as you cross the bridge you seen little old lady and old man.'

It is significant to note that I administered each of these data collection methods in culturally appropriate ways and settings, following AE ways of communicating while speaking to the children in SAE. Making the setting and situation 'culturally appropriate' required me to have an established relationship with the children so they had an expectation of what 'doing things' with me involved. The generosity of the local Aboriginal people employed at the school to assist the children in feeling comfortable in communicating with me also greatly assisted the development of the professional relationship needed to conduct comprehensive language assessments.

When one-on-one time with a child was required, the session occurred in a quiet part of the classroom. It was important not to remove a child to a space or room separate from their classroom, at least not until that child had an expectation of what was going to occur and felt comfortable communicating with the person conducting the assessment. Some Australian Aboriginal children may always feel 'shame' at being 'singled out' and removed from their peers for special treatment. Removing children to separate rooms is what usually happens in assessment situations.

The assessment or data collection sessions were also kept as informal as possible. That is, I maintained the use of informal forms of address and general conversation combined with the playing of games, rather than establishing a more formal SAE communication setting where a distinct difference in power between the child and the assessor is established. All of these considerations contributed to helping the child know what the expectations for behaviour were in these assessment or data collection sessions, thus reducing the likelihood of triggering 'shame' responses. It is important to remember also, that Indigenous children have higher than average incidences of a number of health and social issues (Australian Medical Association, 2005; Zubrick et al., 2004) which may all contribute to how a child participates in language assessment activities on any given day. The significance of chronic ear disease and hearing loss in the lives of Australian Indigenous children requires specific consideration by speech pathologists when conducting speech, language and literacy assessments with Indigenous children. While this may not be of relevance for all Indigenous children being assessed, it is certainly worth considering if a particular child is performing below age expectations or is performing inconsistently.

The most effective sampling strategies

Overall, the free play and group Ghost Story telling and movie discussion situations provided a communication context where the child was able to communicate using AE. This in turn provided ample opportunities for obtaining examples of the children's use of a range of sentence constructions, as well as for examining how the children managed instances of conversation repair and other aspects of taking turns at talk. Additionally, for the free play samples, the children were able to choose their own topics of conversation which provided valuable insights regarding their perceptions of the world and their place in it. Humorous exchanges were also frequent. Observing the children's ability to engage in this important form of spoken interaction was important, because in SAE classroom situations I noted a reduction in the use of humour by AE speaking Aboriginal children. The following speech examples provided by Harold, aged 5 years and 1 month, demonstrate the type of language samples produced by the children in these more appropriate language sampling settings.

> Harold: 'And the other day, she, last night, she, she, she no shush, um she was on the verandah she she open the door slowly and close close it little bit and she went into her room and she try to grab one, yeah and take em to the bush. So don't go up there.'

> Harold: 'Listen to this la, listen to this la. There was a little cat a little human cat and he grew and he grew and he kill Nanna X's brother, the cat, the human cat and he and he was only a cat but he grew up and grew, grew till he was a human, yeah and he stab Nanna X's um brother and he went he went and he went back down into the ground.'

Free play samples were best recorded in AE classrooms or outside of the school context within the child's home or community context. The following conversation between Jimmy aged 6 years and 10 months and myself during a phonological awareness assessment session shows how Aboriginal children will provide spontaneous samples of connected speech as long as the setting either reflects their natural way of communicating or they have sufficient experience with and levels of acceptance of the person conducting the assessment to know what is expected from them within that situation.

> Jimmy: I sawn a snake once, was on my (unin) (unin), was a carpet snake and de, ye, de day before yesterday we we sawn we sawn a big python too, big python. It was a it was a swimmin in water. It was a tree snake. Jack he try nu put it on he arm, he just was pinken it and touchin it.
> Me: Pinken it?
> Jimmy: Yeah and touchin it, try nu, try nu grab it by the tail. He did it lot a snakes.
> Me: Who did that?

> Jimmy: Jack. He did it lots u snakes.
>
> Me: Jack? Who's Jack?
>
> Jimmy: Ding, two Jack, one i my, ah two were my cousin. One my ding, ah fellow who punch my nuther ah ah nuther cousin in de in de in de neck. Dat when dey over de complex.

The least effective sampling strategies

The remaining methods of data collection which included those strategies involving elicitation, retelling or one-on-one conversations with the non-Aboriginal researcher elicited language samples which were not representative of the children's language abilities. When using these methods of data collection, more effort was required from me in relation to encouraging the children to produce any spoken language and what was produced was reduced in sentence length and complexity. Rarely did a child spontaneously produce two or more related sentences. Most often, I had to prompt the children to produce each sentence one at a time. This was especially evident during those tasks involving the use of a picture or photo cue to elicit first person narratives. In these situations, the children tended to use repetitive sentence frames and mostly combined labelling of objects in the picture or photo with a simple descriptive sentence either about the picture or themselves when prompted. It is important to note that spontaneously provided first person narratives can provide very useful data for analysis but, at least for the 4- and 5-year-old Aboriginal children included in this study, they can be difficult to elicit. Felicia's speech samples collected in these two different settings illustrate the differences evident in the children's speech samples.

> Setting One: Elicited sample using photo cue of the Indigenous boy having fallen off his bike.
> Felicia (aged 5 years and 8 months):
> 'Me falled over. Me run and falled over.'
>
> Setting Two: Spontaneously offered sample during an assessment activity with the researcher.
> Felicia (aged 6 years and 6 months):
> 'Me and X seen a big goanna. Big goanna me and X on a (unin). On a bush, on the bush. We left it there on a tree. We left.'

The use of retelling as an elicitation strategy provided some very interesting information. In general, the children did not participate well in the retelling of

Western stories. Once again, a large amount of prompting was required to produce single sentences and the children tended to describe what was on a particular page rather than attempting to re-create the story using a series of connected sentences and ideas. Western stories do not typically reflect Aboriginal ways of structuring stories (Malcolm, 1994), so the researcher created a video of an Aboriginal man telling an unfamiliar traditional Aboriginal story (which was drawn for the children as he told the story) for the children to retell. It is very important for language assessors to understand that expecting Aboriginal children to naturally relate to stories presented in the Western 'orientation, complication, resolution' way is denying them access to the ways they typically structure narratives. While the children were very interested in the AE story and attended well to the telling of the story twice, the children did not retell the story well. Rather, the children preferred to engage in a conversation with me about the story. Most importantly, the aspects of the story the children focused upon were the people, meanings and morals of the story rather than talking about the plot or incidents presented in the story in any kind of linear way. The second retelling task reflected AE ways of structuring and telling stories, and so it may be that the concept of story retelling as a separate language task is more of a Western construct which does not reflect the main purpose of telling stories to children for Aboriginal people. Hence, the children may not have been not practised at this task and were therefore less inclined to participate. I have observed that Aboriginal children participate willingly in language-based tasks which are purposeful and meaningful but tend to show less enthusiasm for participating in tasks which they perceive to be meaningless. This appears to be especially true when the child knows the person asking them for information already knows the answer themselves such as happens in an assessment situation. This may have influenced the children's reduced participation in the task when it was purely a 'Now, you tell me the story' as opposed to us just having a conversation about it because it was an interesting story. I have also observed Aboriginal teachers and teacher aides engaging children in a lot of ongoing discussion and questioning about aspects of a story while that story is being read to them. Rather than focusing specifically upon children being able to remember and then accurately retell a plot once a story has been read, the Aboriginal educators are maybe more concerned to determine what the children have gained from or understood about the story.

The usefulness of the assessment data obtained during conversations with me was variable. Success was mostly dependent upon the topic being discussed and whether the conversation was natural or 'staged'. Often, beginning discussions about photos involving the child or others they knew from the community provided a more suitable way of beginning conversations. The children's participation remained variable, however, especially if the photos had been discussed previously with their teacher, for example, as a class. Perhaps in this situation, the concept of discussing the photos again did not seem purposeful for the child.

Conclusion

The implications of viewing language as separate from culture

A speech pathologist operating within a primarily 'white' Australian perspective who fails to understand the influence of a specific context and, hence, fails to employ an assessment methodology which reflects the child's specific language community is at risk of inaccurately labelling communication differences as communication deficits. Such inaccurate labelling has significant implications for the child and that child's community both in the short and long term. Inaccurate labelling of Indigenous children as language impaired can lead to a child being placed within special education classes or receiving remedial instruction individually, in small groups or as part of a classroom program. None of these situations is likely to benefit the typically developing AE speaking Aboriginal child. The approaches used for English as a Second Dialect speakers and those used for language-impaired children, and the accompanying perceptions of others towards these distinct groups of children, vary considerably.

Speech pathologists will not use the information collected from only one short language sample to diagnose typical or impaired language development. If a speech pathologist continues to keep collecting language samples using the same less effective methods of language sampling, however, the data obtained are likely to remain similar and not truly reflect the language abilities of the child being assessed.

Australian speech pathologists are trained to think of language as an artefact or as a 'thing' which can exist independently of language use. The type of language assessment typically conducted by speech pathologists reflects this view. This theoretical perspective leads speech pathologists to conduct assessments using tests and assessment practices which reflect this theoretical construct.

Australian Aboriginal children are unlikely to perform well when assessed in this way because such assessments do not reflect the ways many Aboriginal people typically use language. These inappropriate assessments are unlikely to be well accepted by Aboriginal people. Aboriginal people recognise that such assessments are highly unlikely to elicit data which provide a true description of an Aboriginal child's language abilities due to their inability to cater for the many culturally specific aspects of Aboriginal communication such as AE 'shame' and context-dependent language use. Considering the cultural nature of language development requires the speech pathologist to understand that language is a vehicle for culture. It requires the speech pathologist to consider how culture is reflected in both the children's language use as well as their own language use and how these come together in spoken interaction to create communication.

Notes

1. The term Indigenous is being used as a collective term to apply to the original inhabitants of a country. The term Aboriginal is the term used to describe a specific group of original inhabitants of Australia and is not inclusive of the other original inhabitants of Australia known as Torres Strait Islanders.
2. All children's names used in this chapter are pseudonyms.
3. Shame is a concept which has specific meaning for Aboriginal speakers of English and is not the same as the SAE concept of 'shame'. This will be discussed in more detail later in the chapter.

References

Anderson, I. (1988). *Koorie Health in Koorie Hands: An Orientation Manual in Aboriginal Health for Health-care Providers.* Melbourne: Koorie Health Unit, Health Department Victoria.

Australian Medical Association. (2005). *Lifting the Weight. Low Birth Weight Babies: An Indigenous Health Burden That Must Be Lifted.* Canberra: Australian Medical Association.

Ball, J., Bernhardt, B. and Deby, J. (2005, 27 Nov–1 Dec, 2005). *Implications of First Nations English Dialects for Supporting Children's Language Development.* Paper presented at the World Indigenous Peoples' Conference on Education, Hamilton, Aotearoa/New Zealand.

Bavin, E. (1991). The acquisition of Warlpiri kin terms. *Pragmatics, 1*(3), 319–44.

Bochenek, C. (1987). *The Kimberley Early Language Scales.* Unpublished.

Botting, N. (2002). Narrative as a tool for the assessment of linguistic and pragmatic impairments. *Child Language Teaching and Therapy, 18*(1), 1–21.

Campbell, T., Dollaghan, C., Needleman, H. and Janosky, J. (1997). Reducing bias in language assessment: processing-dependent measures. *Journal of Speech, Language, and Hearing Research, 40*(3), 519–25.

Carter, J. A., Lees, J. A., Murira, G. M., Gona, J., Neville, B. G. R. and Newton, C. R. J. C. (2005). Issues in the development of cross-cultural assessments of speech and language for children. *International Journal of Language & Communication Disorders, 40*(4), 385–401.

Chaffey, G. W., Bailey, S. B. and Vine, K. W. (2003). Identifying high academic potential in Australian Aboriginal children using dynamic testing. *Australasian Journal of Gifted Education, 12*(1), 42–55.

Cunningham, C. (Undated). *Western Australian Action Picture Test.* Derby, WA: Department of Health.

Curran, L., Elkerton, D. and Steinberg, M. (1996, 12–16 March). *Assessment of American Indian children as Measured by the SON-R and WISC-III.* Paper presented at the National Association of School Psychologists 28th Annual National Convention, Atlanta, GA.

Danzer, V. A., Gerber, M. F., Lyons, T. M. and Voress, J. K. (1991). *DABERON Screening for School Readiness (DABERON-2)* (Second edn). Austin, TX: Pro-ed.

DETE. (2000). *"Children . . . come and Talk": A Communication Assessment for Aboriginal Children and Students.* Adelaide: South Australian Department of Education, Training and Employment.

Diplock, G. and Wommatakimmi, N. (2003). 'The Tiwi Island Language Test'. (Produced with the assistance of Paula Caffrey and Ann Marriot). Unpublished.

Dooly, M. (2005). How aware are they? Research into teachers' attitudes about linguistic diversity. *Language Awareness, 14*(2&3), 97–111.

Eckermann, A., Dowd, T., Martin, M., Nixon, L., Gray, R. and Chong, E. (1992). *Binan Goonj: Bridging Cultures in Indigenous Health.* Armidale, NSW: University of New England Press.

Gould, J. (1999). 'An evaluation of assessment instruments in the measurement of the spoken communication skills of rural indigenous children'. Unpublished MA sub-thesis, Australian National University, Canberra.

Gould, J. (2000). Assessing the spoken communication skills of Aboriginal children. In C. Lind (ed.), *Research, Reflect, Renew.* Proceedings of the 2000 Speech Pathology Australia National Conference. Adelaide: Speech Pathology Australia.

Gould, J. (2001). Joint assessments for Koori children. *Australian Communication Quarterly, 3*(3), 136–38.

Gould, J. (2005). Creating non-standardised assessment tools for use with Indigenous children. *Practicality and Impact: Making a Difference in the Real World.* Paper presented at the Speech Pathology Australia National Conference, Melbourne.

Gould, J. and Chatfield, C. (2000). *The Winanggaay After School Group: Information Package.* Yass, NSW: Yass Community Health Centre.

Gutierrez-Clellen, V. F. and Pena, E. (2001). Dynamic assessment of diverse children: a tutorial. *Language, Speech, and Hearing Services in Schools, 32*(4), 212–24.

Gutierrez-Clellen, V. F. and Quinn, R. (1993). Assessing narratives of children from diverse cultural/linguistic groups. *Language, Speech, and Hearing Services in Schools, 24*(1), 2–9.

Hamilton, A. (1981). *Nature and Nurture: Aboriginal Child-Rearing in North-Central Arnhem Land.* Canberra: Australian Institute of Aboriginal Studies.

Harkins, J. (1990). Shame and shyness in the Indigenous classroom: a case for practical semantics. *Australian Journal of Linguistics, 10*(2), 293–306.

Harkins, J. (1994). *Bridging Two Worlds: Aboriginal English and Cross-Cultural Understanding.* Brisbane: University of Queensland Press.

Harris, S. (1990). *Two-way Aboriginal Schooling: Educational and Cultural Survival.* Canberra: Aboriginal Studies Press.

Jacobs, A. M. (1988). A descriptive study of the bilingual language development of Aboriginal children in the goldfields of Western Australia. *Australian Journal of Human Communications Disorders, 16*(82), 3–15.

James, D. G. H. (2001). Storytelling skills in children aged 3;0 to 5;11 years. *Evidence and Innovation.* Paper presented at the 2001 Speech Pathology Australia National Conference, Melbourne.

Lowell, A., Gurimangu, Nyomba and Ningi. (1996). Communication and learning at home: a preliminary report on Yolngu language socialisation. In M. Cooke (ed.), *Aboriginal Languages in Contemporary Contexts: Yolngu Matha at Galiwin'ku (DEETYA Project Report)* (pp. 109–52). Batchelor, NT: Batchelor College.

Malcolm, I. G. (1992). English in the education of speakers of Aboriginal English. In J. Siegel (ed.), *Pidgins, Creoles and Nonstandard Dialects in Education.* (Occasional Paper no. 12, pp. 15–29). Canberra: ANU Printing Service.

Malcolm, I. G. (1994). Aboriginal English inside and outside the classroom. *Australian Review of Applied Linguistics, 20*(1), 147–80.

Marriot, A. (2003). Amata Activity-Based Oral Language Assessment (AABOLA). Understanding basic questions and directions in context and understanding language concepts. Adelaide: South Australian Department of Education, Training and Employment.

Marshall, J. (2000). Critical reflections on the cultural influences in identification and habilitation of children with speech and language difficulties. *International Journal of Disability, Development & Education, 47*(4), 355–69.

Mattes, L. J. and Omark, D. R. (1984). *Speech and Language Assessment for the Bilingual Handicapped.* San Diego, CA: College-Hill Press.

Moore-Brown, B., Huerta, M., Uranga-Hernandez, Y. and Peña, E. D. (2006). Using dynamic assessment to evaluate children with suspected learning disabilities. *Intervention in School & Clinic, 41*(4), 209–17.

Nippold, M. (2004). Language disorders in school-age children: aspects of assessment. In R. D. Kent (ed.), *The MIT Encyclopedia of Communication Disorders.* Cambridge: The MIT Press.

Oetting, J. B. (2004a). Dialect versus disorder. In R. D. Kent (ed.), *The MIT Encyclopedia of Communication Disorders* (pp. 297–300). *Cambridge:* The MIT Press.

Oetting, J. B. (2004b). Dialect speakers. In R. D. Kent (ed.), *The MIT Encyclopedia of Communication Disorders* (pp. 294–297). Cambridge: The MIT Press.

Philpott, M. (2003). *The Revised Kimberley Speech Pathology Early Language Scales.* Retrieved on 30 August 2007 from <http://www.speechpathologyaustralia.org.au/library/Kimberley%20Scales.pdf>.

Ramage, J. (2004). Early Concepts Photo Assessment Tool for Preschoolers. Adelaide: South Australian Department of Education, Training and Employment.

Seymour, H. N., Roeper, T. W. and de Villiers, J. (2003). *Diagnostic Evaluation of Language Variation.* San Antonio, TX: The Psychological Corporation.

Sharifian, F. (2005). Cultural conceptualisations in English words: a study of Aboriginal children in Perth. *Language and Education, 19*(1), 74–88.

Speech Pathology Australia. (2001). *Working in a Multilingual and Culturally Diverse Society.* Melbourne: Speech Pathology Australia.

Trudgen, R. I. (2000). *Why Warriors Lie Down and Die: Towards an Understanding of why the Aboriginal People of Arnhem Land Face the Greatest Crisis in Health and Education since European Contact.* Darwin, NT: Aboriginal Resources and Development Services Inc.

Westerveld, M. F., Gillon, G. T. and Miller, J. F. (2004). Spoken language samples of New Zealand children in conversation and narration. *Advances in Speech-Language Pathology, 6*(4), 195–208.

Winsa, B. (2000). Defining an ecological niche: the use of 'dialect' or 'language'. *Current Issues in Language Planning, 1*(3), 431–34.

Zubrick, S. R., Lawrence, D. M., Silburn, S. R., Blair, E., Milroy, H., Wilkes, T., Eades, S., D'Antoine, H., Read, A., Ishiguchi, P. and Doyle, S. (2004). *The Western Australian Aboriginal Child Health Survey: The Health of Aboriginal Children and Young People.* Perth: Telethon Institute for Child Health Research. Perth, WA: Telethon Institute for Child Health Research.

10 Indigenous children and conductive hearing loss

Ann Galloway

The classroom was quite noisy; the children moved around and talked in small groups about their projects. Suddenly, through the buzz of the classroom, came the sound of rhythmic drumming. It was Tom, drumming on his desk with a pencil, and rocking on the back legs of his chair. A teaching assistant moved to sit next to him to deter him from drumming and direct his attention to his task. Tom settled to it and the assistant moved away. Shortly afterwards, he started running a toy car across his desktop, calling out and swinging on his chair again, totally disengaged from the task he had been given. The teacher told him to be quiet and get on with his work, but her voice could barely be heard above the noise of the class. Eventually, after repeated infractions, Tom was taken out of class and sent to the Principal. This looks like a behaviour management incident, but it was actually a health incident – Tom has conductive hearing loss as a result of otitis media, and his behaviour results from frustration owing to not being able to hear properly and participate fully in class work. Such incidents are repeated regularly in hundreds of classrooms of indigenous[1] students like Tom.

What is otitis media?

Otitis media is the name for 'all forms of inflammation and infection of the middle ear' (Couzos et al., 2001, p. vii), and is caused by bacterial and or viral infection, often linked to another illness, for example, a cold, influenza, or chest infection (Burrow and Thomson, 2003; Kelly and Weeks, 1991). Hearing loss can occur when a child gets an ear infection and fluid builds up in the ear canal, causing the ear to become blocked, and restricting transmission of incoming sounds (Burrow and Thomson, 2003). This type of hearing loss is known as conductive hearing loss (CHL), and is a consequence of otitis media (OM). OM, sometimes known as 'glue ear', is particularly prevalent among indigenous populations, mainly children, who generally suffer more frequent episodes, occurring earlier and lasting longer than in non-indigenous populations (Boswell, 1997; Kelly and Weeks, 1991). Indigenous people generally suffer from the chronic forms of OM rather than the acute forms that generally affect non-indigenous people (Burrow and Thomson, 2003). Apart from viral or bacterial infections, other risk factors implicated in OM include premature birth; being male; not being breastfed; smoke from cigarettes or wood fires; poor nutrition; poor hygiene; lack of access to clean water; lack of access to medical services; overcrowded living conditions, which may lead to bacterial cross-contamination; and environmental conditions (Kelly and Weeks, 1991; Moore, 1999; WHO/CIBA Foundation, 2000). There is also a high correlation between the incidence of OM and socio-economic and geographic factors. For example, poverty may mean that people cannot afford to visit a doctor, or buy good food, including plenty of fresh fruit and vegetables essential for a healthy diet that will contribute to building up the immune system and resistance to infection, while geographic location may restrict access to services and supplies. These risk factors for OM correlate highly with indigenous populations worldwide, who are often marginalised, relatively poor, and live in more isolated locations.

The statistics for the incidence of OM vary across studies, but the overall picture is consistent – OM is proportionately more prevalent among indigenous populations than non-indigenous. For example, studies of North American Inuit report the incidence of OM to range from 7–78 per cent, while that for First Nations Canadians is 3–17 per cent (Bowd, 2005; Moore, 1999). For Australian Aboriginal children, the prevalence of OM is one of the highest in the world, ranging from around 30 per cent (a level similar to that of the general population) up to at least 80 per cent, with remoteness correlating highly with increased incidence of OM (Burrow and Thomson, 2003; Couzos et al., 2001). It is estimated that Aboriginal children experience middle ear disease for periods totalling about 2.5 years of their childhood, compared with 3 months for non-Aboriginal children (Howard and Hampton, 2006). The significance of these figures (which include several types of OM) becomes clearer when compared with the World Health Organisation's classification of prevalence of one type of OM, chronic suppurative OM (CSOM). Any incidence of CSOM above 4 per cent of the population is a critical public health issue, requiring urgent attention; even 2–4 per cent incidence is considered unacceptably high (Acuin, 2004).

OM is, therefore, a significant problem for indigenous people. Medical interventions such as antibiotics and surgery (e.g. insertion of grommets; Morris, 1998) are usually effective in curing the disease, although it may recur. But there are other impacts of OM, which medical intervention alone cannot cure. These include periodic or ongoing conductive hearing loss (CHL) and associated developmental delays, especially in speech and language, which in turn can have a significant negative impact on educational achievement and social skills, and also future employment and life opportunities (Lowell et al., 1995; Olusanya, 2004). While the level and impact of hearing loss associated with OM varies with factors such as the severity and frequency of episodes of OM, three or more episodes of OM before the age of 3 years may seriously hinder language development (Kindig and Richards, 2000), because this is a time of intense development of oral language skills. These provide the foundation for literacy acquisition (Higgins, 1997), so that educational intervention may be required to address these consequences of CHL due to OM as the impact of speech processing difficulties on children who have or have had OM can have significant impacts upon literacy acquisition.

Conductive hearing loss

The hearing loss associated with CHL is unpredictable and fluctuating, meaning that a child may hear normally at times, but not at others. CHL is therefore much more difficult to cope with than sensorineural hearing loss, where the hearing loss is at a constant level and so compensatory strategies will consistently be effective. The fluctuating nature of CHL has a number of consequences for language development. It means that the language input children with CHL receive will be inconsistent (Walker and Wigglesworth, 2001), so, for example, they hear different forms of the same word at different times, apparently giving several names for the same object. Under these conditions, children's language learning strategies appear to be ineffective, they become easily fatigued and frustrated trying to cope, and frequently give up and withdraw from interaction. Variable language inputs are likely to result in inadequate models and range of language on which to build when learning to read and write (Higgins, 1997), because children may not associate letters with sounds consistently.

Hearing loss will lead to difficulty in discriminating sounds, especially similar sounds, sounds spoken softly, sounds in unstressed positions, and less proficiency at hearing word endings (see section on Phonological awareness). There will also be difficulty in understanding generally what is said. The extent of the impact of hearing loss will be influenced by what the child's home language is, and whether or not they are learning in that language. For Aboriginal children, the language of school is likely to be a second or subsequent language or dialect for them, and often there are issues of power and identity associated with language use (Nienhuys and Burnip, 1988). Further, cultural differences between Aboriginal and non-Aboriginal ways of interacting can 'mask' hearing loss (Howard, 1992; Lowell et al., 1995), for example, not responding to a teacher's question or non-involvement in classroom activities may be attributed to different cultural norms (Moses and Wigglesworth, Chapter 6), or it may be that the child is not participating because they cannot hear what is being said.

The level of hearing loss children experience as a result of OM will vary, but even a low level of loss can seriously impair language development, as the following summary shows:

- 0–15 dB (decibels, a measure of sound) hearing loss is considered within normal limits;
- Up to 25 dB hearing loss is considered mild, but many common sounds will be missed;
- With 30 dB hearing loss, normal conversation sounds like a whisper, and whispers cannot be heard;
- At 60 dB hearing loss, normal conversation cannot be heard, and a shouting voice would sound like normal conversation level (Morris, 1998).

The noisier the classroom, the harder a child with hearing loss will find it to hear the teacher. For ease of hearing, the signal-to-noise ratio (SNR) needs to be at least 15 dB above the ambient noise level (e.g. the level of a speaker's voice in relation to the ambient noise in the room). Noise levels vary according to activity, but in a standard classroom it would be about 60 dB, and 70–90 dB in open plan classrooms, with the SNR between −7 dB and +4 dB, but possibly ranging as widely as –20 dB to +5 dB. Further, the intensity of a speaker's voice diminishes in intensity as distance between speaker and listener increases, so the greater the overall noise level and the greater the distance between speaker and listener, the greater the chance that important acoustic cues will be missed (Massie and Dillon, 2006; McSporran et al., 1997; Pakulski and Kaderavek, 2002). In addition, the level of reverberation in classrooms is often high and compounds the noise problems. Thus, classroom environments represent less than ideal listening conditions. Other consequences of CHL include delays in language comprehension and production; reduced ability to remember what they have heard; poor listening skills; problems with attention and distraction; reduced mathematical skills; reduced scores on intelligence tests; poor social and emotional well-being; and behavioural problems (Howard, 2004b; Partington and Galloway, 2005; Yonowitz et al., 1995; Zubrick et al., 2004). So, language learning problems will have flow-on effects to other areas of education and social life. Much learning in school relies directly or indirectly on written language, so children who have difficulties with written literacy due to oral language problems as a consequence of OM in early life are likely to struggle with most aspects of schooling. This is especially likely to be the case as they move from learning to read to using reading to learn. Children with CHL may have difficulty participating socially because they cannot hear, so their social skills are often diminished, and they may be ostracised by the group. If their educational and social problems are sufficiently great, children may find their school experience so difficult that they leave school early, which can have long-term negative social impacts, including increased likelihood of anti-social behaviour (Howard, 2004a; Nienhuys and Burnip, 1988). Even if students remain engaged with the education system, they may not fulfil their potential, and either leave earlier than they might otherwise have done, or have more restricted employment choices than might have been available with higher qualifications (Howard, 2005).

As children get older, the incidence of ear infections decreases and normally ultimately ceases (Boswell, 1997; Kelly and Weeks, 1991), but the effects of the hearing loss that occurred during bouts of OM remain, and in some cases there can be permanent hearing impairment. So OM and its consequence, CHL, are issues relevant to all teachers, not only to early childhood teachers. Everyone will need to address the consequences of CHL in the classroom through remediation of missing language skills, and through classroom management that enhances listening and hence learning opportunities.

An essential foundation for meeting the needs of students with speech and language impairment is knowing the speech and language skills that are needed for success in written literacy, especially given the integral part that it plays in mainstream learning. The development of these speech and language skills and the use of the classroom management strategies that enhance learning are basic good teaching practices, which will benefit all students in the classroom, but especially indigenous students with CHL. The outline of these skills and strategies that follows draws extensively on outcomes of a longitudinal study [2] undertaken in Western Australia in 16 schools in urban, rural and remote locationsi, one of the few studies undertaken of educational interventions for students with CHL. The study involved 80 teachers and Aboriginal teaching assistants and over 500 Aboriginal students, and investigated effective teaching strategies for developing literacy in Standard Australian English (SAE) with Australian Aboriginal children aged 5–8 years (Preschool to Year 3). The participating education providers had given to the schools a resource book of strategies (Western Australian Department of Education, 2002), and evaluation of their use formed part of the focus of the study. In addition, the researchers drew on strategies that participating staff used with their classes, and additional material from other educational literature. The study found that the students of teachers who, through systematic and explicit teaching, developed the language skills outlined below performed at a level consistent with mainstream age-relevant educational standards.

Speech and language skills underlying written literacy

For success in written literacy, children need to develop a range of phonological, syntactic, discourse, semantic and pragmatic skills. These can be expressed as including:

- phonological awareness, the ability to discriminate and manipulate the sounds of a language;
- text level skills, the ability to use language at sentence level and above;
- the ability to link sounds and written language;
- 'world' knowledge, knowledge of the way language works, of the concepts and content being talked or written about, and how to use language appropriately in different contexts.

Phonological awareness

Phonological awareness is concerned with the reception and production of the sounds of a language, and includes knowledge of rhyme and rhythm; the ability to discriminate sounds in all word positions – beginning, middle and end; blend sounds; divide words into syllables; and manipulate sounds (Yonowitz et al., 1995). These skills will typically be developed in the classroom through activities such as rhymes, songs and poems, rhyming stories, learning letter names and sounds, and playing word games.

There are several issues that Aboriginal children face in terms of the development of phonological awareness in relation to developing written literacy at school. Their home language background is generally Aboriginal English, Kriol, or a traditional Aboriginal language, with Standard Australian English (SAE), the language of school, being a second or subsequent language or dialect. Their home language and literacy experiences are often wholly oral, and may not include the type of oral and written literacy privileged at school, which most children of mainstream, middle-class Anglo backgrounds experience (but see Kral and Ellis, Chapter 7). Then, many Aboriginal children have had extensive hearing loss during their early childhood years due to CHL as a result of OM, and have missed out on much learning in their first language or dialect, so do not have a good foundation to build on in developing skills in a subsequent language or dialect. Further, little is known about the development of phonological awareness in Aboriginal languages, so it is difficult to compare experiences of Aboriginal children and mainstream to know specifically where differences are most likely to occur and where specific attention to development is needed. Even if that information were available, given the prevalence of CHL in some communities, it might be difficult to determine what a normal pattern of development would be anyway. Therefore, phonological awareness needs to be taught explicitly, consistently and over a long period of time, not just at preschool and Year 1 levels. Further, when older students struggle with written literacy, it is likely that they have missed out on vital foundational learning in their early years, and need help to develop those skills and enhance their educational opportunities. For Aboriginal students with CHL, there are several areas of phonology that are likely to cause particular problems, because those sounds are not part of the repertoire of their first language or dialect (e.g. voicing, the difference between 'p' and 'b' or 't' and 'd', is not distinctive in most Aboriginal languages). Also if sounds are generally

Table 10.1 Individual consonants

	Voiceless	as in	Voiced	as in
Plosives	/p/	pig	/b/	big
	/t/	tip	/d/	dip
	/k/	coat	/g/	goat
Affricates	/tʃ/	choke	/dʒ/	joke
Fricatives	/f/	fan	/v/	van
	/θ/	thin	/ð/	then
	/s/	bus	/z/	buzz
	/ʃ/	show	/ʒ/	treasure
Consonant groups				
/t/, /d/, /θ/, /ð/				
/f/, /v/, /p/, /b/				
/s/, /z/, /ʃ/, /tʃ/				

Source: Adapted from Berry and Hudson, 1997.

lower pitch sounds, they are unlikely to be heard by anyone with even a mild hearing loss, especially in a noisy environment. Further, some of these sounds, like 's' and 'd', occur in word final position in SAE, and are obligatory markers of number, tense and possession. However, Aboriginal children, unaccustomed to those sounds in word final position, may miss hearing them. Therefore, when working with Aboriginal students with CHL, the consonants and consonant groups summarised in Table 10.1 require special attention.

Speakers of Aboriginal languages are also likely to have problems with /h/, which does not occur in words initially in Aboriginal languages. Other consonants (e.g. /n/, /m/ and /l/) are unlikely to cause significant problems as they are similar in both Aboriginal languages and SAE. As well, many vowels will also be difficult for Australian Aboriginal students because SAE has far more vowel sounds than Aboriginal languages. Therefore, the vowels and vowel groups summarised in Table 10.2 are likely to be problematic for Aboriginal people if the sounds are not part of their first language repertoire.

Aboriginal children will need explicit teaching in hearing and producing these consonant and vowel sounds in all word positions. Even in the case of sounds that are common to their home language and SAE, students may need explicit instruction in correct production if, due to hearing impairment, they did not learn them properly.

Table 10.2 Individual vowels

Vowel	As in
/i/	bean
/ɪ/	bin
/ɛ/	Ben
/ɜ/	herd
/æ/	hand
/ʌ/	hunt
/a/	hard
/ʊ/	put
/ɒ/	pot
/ɔ/	port
Vowel Groups	
/i/, /ɪ/, /ɛ/	
/ɜ/, /æ/, /ʌ/, /a/	
/ʊ/, /ɒ/, /ɔ/	

Source: Adapted from Berry and Hudson, 1997.

Text level skills

Text level skills, the reception and production of oral and written language at sentence level and above, include vocabulary; meaning of words and concepts; specificity in language use; grammar; sequencing, structure and language of different genres of texts; and language that expresses the relations between entities, and which forms the basis of various genres in SAE. These skills need to be developed first through oral language in the children's home language, as well as the SAE of school, so that there is a solid mental foundation on which children can build when they come to written literacy. Aboriginal children have a rich heritage of oral language skills that can be built on to support the development of written literacy, but will also need to learn new ways of using and organising language. Typically within the classroom, these skills will be developed through activities such as hearing and telling stories; talking about and listening to recounts of events, procedures for doing things, and explanations of what happened; and planning activities, then complementing this oral work with written.

Children with CHL often have very limited vocabularies, due to missing out on language input. Common areas of weakness in SAE identified by educators include description (e.g. adjectives and adverbs), specificity (e.g. use of prepositions, expressing size and distance), and relational language (e.g. reasons/explanations; cause/effect; prediction/justification; speculation/possibility;

similarity/difference; comparison/contrast; problem/solution). Further, Aboriginal languages and culture do not necessarily express these matters in the same way as SAE, so explicit teaching is needed.

Link sounds and written language

As well as learning the sounds of the language, students need to be able to link sounds with their written forms. The links between sounds and written language need to be developed as phonological awareness and text level skills are developed, but it is essential that the teaching be explicit. Important strategies include maintaining a print-rich environment in the classroom, developing students' concepts of print, and helping students to encode the sounds of SAE and to understand that there is no one-to-one sound–symbol correspondence in English.

'World' knowledge

'World' knowledge is another important component of written literacy, that is, knowledge of the way language works (gained from experience with language), appropriate language use for different purposes in different contexts (pragmatics), and of the ideas and concepts that form part of the material being used. A basic element of good teaching is to start with materials and concepts familiar to the student and build from there (scaffolding learning). Many students with CHL may have more limited knowledge of language and life because they are not able to hear properly or to always participate fully in activities. In these cases, to be able to maximise their learning opportunities, they will need input on a variety of topics and concepts. Working thematically will give more intense and prolonged exposure to content that can be used to develop a variety of language skills.

Classroom management

In addition to developing the language skills and knowledge that underlie written literacy, teachers can assist students with CHL by modifying the classroom environment to enhance hearing and learning opportunities. It is much more difficult in a noisy environment for students with hearing impairment to catch on to what is being said, so by modifying the physical environment of the classroom to minimise noise, and organising students to maximise listening, their learning will be better supported. Further, for many Aboriginal students, the culture of school is quite alien, and so teachers also need to interact with students in ways that are compatible with the interaction styles favoured in their communities, as well as making explicit differences between home and school ways so that the children can function more confidently in the school environment.

Modifying the physical environment

To maximise listening and learning opportunities, it is important that teachers try to minimise noise in the external and internal classroom environments. External noise can come from sources such as traffic from adjacent roads; machinery operating near the classroom; and activities of other students or staff close by. Some of these distractions cannot be addressed. However, external noise from other students or the timing of noisy work may be open to negotiation with other staff and contractors. If the external noise is permanent (e.g. traffic), another option may be to try to negotiate a classroom in a quieter area of the school, if only for the part of the day when critical teaching (e.g. explicit teaching of literacy skills) takes place. At the very least, critical teaching should be scheduled for the quietest time of the day so that there is greatest opportunity for children to hear what is going on.

Internal noise, from within the classroom, such as from equipment, people talking or moving around, may be easier to control. A lot of classroom equipment emits low levels of noise, for example, fluorescent lights, air conditioners, fish tanks, and desks and chairs as children move around. Good maintenance (including cleaning) is essential to minimise noise from equipment, so teachers may need to initiate maintenance requests to overcome problems. The noise from classroom movement can be minimised by teaching children to move quietly and carefully, and by putting rubber tips on the end of desk and chair legs. Internal noise can also be minimised by installing sound absorbing materials in the classroom. Classrooms have many hard surfaces from which sound reverberates, making it more difficult for children to hear. If at least 50 per cent of the hard surfaces in a classroom are covered (e.g. soft furnishings, carpet or matting, pin-up boards on walls, and displays of artwork suspended across the classroom), the listening environment can be improved significantly (Education Queensland, 2002). Another useful tool to improve the listening environment for children with CHL is sound field amplification (SFA), which will increase the signal-to-noise ratio, enabling children to hear more clearly and with less effort what is being said (Education Queensland,

2002; Massie and Dillon, 2006; McSporran et al., 1997). The SFA unit does not need to be used all day, but should at least be used when explicit teaching to the whole class is in progress. As with any other equipment, it is essential that SFA units are well maintained, for example, batteries are fresh and the unit is correctly tuned for the room where it is situated.

Organising children to maximise listening

The second major area of classroom management to enhance learning for children with CHL is organisation of teaching and learning activities within the classroom. Children who are known to have a hearing impairment should be seated close to the speaker to make it easier for them to hear what is being said, and hence participate in whatever is happening at the time. In addition to seating children with CHL close to the speaker, they should also be positioned in a close group when instructions are being given or explicit teaching is taking place, for example, seating them on a specially designated carpeted area of the classroom ('a mat session'), before sending them to work individually or in small groups. When speaking to children, face the group, wait for silence and ensure everyone is listening before speaking so everyone has maximum chance of hearing what is said. Also, children with CHL may have got into the habit of being inattentive to language (Ford, 1993), and so need to learn to pay attention to what is being said. Making sure the speaker's face is visible enables children with CHL to utilise visual cues, including lip reading, which will assist them in understanding what is being said. Speaking clearly; repeating (or re-phrasing) if necessary; giving short, sequenced instructions; and using non-verbal language as well also help. As part of ensuring a speaker's face is visible, it is important to check that the lighting in the room is adequate, so that children who need to rely on visual cues can see clearly (Ford, 1993).

Teachers of students from cultural backgrounds different from theirs need to be sensitive to different listening styles and negotiate with their classes culturally appropriate listening behaviours. In mainstream Australian classes, it is normal to face the speaker, maintain eye contact and stay still during an interaction. This is not necessarily the norm for all Australian Aboriginal people. For example, in some parts of Australia, lowered eyes are a mark of respect and maintaining eye contact might be considered disrespectful. Similarly, remaining still while someone is speaking may not be the usually expected behaviour, and people may move in and out of a conversation, and still be listening. Indeed, in school contexts where teachers find Aboriginal students sitting still and listening carefully, it may indicate that the children involved have hearing problems and are trying hard to pick up what is going on (Lowell et al., 1995). Aboriginal support staff and local community members can provide advice about protocols and help negotiate culturally appropriate ways for students to signal to the teacher that they are listening.

In addition to the strategies outlined above, there is a need for additional support structures to be in place in the classroom to help children with CHL. Among the possibilities are establishing a 'buddy' system, whereby designated students help each other, following pre-determined guidelines set by the teacher. The 'buddy' of a student with CHL is responsible for making sure the student has heard instructions, for example, and knows what to do, and it is to the buddy that the student with CHL turns in the first instance for help. A different version of the buddy system is having older students tutor younger ones. Older students could be taught the same material as the younger ones are learning so they can tutor appropriately. This would help older students develop further essential foundational language skills (which they may have missed out on due to hearing loss when younger) in a way that does not cause embarrassment, and provides a way of helping younger children which may be culturally relevant. In classrooms where an Aboriginal teaching assistant is available, they will also be able to help monitor children with CHL and help them participate. Small group work and one-to-one teaching are other useful ways of increasing opportunities for hearing and learning by students with CHL. In these contexts, the listening demands are reduced compared with a large one, it is easier for students to attend to non-verbal cues, and there are more opportunities for seeking clarification if they do not understand.

Introduction of new material is a particular problem for children with CHL. If students are not familiar with key words and concepts, they cannot use those as 'pegs' to help make sense of what is going on. Teachers can help to alleviate these problems by preteaching key words and concepts to these students, ahead of introducing the material to the class (Pakulski and Kaderavek, 2002). This preteaching will provide a foundation they can build on when the class session comes round. Consequently they will be better able to participate in the lessons and gain more from them. Teaching sessions should be followed up to check children's understanding and grasp of information and concepts presented, and reinstruction provided when necessary.

A particularly critical part of classroom organisation for children with CHL is establishment and maintenance of routines. If there is predictability about the way that things are done in the classroom, children will be able to follow and participate appropriately, even if they have not heard all the instructions properly. This will enable them to remain engaged, and minimise the chances of ostracism by others due to inappropriate responses.

This discussion of classroom management strategies has largely focused on the teacher's role in helping to improve the quality of the learning environment for children with CHL. Students can also play a role in this if teachers raise awareness of hearing problems and the consequences of them for learning. Hearing and ear health can be a focus of health and science lessons, and as part of that children can learn about the problems that children with CHL face, and the role of good nutrition, hygiene and physical activity in promoting ear health. Lessons can also include discussions of ways students can minimise classroom noise and take responsibility for the quality of their learning environment. As children get older, they can also be helped to take responsibility for recognising the symptoms of a CHL episode and alerting their teacher to the fact that they are having a bad hearing day, as well as organising themselves for optimum listening.

Identifying hearing problems

Teachers often face the dilemma of being aware that hearing problems may exist, but not knowing if any of their students is affected – hearing problems are not usually seen (unless perhaps a student has ear discharge, or wears a hearing aid). And because of the fluctuating nature of CHL, when a child is hearing normally, they are likely to be participating normally within the classroom, yet at other times appear totally disengaged and withdrawn in ways that might mistakenly be attributed to misbehaviour, as in the case of Tom, above. Also, some children become quite adept at compensating for their hearing loss or masking the fact that they are not coping with classroom demands. Again, the real cause of the problem is not evident.

There are a number of ways teachers can find out about the hearing status of children in their classes. One avenue is checking the children's school health records, following the standard school protocols for access. Often in the early years of school children will have had a basic health screening, normally including screening for hearing problems, generally using otoscopic and audiometric screening. If there has been a history of ear disease, that may have been recorded there. However, caution is needed in that a child may have had normal hearing at the time a hearing assessment was done, but still have some hearing impairment, or may have a mild hearing impairment that will impact negatively on speech and language development and learning but be below the health authority's threshold for normal hearing. Such a result might not be noted on the health record. Screening tools are another useful source of information about the possible presence of CHL. There is a range of tools available, which list physical, speech, learning and behavioural indicators (e.g. Education Queensland, 2002; Higgins, 1997). Each child in a group can be monitored over a week or two for evidence of these symptoms. If a number of symptoms are present, it may be that the child has hearing impairment as a result of CHL. This can alert the teacher to seek help for the child, following the school protocols applicable for suspected medical problems. This may mean talking with the school nurse or health worker, who will then work with the parent and the child to arrange further more specialised help. The information from the screening tool can also be utilised to assist in classroom management, as it will identify students who may be at risk and therefore need extra support and other educational interventions. Another type of screening tool is one that helps to identify who may be suffering from hearing loss at different times of the day. One widely used tool is 'Blind man's Simon says' (Howard, 1992), whereby the teacher or an assistant stands at the front of a small group of children that includes hearing and suspected hearing-impaired students and gives instructions for actions, initially in a voice that all can hear, but gradually more softly. Children with hearing problems will not be able to follow and respond appropriately, which can be noted by an assistant and the information passed onto the teacher discreetly later. The teacher can then make sure that those children receive additional support during learning sessions.

Information about the possibility of hearing problems may also come through informal routes, such as comments from a parent or community member or even another child about a child having sore ears or being sick. It is wise for teachers, especially those working in high-risk areas, such as remote locations, to work from the premise that all children in the class might have had ear disease at some time, and consequently some level of hearing impairment that will have impacted negatively on speech and language development.

As well as being aware of students who have hearing problems as a result of CHL, teachers also need to know what gaps are present in their language learning. Taping and analysing children's oral language and analysing samples of written language are helpful ways of identifying these and providing information on which to base interventions. The types of oral language recorded should include conversations with peers and with adults, as well as sequentially ordered texts, such as narratives. Getting children to tell a story based on a series of a few pictures can be a useful scaffold for them and provides a framework for analysis of grammar and genre structures, as well as pronunciation, although this may have some limitations in terms of the quality and quantity of language produced by the child, and examples of the child's extended oral language need to be gathered from other sources as well. When analysing written language, errors of spelling, grammar and discourse sequencing can be noted in the samples, and patterns identified. It is important to seek the help of an Aboriginal teaching assistant when analysing language samples, to be sure that features that reflect the student's home language patterns are not incorrectly coded as errors due to CHL, even though they may indicate a need for intervention to help the child master SAE conventions. There is a range of other assessment tools – commercially produced or teacher generated – that can also be used in the classroom to monitor and inform language development. The information from screening tools can be used by teachers to develop interventions and learning programs for children with CHL, keeping in mind the need to develop the skills that underlie written literacy. The information from screening tools can also be used as the basis for discussions with education and health support staff for further help and ideas about working with children with CHL.

Conclusion

Otitis media, and its resultant conductive hearing loss and speech and language development delays, is a significant problem for indigenous people and requires both medical and educational interventions. Good oral language skills are essential for success in written literacy, and this is as true for older students as for those in the early years, so it is important that students receive a firm grounding in those skills. It is also essential that the language skills that underlay written literacy be taught explicitly, especially when children are learning in a second language, as well as incidental teaching opportunities being exploited through integrating language skills with all learning areas and through language games. Teachers have a lot of expertise in developing language skills, but should work in partnership with indigenous teaching assistants and community-school liaison people to ensure culturally appropriate interventions, as well as drawing on the resources available from specialist education staff and through print and web-based resources. In addition, to address this important issue of developing the language and literacy skills of indigenous students with CHL, teachers, schools and their communities also need ongoing support and professional development from education providers and support services so that educational outcomes, and consequently life opportunities are enhanced for students with CHL.

Notes

1. 'indigenous' is used when referring to indigenous people generally, and 'Aboriginal' or 'Aboriginal Australian' when referring specifically to indigenous Australian people.
2. The project "Teaching Indigenous students with conductive hearing loss in remote and urban school in Western Australia" was conducted by Edith Cowan University, Western Australia, under the leadership of Professor Gary Partington and funded by Australian Research Council [SPIRT] Grant #C00107680 and industry partners the Department of Education and Training Western Australia, Catholic Education Office Western Australia, and Association of Independent Schools Western Australia.

References

Acuin, J. (2004). *Chronic Suppurative Otitis Media: Burden of Illness and Management Options.* Geneva: World Health Organisation.

Berry, R. and Hudson, J. (1997). *Making the Jump.* Broome, WA: Catholic Education Commission of Western Australia, Kimberley Region.

Boswell, J. (1997). Presentation of early otitis media in 'Top End' Aboriginal infants. *Australian and New Zealand Journal of Public Health, 21*(1), 100–02.

Bowd, A. D. (2005). Otitis media: health and social consequences for Aboriginal youth in Canada's north. *International Journal of Circumpolar Health, 64*(1), 5–15.

Burrow, S. and Thomson, N. (2003). Ear disease and hearing loss. In N. Thomson (ed.), *The Health of Indigenous Australians* (pp. 247–72). Melbourne: Oxford University Press.

Couzos, S., Murray, R. B. and Metcalf, S. (2001). *Systematic Review of Existing Evidence and Primary Care Guidelines on the Management of Otitis Media in Aboriginal and Torres Strait Islander Populations.* Canberra, ACT: Indigenous and Public Health Media Unit, Commonwealth Departement of Health and Aged Care.

Education Queensland. (2002). *Specific Teaching Emphasis for Aboriginal and Torres Strait Islander Students with a Conductive Hearing Loss.* Retrieved 29 December 2006, from http://education.qld.gov.au/curriculum/learning/students/disabilities/resources/information/hi/stea.html

Ford, L. (1993). Teaching Aboriginal learners with hearing difficulties and special communication needs. *Ngoonjook: A Journal of Australian Indigenous Issues, 8*(14), 14–20.

Higgins, A. H. (1997). *Addressing the Health and Educational Consequences of Otitis Media among Young Rural School-Aged Children*. Townsville, QLD: Australian Rural Education Research Association Inc.

Howard, D. (1992). Knowing who may have a hearing loss: a simple speech reception game for use by teachers and parents. *The Aboriginal Child at School, 20*(4), 37–47.

Howard, D. (2004a, June). *Social Outcomes of Conductive Hearing Loss*. Paper presented at the Office of Aboriginal and Torres Strait Islander Health Berrimpa Conference, Brisbane, QLD.

Howard, D. (2004b). Why we need more Aboriginal adults working with Aboriginal students. *The Australian Journal of Teacher Education, 29*(1), 14–22.

Howard, D. (2005). *Scoping Project: Indigenous New Apprentices' Hearing Impairment and its Impact on their Participation and Retention in New Apprenticeships*. Darwin, NT: Phoenix Consulting.

Howard, D. and Hampton, D. (2006). Ear disease and Aboriginal families. *Aboriginal and Islander Health Worker Journal, 30*(4), 9–11.

Kelly, H. A. and Weeks, S. A. (1991). Ear disease in three Aboriginal communities in Western Australia. *Medical Journal of Australia, 154*(4), 240–45.

Kindig, J. S. and Richards, H. C. (2000). Otitis media: precursor of delayed reading. *Journal of Pediatric Psychology, 25*(1), 15–18.

Lowell, A., Budukulawuy, Gurimangu, Maypilama and Nyomba. (1995). Communication and learning in an Aboriginal school: the influence of conductive hearing loss. *The Aboriginal Child at School, 23*(4), 1–7.

Massie, R. and Dillon, H. (2006). The impact of sound-field amplification in mainstream cross-cultural classrooms: part 1 educational outcomes. *Australian Journal of Education, 50*(1), 62–77.

McSporran, E., Butterworth, Y. and Rowson, V. J. (1997). Sound field amplification and listening behaviour in the classroom. *British Educational Research Journal, 23*(1), 81–96.

Moore, J. A. (1999). Comparison of risk of conductive hearing loss among three ethnic groups of Arctic audiology patients. *Journal of Speech, Language, and Hearing Research, 42*(6), 1311–22.

Morris, P. S. (1998). The diagnosis and treatment of middle ear diseases in high risk populations: a user's guide. *Aboriginal and Islander Health Worker Journal, 22*(3), 19–23.

Nienhuys, T. and Burnip, L. (1988). Conductive hearing loss and the Aboriginal child at school. *Australian Teacher of the Deaf, 29*, 4–17.

Olusanya, B. O. (2004). Classification of childhood hearing impairment: implications for rehabilitation in developing countries. *Disability and Rehabilitation, 26*(20), 1221–28.

Pakulski, L. A. and Kaderavek, J. N. (2002). Children with minimal hearing loss: interventions in the classroom. *Intervention in School and Clinic, 38*(2), 96–103.

Partington, G. and Galloway, A. (2005). Effective practices in teaching Indigenous students with conductive hearing loss. *Childhood Education, 82*(2), 101–06.

Walker, N. and Wigglesworth, G. (2001). The effect of conductive hearing loss on phonological awareness, reading and spelling of urban Aboriginal students. *Australian and New Zealand Journal of Audiology, 23*(1), 37–51.

Western Australian Department of Education. (2002). *Do You Hear What I Hear? Living and Learning with Conductive Hearing Loss*. Perth, WA: Western Australian Department of Education.

WHO/CIBA Foundation. (2000). *Prevention of Hearing Impairment from Chronic Otitis Media.* Report of a WHO/CIBA Foundation Workshop, London, 19–21 November 1996. Retrieved December, 2006, from http://www.who.int/pbd/deafness/en/chronic otitis media.pdf

Yonowitz, L., Yonowitz, A., Nienhuys, T. and Boswell, J. (1995). MLD evidence of auditory processing factors as a possible barrier to literacy for Australian Aboriginal children. *The Australian Journal of Education of the Deaf, 1*(1), 34–41.

Zubrick, S. R., Lawrence, D. M., Silburn, S. R., Blair, E., Milroy, H., Wilkes, E., Eades, S., D'Antoine, H., Read, A., Ishiguchi, P. and Doyle, S. (2004). *The Western Australian Aboriginal Child Health Survey: The Health of Aboriginal Children and Young People.* Perth, WA: Telethon Institute for Child Health Research.

Section 4

Language mixing and language shift in Indigenous Australia

11

Patrick McConvell

Australian Indigenous languages are undergoing rapid loss through language shift to English and English-based creoles, particularly in the last 50 years. Less than 20 traditional languages are now being learnt fully by children. Many people in education add to this trend by emphasising English-only schools and disregarding Indigenous languages, failing to understand how normal and advantageous bilingualism is. It is important to understand the language ecologies in Indigenous communities that are leading to language shift and radical language change, as this may be a key to preventing further losses. This chapter reviews ways of looking at how languages relate to each other in multilingual situations, and hypotheses about outcomes which flow from them, including the domains approach of Fishman, and the approaches to social meaning in code-switching of Gumperz and others. Then a number of earlier and recent studies of language change and language shift in Indigenous communities are examined including the following situations (1) where the old language is retained but with minor changes and loss of dialect diversity; (2) where the new language (an English variety or creole) becomes mixed with the traditional language yielding a new hybrid language; (3) where language shift to English or a creole is more thorough but words and phrases from the old language are still occasionally inserted. A hypothesis is proposed that the difference between the outcomes (2) and (3) may relate to a single dominant traditional language in (2) and a number of languages in the community in (3). However even where there is a single language, a language ecology in which a mixed language is only used by a segment of the community can lead fairly quickly to the outcome (3), total language shift to English or a creole.

Introduction

In 1788 when Europeans arrived in Sydney, Australia had about 300 Indigenous languages. Since then the number of languages spoken has declined, with the most rapid decline occurring in the last 50 years. Australia holds the unenviable world record for the greatest loss of languages in the world, in the recent period (Nettle and Romaine, 2000, p. 4). Of the remaining languages, fewer than 20 are being fully passed on to the next generation (McConvell et al., 2005; McConvell and Thieberger, 2006). Now there is a risk that these will also be lost in this century.

This is not an inevitable outcome and measures can be taken to avoid this. What leads to language shift – when people take on a new language and stop speaking their old one? Conversely what leads to language maintenance? If we knew more about this, Indigenous people would be able to plan strategies which would imitate the natural conditions of language maintenance and avoid the conditions of language shift.

There is no reason why people who learn a new language should lose their old language. Unfortunately many of those who control language policy (for instance, in education) seem to believe, contrary to evidence around the world, that people must inevitably learn only one language (the national language, English, in this case) and that use of other languages will be damaging to their education and job prospects.

The majority of people around the world are bilingual or multilingual, living in stable language situations where they use both or all their languages without problems. For many years, many Indigenous Australian communities were bilingual in a local language or languages and a variety of English without shifting to English completely. For some time, however, Indigenous children have been shifting to English or an English-based creole variety, and this trend seems to be sweeping the board.

Even in the cases where traditional languages have been maintained, change has occurred in the variety used by children, which can include more use of English vocabulary, some simplification of grammar, and loss of dialect forms. While this is probably to be expected as part of normal language change, some change includes radical changes in grammar as compared to traditional norms. In some cases the newly emerging languages can be said to be 'mixed' or 'hybrid' languages, combining features of the traditional languages and an English-based variety or creole. In such cases the outcome is neither shift to another (existing) language or language maintenance, but birth of a new language. In many other cases however, children have shifted and are learning English or a creole and, with the exception of a few words and phrases, not learning the traditional language.

In this chapter the focus will be on how people use the languages in a multi-lingual *language ecology*, and how different ways of using language may be connected with whether the languages survive or die, and whether they change radically and rapidly or hybridise with other languages or not.

Language ecology and language transmission

The notion of language ecology has been found useful in sociolinguistics at least since Haugen's work (1953; 1972) on the status and functions of Norwegian in the USA, and recent work in 'ecological linguistics' has also brought it to the fore (Croft, 2000; Mufwene 2001). A basic notion is that different species (in this case languages) can be part of a community and share the resources by taking on differing habits and roles. Competition may also be part of the picture and this can be a stable feature or can lead to erosion of the basis of one competitor and eventual extinction from the area – as with language shift (compare with the 'linguistic market' concept proposed by the anthropologist Bourdieu (1991)).

The actual mechanism of language shift is failure of intergenerational transmission, that is, at a certain stage children no longer learn the old language, or else do so imperfectly, with the result that they cannot speak it. This ensures that their children will definitely not learn it. So language acquisition by children has to be built into a language ecology model. The nature of this 'failure' can be of several different kinds. The parental generation may speak the old language but only in very restricted environments so that it does not impact on the children enough for them to learn it. This may be a deliberate choice on the part of caregivers for various reasons, or an accidental by-product of the way in which use of the old language is restricted (McConvell, 1991b).

A variation on this scenario is that children are exposed to elements of the old language but it is always heavily mixed with other languages (primarily the new language) so that children do not have sufficient unmixed input to reproduce the old language fully, even if they had motivation to do so. This type of situation can lead to the adoption of the mixed speech input as the basis of a new mixed language, as discussed below.

Failure of perfect or near-perfect transmission of the language of previous generations does not solely result from interaction between young children in the early acquisition phase and the parental generation. The young children are also subject to linguistic input from older children, and this peer influence can eclipse that of the parental and grandparental generation. Children and teenagers may deliberately choose not to emulate parents or the old language. Instead they select or build a language variety of their own from among the models available. If there is no counter-weight from the old language, then this peer-group talk can form the basis of the language of the rising generation. In the case of the younger generation of Dyirbal (spoken in the rainforests of north Queensland (Schmidt, 1985)), it was not one norm that emerged but different ones in different groups or gangs, fragmenting the language even more.

Code-switching and code-mixing

Domains theory and the role of switching in language shift

An influential theory in the field of 'language ecology' has been the 'domains' theory use of languages, developed by Joshua Fishman, a leading figure in the fight for maintenance of endangered and minority ethnic languages and cultures. In combining these two interests he proposed a plan for 'reversing language shift' which drew on the Domains theory (Fishman, 1991).

A language or linguistic variety ('lect' or 'code') is said to be confined to 'domains' where more than one language or variety is spoken in a community and the languages or varieties are generally only used in specific circumstances such as with specific types of people (interlocutors), in particular settings or when talking about a particular topic. For example, in a bidialectal situation, such as exists in many Australian Indigenous communities, you may speak an Indigenous form of English to your mates, but in speaking to a school principal you may instead use Standard English. Or around the school, you may use Standard English if the school is a 'Standard English domain'. Or you may talk about chemistry in Standard English and sports in your own dialect. Often language choice is not so easily predicted by such external factors, however, and other theories have been brought into play.

Fishman (1967) went on to define the term 'diglossia' (already in use in sociolinguistics) in terms of the domains idea. Diglossia is the situation where two different varieties of one language, or two languages are used, each in its own distinct domains, like Classical Arabic and local dialects in many parts of the Arab world – these varieties are usually known as 'High' and 'Low'. Classical Arabic is used throughout the Arab world in 'high' public functions – domains such as sermons, most media news, official proceedings, etc., while the local dialects are used in 'low' family and community settings – the home, in informal situations at work, in the market and so on. The situation of an Australian community referred to above could be argued to be one of 'diglossia' in the original sense with Standard English being the 'high' variety and Indigenous English the 'low' variety of a single language. In some Indigenous communities in Australia, a diglossia exists with English used in the school, office, etc., but a local traditional language or languages used in the home and other situations.

Fishman believes that diglossia is a stabilising force in maintaining languages. On the other hand 'bilingualism without diglossia', where people use more than one language in particular domains, is unstable and can rapidly lead to the loss of the minority language (Fishman, 1991, 2001). (For different perspectives on these ideas see McConvell (1992); Romaine (2002); Schiffman et al. (2006)).

This 'language maintenance through diglossia' hypothesis has been fairly widely accepted although there is some criticism of it both in terms of whether loss of languages is actually related to loss of diglossia, and more generally about whether the domains theory is the best explanatory tool in investigating language ecology. Many approaches stress how people use language choice to express their different identities and perform other functions in conversation (e.g. Gumperz, 1982; Myers-Scotton, 1993). LePage and Tabouret-Keller

(1985, p. 247) call these language (or 'code' or 'lect') choices 'acts of identity' and state

> linguistic tokens [are] socially-marked – that is, as being used by an individual because they are felt to have social as well as semantic meaning in terms of the way in which each individual wishes to *project his/her own universe and to invite others to share it*

This kind of explanation throws a different light on the ways people switch between language varieties when talking. This practice is known as 'Code-switching' (defined as 'an individual's use of two or more language varieties in the same speech event' (Woollard, 2006, p. 74)). In this definition 'language varieties' includes separate languages.

For instance in the situation of an Indigenous community where Standard and Indigenous English are spoken, an Indigenous student may depart from the 'domain-determined' language to express social meaning. She may switch into Indigenous English in a formal class to express her Indigenous identity as a form of 'resistance' against something going on in the school. She may switch into Standard English in an informal context to express authority or as a joke. If the Indigenous dialect or separate language is not intelligible to non-Indigenous people it can be a way of making some expressions private within a select in-group.

This freer more expressive use of language choice may actually be a valuable function of bilingualism which can support the maintenance of languages despite absence of strict diglossia. Moreover there appear to be significant numbers of cases around the world where groups have practiced pervasive code-switching for decades or even hundreds of years without language shift removing one of the languages from the repertoire, as in the case of Tagalog and English in the Philippines.

Jernudd (1969; 1971) reviewed the situation of languages in Indigenous Australia from a sociolinguistic viewpoint. For many places he regarded Aboriginal traditional languages (called here TIL's – Traditional Indigenous Languages) and English as being in a diglossic situation, with English used in most public contexts and the traditional languages in home and family situations mainly. However for the English-based creoles and codes involving mixtures of English and TIL's, on the one hand, and the traditional Indigenous languages on the other, he could see no diglossia between them. They were, he thought, used in the same range of situations. Applying Fishman's theory, Jernudd related this situation to rapid social change and pointed to wide individual variation and uncertainty and flexibility of norms as other symptoms of lack of clarity in the community about domains (Jernudd, 1971, pp. 17, 21).

Jernudd describes the use of languages at Bagot, an Aboriginal reserve in Darwin, and in the Aboriginal communities of Oenpelli and Bamyili in the 'Top End' of the Northern Territory. Here he points out different functions of the TIL and the pidgin/creole/mixed speech but also identifies the limitations of the domains approach in describing this difference. He points out the advantages of the 'metaphorical' approach to code-switching, citing Blom and Gumperz (1972), which was a precursor to the 'social meaning' approaches cited above, where functions of code choice are not tied to 'domain'. One example is the use of English in abuse and quarrels in a normally TIL community domain (Jernudd, 1971, p. 19). In general the only aspect which can be described in terms of domains, according to Jernudd, is the difference between older and younger people 'determined exclusively by the generational language shift' which was going on in many places between the TIL(s) and the creole.

Northern Territory bilingual education and domains

In 1974, a major event occurred in Australian language policy – the institution of bilingual education for some of the Indigenous languages of the Northern Territory (NT; Hoogenraad, 2001; O'Grady and Hale, 1974), the first and only large-scale move to support Indigenous languages in Australia. The NT Education Department targeted only languages which were judged to be 'strong' and even then not in all communities.

Initially, the NT Bilingual Education program was well staffed and resourced (although that declined until the announcement of its closure in 1998). Stephen Harris, who had done fieldwork among Yolngu people in north-east Arnhem Land was one of the original senior staff and helped to build the program and its policies (Harris, 1984). The guidelines called for strict separation of languages (English and the local vernacular). Fishman's domain theory was the motivation for this – if diglossia can be maintained then there is a greater chance for the vernacular language to be maintained.

Ironically, similar arguments were also used to support the closing down of bilingual education first in South Australia, then in the Northern Territory. In these cases it was argued that the relevant domains were not two domains in school for English and the vernacular, respectively, but the school for English and the home for the vernacular (see McConvell, 1992 for a critique of such ideas). These somewhat subtle arguments for English-only schools dovetail with cruder assimilationist undercurrents and arguments based on the higher cost of bilingual programs to produce quite powerful resistance to bilingual education in the bureaucracy and among politicians (Hoogenraad, 2001). Today echoes of these arguments are to be heard in the strong endorsement of English-only school programs by current governments, and some Indigenous leaders (Pearson, 2007). Generally such arguments fail to cite the positive results from bilingual education programs or the advantages of bilingualism for general cognitive skills (O'Shannessy, Chapter 12).

There was also debate between groups which equally supported bilingual education but had differences over the philosophy and implementation (McConvell, 1991a, 1994). One issue was the one alluded to – the applicability of the domains separation approach of Fishman. Another related issue in the debate was the interpretation of the idea of 'two-way education', a concept which was developed in the Indigenous communities themselves. Harris argued that 'two-way', two separate ways – Indigenous and European reflected incompatible conceptual systems, which should be kept separate. Another interpretation however stressed the 'exchange' aspect of 'two-way' and how aspects of Indigenous and European–Australian could work together (Raymattja, 1999; Tamisari and Milmilany, 2003).

Code-switching and language ideology

A problem for trying to enforce strict domain separation in schools is that 'code-switching' between forms of English and TILs is very common in many Indigenous communities. The effort needed to make this cultural change would need at least an equivalent pay-off in terms of language maintenance and no other negative consequences.

A negative stance towards code-switching as being an undesirable 'mixing' of languages is characteristic of authorities in many Western contexts (e.g. Weinreich, 1953, pp. 73–74), and may be part of what Irvine and Gal (2000) describe as 'the erasure of differentiation' in many language ideologies. 'Purist' attitudes towards language, and negative evaluations of code-switching and code-mixing are not confined to Western ideologies which equate a nation-state with a language variety. This also occurs for instance among the Arizona Tewa (Kroskrity, 1993), and is apparently a long-standing pattern among them, but is not reported from Australian Indigenous groups. 'Purism' is also characteristic of some registers of Indigenous or minority language speech through which speakers are resisting a dominant 'syncretic' or highly mixed register (Hill and Hill, 1986; Wertheim, 2003). Virtual absence of code-switching in some situations of societal bilingualism, is sometimes coupled with an ideology of language separation. Again this seems very rare in Australian Indigenous contexts.

Code-switching in Australian Indigenous situations

Code-switching practices in Indigenous Australia have been noted – switching in the same sentence between TILs at Maningrida (Elwell, 1982), and between Kalaw Lagaw Ya and English or Torres Strait Creole (Bani, 1976). In the Victoria River District, NT, code-switching between the traditional language Gurindji and Kriol in the same sentence, or across sentences was also pervasive in the 1970s and 1980s. Most adults used this kind of speech to each other as the normal mode, although people over ages 30–40 could speak pure Gurindji fluently and did so sometimes. Language shift appeared to be already under-way then as children no longer appeared to be speaking traditional Gurindji.

McConvell (1985; 1988) describes the social motivations of language choice in conversation among middle-aged and older men. Different languages are mixed in a single discourse where the situation, interlocutors, location and topic are the same so 'domain' analysis cannot explain language choice. Nevertheless the choices are not random and have social meaning and prag-matic function. This analysis is situated within the tradition of Gumperz and associates (e.g. Blom and Gumperz, 1972)in terms of 'metaphorical code-switching'. That is, using a particular language appeared in many cases to add a 'social meaning' about the 'social arena' in which the literal meaning of the utterance was to be construed – in this case the local dialect group, the com-munity, the wider group of Aboriginal people in the 'cattle belt' region, and Australian society in general (McConvell, 1988, p. 110). As in much code-switching around the world, the choice of language has additional pragmatic force. Using a language like a shared local dialect calls up a set of rights and responsibilities associated with the speaker's and other participants' position in the social arena – for instance that people who belong to the same dialect group should share resources. A statement or question in such a dialect can have the force of a request. In contrary fashion, use of another variety can deny any such implications. Switches between Kriol (the regional English-based creole) and Gurindji also occurred frequently in Gurindji speech, with prag-matic force (e.g. see McConvell, 1988).

Clearly such a language ecology including code-switching with social mean-ing gives extra dimensions to forms of expression in conversation. These sty-listic and social uses of code-switching indicate that, far from being a problem, code-switching is a resource in bilingual and multilingual communities, as Myers-Scotton (1993) has argued.

Code-switching, intergenerational language transmission and language shift

Code choice in code-switching which does have a social or discourse meaning has been called 'marked' switching. In contrast, random switching without any meaning has been called 'unmarked' switching (Myers-Scotton, 1993) and 'code-mixing'. It has been argued that this form of speech can become the variety characteristically used by a social group. This may well be the situation in many Indigenous communities with code-mixing between a TIL and English or a creole being the pervasive mode of speech, with code choices within the code-switching no longer having expressive meaning.

If this kind of 'code-mixing' is pervasive in the speech that young children hear, they may miss the meanings associated with switching language. If, as well, the children have little exposure to the TIL without admixture of another language, then the conditions for transmission of the TIL may be compromised. Two results might be expected – the children may develop a new mixed language based on the input of code-switching, (Meakins, Chapter 13) and/or, as the new language is used as the main language of talk,, language shift to the new language takes place with just a few words and phrases from the old TIL still remembered and inserted. These outcomes are further discussed below.

Pervasive and relatively indiscriminate code-switching or 'code-mixing' can contribute significantly to language shift when it is the only model that young children have as input when learning language. However code-switching by itself does not automatically lead to language shift. Nor is the reason for language shift primarily lack of adherence to domain separation of the languages in the bilingual ecology.

Some types of change in Indigenous languages

The following sections examine briefly some changes that have been studied in Australian TILs in recent times. These are divided into three major types:

1. Maintenance of languages with relatively minor changes: this is illustrated by Dhuwaya, a new Yolngu variety spoken in Arnhem Land, and Teenage Pitjantjatjara spoken in the north of South Australia and the south of the NT.

2. Radical change in languages which may be classed as hybridisation (the development of a mixed language) illustrated by Modern Tiwi spoken on Melville and Bathurst islands near Darwin in the NT, Light Warlpiri and Gurindji Kriol, the latter two briefly as they are dealt with separately in this book (O'Shannessy for Light Warlpiri (Chapter 12), and Meakins for Gurindji Kriol (Chapter 13)). Young People's Dyirbal is partially in this category but moving towards full language shift.
3. Language shift to a variety of English or an English-based creole but with retention of a few elements from the old language.

Other studies not discussed here include work on language obsolescence (Austin, 1986; McGregor, 2002) and rapid language change (Richards, 2001).

Maintenance with minor change

Dhuwaya

The case of Dhuwaya among the Yolngu people of Yirrkala is where a 'baby talk' 'motherese' variety (the way caregivers speak to children) has become the language of the young people (Amery, 1993). At the stage that Rob Amery studied it (Amery, 1985) this was the situation; now, over 20 years later, middle-aged people also speak it much of the time. One of the striking aspects of it is that all the youth of the Yirrkala community speak this same variety whereas the traditional situation was for several 'patrilects' to be spoken – each dialect being distinctive of a clan. In this respect, the change here to one 'communilect' from a group of patrilects is parallel to the takeover among the Yolngu people of Galiwin'ku of Djambarrpuyngu from former patrilects. The difference is the source – Djambarrpuyngu was one of the patrilects whereas Dhuwaya is not. Although it is sometimes referred to as 'Baby Gumatj' it is not particularly related to the clan dialect Gumatj. In fact Amery believes that it represents a merger of the motherese varieties of all the Yirrkala dialects. Mergers of dialects are known as 'koines', and the process of formation of such a language is called koineisation.

The other interesting aspect of the situation is that the new language Dhuwaya as well as the patrilects were still spoken by the community, including the young children, at least at the time of Amery's research (although more recently Yolngu elders feel that quite a number of the patrilects have become endangered). Amery (1985, p. 135) describes the situation as 'diglossia turned on its head' because unlike with the example of Arabic above, in Yirrkala it is the 'local dialects' – the patrilects – which are the H (High) varieties, and the language which straddles all the groups (Dhuwaya) which is the L (Low) variety. He illustrates this in terms of the domains in which each of these are typically used: patrilects are used in meetings and in church, for public announcements, talking to distant kin and, perhaps incongruously, drunken talk (but recall Jernudd's finding that English is used for fighting and abuse in other communities). Talk at home, among peer groups and close kin, and in sports contexts is in Dhuwaya on the other hand.

The actual differences between Dhuwaya and the patrilects are fairly minor, consisting of changes to a few consonants to weaker sounds (as in the change of 'l' to 'y' in the language name Dhuwaya compared to Dhuwala, meaning 'this'); reduction of suffixes like -*mirri* 'having' to '-*mi*'; and simplification and regularisation of the forms of verbs. To judge by Amery's examples, there is little influence of English or importation of English vocabulary into Dhuwaya, although code-switching into English is rife in spoken Yolngu of most varieties.

Yolngu elders have been concerned about the rise of Dhuwaya even though the actual changes seem minor to the outside observer. In part this is because they see this as the 'thin end of the wedge' which may lead later to more radical change and language shift, and, in the north-east Arnhem Land case, they see a link to loss of clan dialects which are the media for much sacred lore and local knowledge.

Teenagers' Pitjantjatjara

Like Yolngu languages in general, the chain of dialects known as the Western Desert language remains a 'strong language' in the sense that it is still learned by children in a number of areas. However there has been shift to English on the part of speakers of a number of Western Desert dialects, for example, Wangkatha and other south-western dialects, and other desert-fringe languages are showing signs of endangerment (Bucknall, 1997). Changes in young people's speech, including heavy English influence, preceded such shift, so it is reasonable for speakers to see these sorts of changes as possible signs of shift ahead. Such changes also tend to go hand-in-hand with loss of words for things in the environment such as bush medicines and water features, and aspects of Indigenous knowledge systems as demonstrated by Lizzie Ellis, a researcher who is a native speaker of a Western Desert dialect (Ellis, 2000).

When carrying out a survey of South Australian languages (McConvell et al., 2002) our team gathered many expressions of worry from Pitjantjatjara-Yankunytjatjara speakers in the north of the state about current changes in the language. These expressions were often linked to complaints about the closing down of bilingual education in Pitjantjatjara schools referred to above. People believed that the bilingual education system helped to maintain standards in the Pitjantjatjara language and Indigenous knowledge and that these had gone into decline since the institution of English-only school. The research has not been done to establish this link, but it could well be so (Eickelkamp, 2006).

Langlois' (2004) study shows that Pitjantjatjara was used by young people at Areyonga in 1994–1995 as their major mode of communication and is a vibrant language open to some innovation and change. Such changes, as there are, are relatively minor and are not seen as a symptom of language shift or language death. Some of the changes are not related to English 'interference', while others may be, but are of a kind also commonly found in different contexts. For instance, in traditional Pitjantjatjara, as in many Australian languages, the way to express ownership of a body part 'my stomach' is to juxtapose the owner and the body part 'me stomach', while the way to express ownership of other things is to use a suffix -*ku* on the owner 'me -*ku* book' = 'my book'. But young people are now extending the suffix -*ku* for ownership of body parts. In teenage Pitantjantjatjara Example 1(a) is found

Example 1

(a)   ngayu-ku tjuni pika
      my stomach sick   'I have a sore stomach'

as opposed to the traditional

(b)   ngayulu tjuni pika
      me stomach sick

However there are examples of just this kind of change in many languages that are not in contact with English, around the world, and it seems likely that the alienable/inalienable distinction is somewhat fragile and easily lost (McConvell, 2005; Nichols, 1988). This is the kind of 'grammatical error' in young people's speech which does often disturb older speakers and is sometimes pointed to by non-Indigenous commentators as indicating a change in the conceptualisation of the world. However this and similar grammatical adjustments are not radical changes and are not necessarily an omen of impending language shift.

Radical change and hybridisation

Young people's Dyirbal

The most well-known study of the sociolinguistics of a severely endangered language in Australia is Annette Schmidt's study of Young People's Dyirbal (YD), spoken in the North Queensland region around Cardwell and Tully in the 1970s and 1980s. Dyirbal underwent radical change among young people in the 30 years before Schmidt's study. Although a local form of Aboriginal English has been used for many years whenever white people or strangers were around, the changes in YD are not studied in terms of contact with English, and indeed some do not appear to be related to English or Pidgin influence directly.

However clearly much of the structure and content of YD is related to local Aboriginal English, but grammatical elements are retained from traditional Dyirbal beyond simply vocabulary items. These include Dyirbal case-marking (albeit in a simplified form) including the 'ergative' or 'actor' case, which distinguishes the subjects of transitive verbs (**Dogs-Ergative** bite cats), from the subjects of intransitive verbs (**Dogs** bark). Ergative case-marking is common in Australia but unknown in English and most other European languages (O'Shannessy 2005, Chapter 12).

One of the most interesting things about Schmidt's study is that she uses a sociolinguistic approach and shows that the changes are not uniform across the young people in the community but vary in different 'gangs'. The two that she studied were the Buckaroos, who favour a 'cowboy' style of dress, music and behaviour, related to those Aboriginal people in the region who have been in the cattle industry, and the Rock'n'Rollers who, as the name implies, favour rock and roll music and have more attachment to some traditional styles and beliefs of the Aboriginal people of the region, including the Dyirbal language. These stylistic preferences are also reflected in the lects which they adopt when speaking their version of 'Dyirbal'.

The use of the ergative case-marker, is very high (around 90 per cent) in the Rock'n'Rollers whereas it is very low (around 10per cent) among the Buckaroos. On the other hand, the past tense marker *bin* from nearby varieties of Aboriginal English (also found in Kriol) is entirely absent from Rock'n'Rollers speech but present in about 50 per cent of the Buckaroos' past tense clauses.

Schmidt (1985, pp. 133–134) found that use of ergative was even more frequent in peer-group conversation than in test situations with stimulus sentences,, indicating perhaps that this is a strong social marker of loyalty to Dyirbal language which characterises this gang.

Schmidt's study was framed as a study of 'language death' and as such was in part allied to other studies which were carried out of 'dying languages' where what was happening in the forms of speech used was ascribed to the fact that the language was dying. Most of the 'symptoms' noted in the 'language death' framework are not inevitable signs of impending death of the language, but phenomena that can otherwise occur in language change, such as loss of case-markers and simplification of irregular forms. We need to understand why these changes are happening, in terms of prior and current conditions, not a projected end-point. If a particular constellation of features are found which have always led to language death, then that is a worthwhile finding but this must be discovered on a comparative basis, not simply assumed to exist in an individual case being studied.

However, it has proved true that Dyirbal and related dialects are indeed now spoken only by a small handful of older people and even the kind of YD spoken by the Rock'n'Rollers is extremely unlikely to extend its life into the next generation. Perhaps the fact that young people's speech was not gener-alised in the community but fragmented between different groups has not helped.

Modern Tiwi

In contrast the language called 'Tiwi' is still spoken by children and young people, on Melville and Bathurst Islands off shore from Darwin in the NT, even though it has undergone radical change away from its original form. The traditional form of the language had extremely complex verb forms (of a type known as 'polysynthetic'). It was spoken with little change until around the 1950s when the language of the younger people began to display major differ-ences from that of the older generations, including simplification of verb forms and many more words imported from English and Pidgin.

This dramatic change coincided largely with the full impact of the Catholic mission regime, along with the housing of children in dormitories. In other cases such isolation from parents and their language in institutions has been seen as responsible for shift to Kriol and English. The children, however, did not suffer complete removal from interaction with Tiwi speakers. While the story of how the radical changes in Tiwi came about is not clear, there is known to have been some kind of interlanguage used by priests and brothers with influences of Pidgin English and Tiwi insertions which may have played a role. Another idea is that there was a motherese or developmental style of Tiwi traditionally which had simplified verb forms, and children who had their further development hindered, perhaps by the dormitory experience, did not acquire full adult competence but retained features of the children's variety. Another possibly relevant factor is the pervasiveness of code-switching between Tiwi and Pidgin or English both today and at the time when Modern Tiwi, as Lee calls the new variety, arose.

Although the genesis of Modern Tiwi is cloudy, the nature of the language and the subsequent changes which produced Ultra-Modern Tiwi in the children of the 1970s–1980s are described in detail by Lee (1987). The examples below give some idea of some of the kinds of changes in Modern Tiwi.

Example 2: Prepositional phrasesModern Tiwi

Traditional Tiwi

(a) ngu-mpu-nginji-kuruwala
I – NPST-you DAT-sing
'I will sing for you'

(c) a-wuni-marri-kiji-ja manjanga
heNPST-LOC-COM-stick-go
'He came with a stick'

Modern Tiwi

(b) yi-kirimi jurra **fu ngawa**
hePST-make church for us
'He made a church for us'

(d) wokapat a-mpi-jiki-mi **with layt**
walk she-NPST-DUR-do with stick light
'She is walking with a light'

Traditional Tiwi verbs are complex. A verb or helping verb occurs at the end of the word, and is preceded by prefixes which represent the time of the event (*mpu* non-past i.e. is happening or will happen in (a)), the subject of the sentence (*ngu* 'I' in (a)), and other elements of the sentence including indirect objects. Modern Tiwi verbs keep the subject prefixes (*yi*-'he' in (b)), the time prefixes (-*mpi*- in (d)), and whether the event keeps going (-*jiki*- 'durative' in (d)). But it does not keep the prefixes for objects and other elements; so in (b) 'for us' is expressed as a prepositional phrase, contrasting with Traditional Tiwi (a) where 'for you' is expressed in the verb (*nginji*'you'), and similarly for (c) and (d). In Traditional Tiwi these complex verbs could be accompanied by number of free form verb stems, provided the complex verb ended in a 'helping verblike -*mi*"do"'. This construction has now swept the board pushing out most of the non-compound verb forms and providing a welcoming environment for much borrowing of verb stems from English and Pidgin (as in the case of *wokapat*'walk' above in Example 2(d) which is accompanied by a complex verb *a-mpi-jiki-mi* ending in the helping verb -*mi*'do').

Clues to possible scenarios leading to the Tiwi situation can be found in contemporary code-switching in communities where people speak languages with similarly complex prefixing verbs, such as the non-Pama-Nyungan languages of northern Australia. From the limited data so far available (Leeding 1993), young people's code-switching shows a strong tendency to retain verb morphology from the Aboriginal language while adopting vocabulary and nominal related features from English or Kriol. In the following Burarra example the English/Kriol verb 'wait' is borrowed but is followed by a Burarra complex verb consisting of a subject prefix *ngu-* and a helping verb -*nirra*.

> ## Example 3: Burarra
> Ngaypa /WAIT/ ngu-nirra nula /MY HUSBAND
> I I /WAIT/   - be for him /MY HUSBAND
> 'I waited for my husband'

The pattern for languages with similarly complex verbs in North America (e.g. Michif (Bakker, 1997) and Montagnais (Drapeau, 1995)) seems to be for speakers when code-switching is used to retain the old language verb forms, and for a similar pattern to emerge when contact leads to a new mixed type of language.

Light Warlpiri and Gurindji Kriol

The change in Tiwi is in some ways the same process as has occurred with the new mixed languages Light Warlpiri (LW; O'Shannessy Chapter 12) and Gurindji Kriol (GK; Dalton et al., 1995; Meakins, Chapter 13), but the 'split' in the respective contributions of the languages to the hybrid is opposite – in LW and GK the tense, aspect and mood inflections are not retained from the old language, but come from the new language Kriol. Nominal inflections such as case-marking are retained from the old languages Warlpiri and Gurindji, respectively. LW and GK are not discussed further in this chapter, as they are more fully described in the chapters by O'Shannessy and Meakins.

Language shift with retention of some vocabulary

Many of the languages in Australia may have gone through stages of minor change, and/or stages of radical change or hybridisation, but these stages were short-lived and mostly not recorded, (exceptions include Donaldson (1985) and Austin (Austin, 1986)). Most language groups have ended up shifting to an English variety or an Indigenous English-based creole. In many cases they have retained words and phrases from the old language or from a regional group of old languages which they insert into their English or Kriol speech in in-group contexts. The examples below are of neo-Nyungar, and Nunga English and 'slang' of the south of South Australia.

Neo-nyungar

Douglas (1976) reports on a variety known as neo-Nyungar current among Aboriginal people in the south-west of Western Australia. Little detail is given but it appears to be mainly a regional Aboriginal variety of English with Nyungar words (apparently mainly nouns) inserted as in

> yer gotta *yok*?
> Have you got a woman? [are you married?] (Douglas 1976, p.16).

Nunga English and 'Slang'

Nunga English is the variety of English used by many Aboriginal people of the Adelaide Plains and York Peninsula ('Nungas'). Words from specific local languages are also inserted into this dialect and sometimes include words from Ngarrindjeri of the Murray and other languages. This kind of mixture is locally called 'slang'. Some local Aboriginal people are not happy with it as it mixes different languages too much (McConvell et al. 2002, pp. 51–52).

Reasons for language maintenance, language shift and language hybridisation

The four communities focused on in the Aboriginal Child Language Acquisition project (ACLA) (Simpson and Wigglesworth, Chapter 1) show different scenarios. In Lajamanu and Kalkaringi, mixed languages have arisen from a hybridisation of the traditional Indigenous language and Kriol as noted above. In the case of Walmajarri in the central Kimberleys, language shift to an Aboriginal English/Kriol with retention of some old language vocabulary occasionally inserted appears to have occurred, although it is possible that other scenarios occurred in some groups. In the case of Warumungu in the Tennant Creek area of the NT, the scenarios appear to have differed according to where the speakers grew up. Most people have shifted to an Aboriginal English/Kriol with some Warumungu words and suffixes. However some middle-aged speakers from the Barkly Tablelands show evidence of using a mixed language resulting from hybridising Kriol and traditional languages (Disbray, Forthcoming).

Why have these different outcomes occurred in communities which otherwise have quite similar backgrounds? It has been suggested that 'mixed language genesis' – a fairly rare event according to most authorities – is associated with a group of people who have a strong desire to forge a separate identity (new or ancestral), rather than be subsumed into a more general grouping (Thomason, 2003). The Gurindji certainly have had a recent history as leaders in the cattle station strike movement and the land rights movement which might fit them for this kind of aspiration. The Lajamanu Warlpiri however do not have the same kind of profile yet also went down this road.

There is a striking difference which does appear to correlate with the divergence in paths of the different groups. The two groups which hybridised have basically only one language group in their communities – Gurindji and Warlpiri, respectively. Other probable cases of hybridisation like Modern Tiwi have also occurred in communities with single TIL's in conformity with the above hypothesis.

The Warumungu however live in multi-ethnic communities, with several languages competing. In the latter context, I have argued, there is stronger pressure towards straight forward shift to the 'neutral' language Kriol/Aboriginal English than any mixed language which continues the heritage of only one language (McConvell, 2007).

This does not necessarily mean that language identity can only be maintained in isolation from other ethnic groups – in fact linguistic identity can sometimes be asserted precisely in the context of being cheek-by-jowl with other groups. In many cases however the need for a common medium of communication overrides this need for assertion of identity, which in any case can be carried out by 'acts of identity' which may only require use of a few distinctive words in a discourse using the more general lingua franca.

Of course hybridisation is only language maintenance to a degree, at the price of merging with a more widely spoken language. We need to talk also of the conditions needed for full maintenance of TIL's, or at least maintenance with minor change and loss of dialect distinctions as in our first cases above of Yolngu Matha (Dhuwaya) and Pitjantjatjara. These are relatively isolated places with relatively large numbers of speakers of a single language in the communities in the region. Neither Kriol nor any other form of Indigenous English has made much inroad into the community.

The case of Light Warlpiri is one of hybridisation at one end of a large rather homogenous Warlpiri area. In line with this is the fact that O'Shannessy (2005; Chapter 12) reports that Lajamanu children still can speak old Warlpiri, unlike Gurindji young people who cannot fluently speak old Gurindji in most cases. The Warlpiri situation may be a case of the value for language maintenance of having a 'homeland' where the language is fully spoken – a circumstance cited to explain the relative vitality of Arrernte in Alice Springs compared to the loss of the Indigenous languages of all other Australian cities.

It is quite likely that hybridisation occurs during short periods and perhaps with some fractions of the populations (as suggested for some Warumungu speakers) but is in the end overwhelmed by the tide of language shift. Unless there has been some record of this we may not know of the hybrid phase. The Dyribal case suggests that there may be splits in the population, especially among the youth, between those taking the hybridisation path and those moving more directly towards shift. It has been noted that young peer groups more generally around the world tend to take opposite stands in linguistic styles, for instance some 'gangs' favouring code-switching, and some gangs favouring purism in one language, especially in 'performances' (Jørgensen, 1998; Kyratzis, 2004). In the Dyirbal case – and one might surmise, in most cases – the language shift alternative, with retention of a little traditional vocabulary, wins out in the end. However in just a few cases, especially perhaps where there is less competition between languages, the push to maintain a localised hybrid is strong enough to resist total shift for at least a few generations.

Conclusions

Code-switching does not in and of itself cause language shift, even if it is used in ways that go beyond diglossia and domains separation. However it can be, and has been sometimes in Australia, an impediment to children learning the traditional Indigenous language, if it becomes pervasive to the exclusion of TIL speech and if it is dominated by forms which use English or Kriol as the framework for sentences. Children do not then have enough exposure to the full TIL grammar and can no longer form fully grammatical sentences in the old language. Their feeling of lack of competence can sometimes be reinforced by adults who criticise the mistakes they make, and their own feeling that the old language belongs to a bygone era, an attitude often articulated explicitly or implicitly by schools and other non-Indigenous institutions.

There are two outcomes of this situation which we have looked at: language hybridisation; and language shift to English/Kriol with just some elements of the TIL left over. We have discussed cases of each and possible reasons why one or other might have occurred.

Code-switching between the TIL and varieties of English also occurs in the other cases we have looked at where the TIL is being maintained (so far) without signs of language shift or hybridisation. There may be some influence of English in some of the changes in these strong languages, but there are also other minor changes which are more just the kind of changes one might expect in any language. In the words of one of the authors, these languages are 'alive and kicking' all the more so perhaps by being used and adapted by young people in their everyday life.

References

Amery, R. (1985). 'A new diglossia: contemporary speech varieties at Yirrkala in North East Arnhem Land'. Unpublished MA dissertation, Australian National University, Canberra.

Amery, R. (1993). An Australian koine: Dhuwaya, a variety of Yolngu Matha spoken at Yirrkala in North East Arnhemland. *International Journal of the Sociology of Language, 99*, 45-64.

Austin, P. (1986). Structural change in language obsolence: some eastern Australian examples. *Australian Journal of Linguistics, 6*, 201–30.

Bakker, P. (1997). *A Language of Our Own the Genesis of Michif, the Mixed Cree-French Language of the Canadian Métis*. Oxford: Oxford University Press.

Bani, E. (1976). The language situation in the Torres Strait. In P. J. Sutton (ed.), *Languages of Cape York*. Canberra: Australian Institute of Aboriginal Studies.

Blom, J. P. and Gumperz, J. J. (1972). Social meaning in linguistic structures: Code switching in Norway. In J. J. Gumperz and D. H. Hymes (eds), *Directions in Sociolinguistics: The Ethnography of Communication* (pp. 407–34). New York: Holt, Rinehart & Winston.

Bourdieu, P. (1991). *Language and Symbolic Power* (G. Raymond and M. Adamson, Trans.). Cambridge: Polity.

Bucknall, G. (1997). Nyangumarta: alive and adapting. *Australian Review of Applied Linguistics, 20*(1), 43–56.

Croft, W. (2000). *Explaining Language Change: An Evolutionary Approach*. New York: Longman.

Dalton, L., Edwards, S., Farquharson, R., Oscar, S. and McConvell, P. (1995). Gurindji children's language and language maintenance. *International Journal of the Sociology of Language, 113*, 83–96.

Disbray, S. (Forthcoming). 'More than one way to catch a frog: children's discourse in a contact setting'. Unpublished PhD thesis, University of Melbourne, Melbourne.

Donaldson, T. (1985). From speaking Ngiyambaa to speaking English. *Aboriginal History, 9*, 126–47.

Drapeau, L. (1995). Code switching in caretaker speech and bilingual competence in a native village of Northern Quebec. *International Journal of the Sociology of Language, 113*, 157–64.

Eickelkamp, U. (2006). On a positive note: the Anangu Education Service Conference. *The Australian Anthropological Society Newsletter*(103), 14–15.

Ellis, L. (2000, 6 March 2000). 'Threatened languages and threatened species'. Paper presented at the AIATSIS seminar. Unpublished paper. Canberra: AIATSIS.

Elwell, V. M. R. (1982). Some social factors affecting multilingualism among Aboriginal Australians. *International Journal of the Sociology of Language, 36*, 83–103.

Fishman, J. A. (1967). Bilingualism with and without diglossia; diglossia with and without bilingualism. *Journal of Social Issues, 32*(2), 29–38.

Fishman, J. A. (1991). *Reversing Language Shift: Theoretical and Empirical Foundations of Assistance to Threatened Languages*. Clevedon: Multilingual Matters.

Fishman, J. A. (2001). *Can Threatened Languages Be Saved: Reversing Language Shift, Revisited: A 21st Century Perspective*. Clevedon: Multilingual Matters.

Gumperz, J. J. (1982). *Discourse Strategies*. Cambridge: Cambridge University Press.

Harris, S. (1984). *Culture and Learning: Tradition and Education in North-east Arnhem Land*. Canberra: Australian Institute of Aboriginal Studies.

Haugen, E. (1953). *The Norwegian Language in America: A Study in Bilingual Behavior*. Bloomington: Indiana University Press.

Haugen, E. (1972). *The Ecology of Language: Essays by Einar Haugen*. Stanford: Stanford University Press.

Hill, J. H., & Hill, K. C. (1986). *Speaking Mexicano: Dynamics of Syncretic Language in Central Mexico*. Tucson: University of Arizona Press.

Hoogenraad, R. (2001). Critical reflections on the history of bilingual education in Central Australia. In J. Simpson, D. Nash, M. Laughren, P. Austin and B. Alpher (eds), *Forty Years On: Ken Hale and Australian Languages* (pp. 123–50). Canberra: Pacific Linguistics.

Irvine, J. T. and Gal, S. (2000). Language ideology and linguistic differentiation. In P. Kroskity (ed.), *Regimes of Language: Ideologies, Polities, and Identities* (pp. 35–84). Santa Fe: School of American Research Press.

Jernudd, B. (1969). Social change and Aboriginal speech variation in Australia. *University of Hawai'i Working Papers in Linguistics, 4*, 145–68.

Jernudd, B. (1971). Social change and Aboriginal speech variation in Australia. *Anthropological Linguistics, 13*(1), 16–32.

Jørgensen, J. N. (1998). Children's acquisition of code-switching for power wielding. In P. Auer (ed.), *Code-switching in Conversation: Language, Interaction and Identity* (pp. 237–58). London: Routledge.

Kroskrity, P. V. (1993). *Language, History, and Identity: Ethnolinguistic Studies of the Arizona Tewa*. Tucson, AR: University of Arizona Press.

Kyratzis, A. (2004). Talk and interaction among children and the co-construction of peer groups and peer culture. *Annual Review of Anthropology, 33*(1), 625–49.

Langlois, A. (2004). *Alive and Kicking: Areyonga Teenage Pitjantjatjara*. Canberra: Pacific Linguistics.

Le Page, R. B. and Tabouret-Keller, A. (1985). *Acts of Identity: Creole-Based Approaches to Ethnicity and Language.* Cambridge: Cambridge University Press.

Lee, J. (1987). *Tiwi Today: A Study of Language Change in a Contact Situation.* Canberra: Pacific Linguistics.

McConvell, P. (1985). Domains and codeswitching among bilingual Aborigines. In M. Clyne (ed.), *Australia, Meeting Place of Languages.* Canberra: Pacific Linguistics.

McConvell, P. (1988). Mix-im-up: Aboriginal code switching, old and new. In M. Heller (ed.), *Codeswitching: Anthropological and Sociolinguistic Perspectives* (pp. 97–149). Berlin: Mouton de Gruyter.

McConvell, P. (1991a). Cultural domain separation: Two-way street or blind alley? Stephen Harris and the neo-Whorfians on Aboriginal education. *Australian Aboriginal Studies* (1991.1), 13–24.

McConvell, P. (1991b). Understanding language shift: a step towards language maintenance. In S. Romaine (ed.), *Language in Australia* (pp. 143–55). Cambridge: Cambridge University Press.

McConvell, P. (1992). Review of Fishman reversing language shift. *Australian Journal of Linguistics,* 12(1), 209–19.

McConvell, P. (1994). Two-way exchange and language maintenance in Aboriginal schools. In J. Henderson and D. Hartman (eds), *Aboriginal Languages in Education* (pp. 235–56). Alice Springs, NT: IAD Press.

McConvell, P. (2005). Language contact interaction and possessive variation. *Monash University Linguistics Papers,* 4(2), 87–105.

McConvell, P. (2007,). *Mixed Language vs. Language Shift Outcomes in Australian Indigenous Language Contact: The Role of Language Ecology.* Paper presented at the 6th International Symposium on Bilingualism (30 May–2 June), University of Hamburg, Hamburg.

McConvell, P., Amery, R., Gale, M. A., Nicholls, C., Nicholls, J., Rigney, L. and Tur, S. (2002). '"Keep that language going." A needs-based review of the status of indigenous languages in South Australia'. Unpublished report. Canberra: AITSIS.

McConvell, P., Simpson, J. and Wigglesworth, G. (2005). *Mixed Codes: a Comparison Across the Four Field Site.* Nijmegen: Max Planck Institute.

McConvell, P. and Thieberger, N. (2006). Keeping track of language endangerment in Australia. In D. Cunningham, D. Ingram and K. Sumbuk (eds), *Language Diversity in the Pacific: Endangerment and Survival.* Clevedon: Multilingual Matters.

McGregor, W. (2002). Structural changes in language obsolescence: a Kimberley (Australia) perspective. *SKY Journal of Linguistics,* 15, 145–85.

Myers-Scotton, C. (1993). *Social Motivations for Code-Switching.* Oxford: Oxford University Press.

Mufwene, S. (2001). *The Ecology of Language Evolution.* Cambridge: Cambridge University Press.

Nettle, D. and Romaine, S. (2000). *Vanishing Voices: The Extinction of the World's Languages.* Oxford: Oxford University Press.

Nichols, J. (1988). On alienable and inalienable possession. In W. Shipley (ed.), *Studies in Honor of Mary Haas* (pp. 475–521). Berlin: Mouton de Gruyter.

O'Grady, G. and Hale, K. (1974). *Recommendations Concerning Bilingual Education in the Northern Territory.* Darwin: NT Department of Education.

O'Shannessy, C. (2005). Light Warlpiri: a new language. *Australian Journal of Linguistics, 25*(1), 31–57.

Pearson, N. (2007). Native tongues imperilled. *The Australian, 10 March 2007.*

Raymattja, M. (1999). Milthun latju wanga romgu Yolngu: valuing Yolngu knowledge in the education system. *Ngoonjook: A Journal of Australian Indigenous Issues, 16,* 107–20.

Richards, N. (2001). Leerdil Yuujmen bana yanangarr (Old and New Lardil). In J. Simpson, D. Nash, M. Laughren, P. Austin and B. Alpher (eds), *Forty Years On: Ken Hale and Australian Languages* (pp. 431–45). Canberra: Pacific Linguistics.

Romaine, S. (2002). Can stable diglossia help to preserve endangered languages. *International Journal of the Sociology of Language, 157,* 135–40.

Schiffman, H. F., Garcia, O. and Peltz, R. (2006). *Language Loyalty, Continuity And Change: Joshua A. Fishman's Contributions to International Sociolinguistics.* Clevedon: Multilingual Matters.

Schmidt, A. (1985). *Young People's Dyirbal. An Example of Language Death from Australia.* Cambridge: Cambridge University Press.

Tamisari, F., & Milmilany, E. (2003). Dhinthun wayawu – looking for a pathway to knowledge: towards a vision of Yolngu education in Milingimbi. *The Australian Journal of Indigenous Education, 32*(1), 1–10.

Thomason, S. G. (2003). Social factors and linguistic processes in the emergence of stable mixed languages. In Y. Matras and P. Bakker (eds), *The Mixed Language Debate: Theoretical and Empirical Advances* (pp. 21–40). Berlin: Mouton de Gruyter.

Weinreich, U. (1953). *Languages in Contact.* The Hague: Mouton.

Wertheim, S. (2003). 'Linguistic purism, language shift and contact-induced change in Tatar'. Unpublished PhD dissertation, University of California, Berkeley.

Woollard, K. (2006). Codeswitching. In A. Duranti (ed.), *A Companion to Linguistic Anthropology* (pp. 73–94). Oxford: Blackwell Publishers.

Children's production of their heritage language and a new mixed language

Carmel O'Shannessy

12

Chapter Outline

Children in Lajamanu community grow up in a complex linguistic environment in which people around them talk in several languages and code-switch between them. They learn two Indigenous languages in the home – Light Warlpiri, which they use on a daily basis from when they first start to talk, and Warlpiri, which they begin to produce between the ages of 4 and 6 years. Light Warlpiri and Warlpiri share a lot of vocabulary and grammatical patterns. They differ mainly in the use of verb systems, and in the distribution of certain types of suffixes on nouns. The similarities and differences in the two languages lead to intriguing questions about how the children in the community deal with such complex and variable input. In this paper I discuss the children's development in speaking each language, by examining their production of a set of stories told in both Light Warlpiri and Warlpiri. Analysis shows that they can identify and reproduce quite finely differentiated patterns within and between languages.

Introduction

Children growing up in remote Indigenous communities in Australia often learn to speak in complex linguistic environments, such as in Example 1, in which Adult 1 is code-switching between Warlpiri and English, and Adult 2 is speaking a new mixed language, Light Warlpiri.

Example 1

ADULT 1: *nyarrpara* modika *yirra-rnu* ? weya modika?
  where car put-NPST where car
  'Where is the car? Where did you put it?'

ADULT 2: angkulu-*ng* i-m *puntarn*-im fo mi
  uncle-ERG 3sg-NF take:from-TRN DAT me
  'Uncle took it from me'

ADULT 2: rabish i-m jak-ing it
  rubbish 3SG-NF throw-PROG 3SG
  'he's throwing out the rubbish.'

Often people fear that exposing children to two or more languages will lead to the children being confused about the different languages and not be able to tell them apart (Lanza, 1997). Parents and carers of the children in the community, in the study reported here, want the children to learn both their traditional language, Warlpiri, and English, the language of the wider society (Ross, 1999). Being bilingual or multilingual themselves, they know that it is realistic for their children to be proficient in both Warlpiri and English. That the children speak Warlpiri is very important to them because it is their heritage language and speaking it expresses a Warlpiri identity. That the children speak English is also important to them so that the children can operate effectively in the wider society as well as in the local community.

More people in the world grow up speaking two or more languages than only one (Baker, 2006). When people are learning languages that are high in status or have large numbers of speakers, speaking several languages is seen as a resource rather than as a problem (Baker, 2006). This resource is valued socially, economically and politically. In some situations, the languages may not be equally valued, and where one language is dominant, a person's bilingual ability might not be valued so highly. In these circumstances, most attention is given to the development of the dominant language. For the bilingual, the social benefit is in being able to communicate effectively in situations involving more than one culture and more than one language. In areas where the two (or more) languages are both highly valued by most people in the society, such as English and French in Canada, or Dutch, German and French in parts of Europe, the positive social benefit of being bilingual or multilingual is well accepted. Monolingual speakers of English from the UK, USA or Australia often express feelings of linguistic inadequacy when they travel to Europe and talk to people who can easily switch between fluent German, English, Spanish, French or Dutch, for example.

In addition to the social benefits, psycholinguistic research shows that being bilingual has some cognitive benefits over being monolingual (Bialystok, 2007). In some linguistic tasks bilinguals perform more slowly than monolinguals (Gollan et al., 2002), but on higher level functions they perform better. Research shows that the representations of both languages in the brain are active even when only one language is being used (Brauer, 1998; Chen and Ho, 1986; Dijkstra et al., 1999; Gollan et al., 1997; Hermans et al., 2003; van Heuven et al., 1998).

A bilingual person must be able to pay attention to each language, inhibit the language not being used in the conversation, monitor both languages and switch between languages. In combination, these functions are part of what is called executive processing (Bialystok, 2007; p. 212). Executive processing is part of all of our thinking – controlling our attention, planning and categorising, and knowing how to avoid responding inappropriately. Bilingual children develop control of this function earlier than monolinguals, show superior control in adulthood, and lose the control later than monolinguals as they age (Bialystok, 2007 pp.291, 220). The reason for their enhanced performance is probably that they practise these functions more often because from an early age they need to manage two languages. Bilinguals have been shown to perform better than monolinguals on spatial tasks (McLeay, 2003), have better metalinguistic knowledge (Ransdell et al., 2006), and perform better in tasks requiring memory (Haritos, 2002). The participants in the studies had a high level of ability in each language that they spoke, and Cummins (1978, 1991) suggests that cognitive advantages for bilinguals only come into play when the bilingual has reached a high level of performance in both languages.

In areas where most people in the society do not value both or all of the languages equally, the value of being bilingual or multilingual is sometimes not recognised. When people are bilingual in English and a minority language, the social and cognitive benefits of being bilingual are not always appreciated by the dominant English-speaking group in the society. Similarly they might not be recognised by all of the professionals who work with bilingual children, for instance, as educators in schools. A greater understanding of the linguistic complexity that some children deal with can help visiting professionals such as teachers be aware of the kinds of language knowledge and skill that children in multilingual communities have, and what they are already learning. In this chapter, I present the complex language learning situation in one remote Indigenous community in northern Australia and show that primary-school-aged children have already learned at least two different ways of speaking (other than English) and are able to recognise fine distinctions in the linguistic properties of each.

Sociolinguistic background

In the Warlpiri community of Lajamanu, in northern Australia, people speak in several different ways, or codes. The main language spoken is Warlpiri, the traditional Indigenous language. Warlpiri is also spoken in other Warlpiri communities – in Yuendumu, Willowra and Nyirrpi. There are Warlpiri people living and speaking Warlpiri in each of the towns in the Northern Territory (NT) and in other communities in the NT and Western Australia. There are an estimated 4,000 speakers of Warlpiri in Central Australia (Laughren et al., 1996, p. 1). Before describing the language learning situation in Lajamanu community in detail, I provide some information about the social and geographical networks of people in the community, because they are relevant to the ways in which people speak.

Lajamanu is a remote community, nearly 600 km south-west of Katherine, the nearest commercial centre. There are few flights in and out of the community and not all of the roads leading to it are in good condition – only the road to the north can be travelled on all year round. Many government centres for services to Lajamanu are in Katherine, so people who live in Lajamanu travel to Katherine frequently. The other main Warlpiri-speaking communities are to the south. The nearest is Yuendumu, also about 600 km distant. People can only travel directly by road to the other Warlpiri communities to the south in the 'dry season', from about June to November. During these months people from the Warlpiri communities travel to each other's communities often for sporting events and cultural and family reasons. The remote locality of Lajamanu community, the differing road conditions and the delivery of services from Katherine mean that people in Lajamanu travel to the north frequently for economic and service reasons, and to the south for family and cultural reasons.

The languages Lajamanu people use when interacting with others differ depending on whether they travel to the north or to the south. When they travel to the south and interact in other Warlpiri communities they mainly speak Warlpiri because they are speaking to other Warlpiri people. But when they travel to the north they interact both with other Warlpiri speakers and also with speakers of many other Indigenous languages and speakers of English. The common languages used with Indigenous people who do not speak Warlpiri are Kriol and Aboriginal English. Kriol and Aboriginal English are also often used when speaking to people in the community closest to Lajamanu, Kalkaringi-Daguragu, often with switching between them and Warlpiri. Kriol is the first language of approximately 20,000 people, and the second language of many others (Munro, 2004). It is an English-based creole, that is, a language, distinct from English that developed from contact between English and several Indigenous languages. It draws its vocabulary mainly from English but much of its grammar and sound patterns from Indigenous languages (Hudson, 1985, p. 22; Sandefur, 1991, p. 29). Kriol itself has different varieties and can, broadly, be spoken in two ways: a basilectal variety that has relatively more features from Indigenous languages; or an acrolectal variety with fewer features from Indigenous languages and more from standard English (Simpson, 2007). Aboriginal English (Malcolm and Kaldor, 1991, p. 67) is a variety of English with elements of grammar and sound patterns from Indigenous languages. There is debate about where to draw a division between acrolectal Kriol and Aboriginal English, because they have some elements in common – words from English, and elements of grammar and sound patterns from Indigenous languages. When people from Lajamanu travel to Katherine and the north they hear Kriol spoken around them a lot, and interact with Kriol speakers in acrolectal varieties of Kriol or Aboriginal English. Warlpiri people also speak Standard Australian English (SAE), or a variety close to SAE, to non-Indigenous people, wherever they are.

As a result, Warlpiri people from Lajamanu frequently switch between speaking in Warlpiri, Aboriginal English, SAE and acrolectal Kriol, or varieties of these. Because it is sometimes difficult to distinguish between acrolectal Kriol and Aboriginal English, from now on I will refer to AE/Kriol when I refer to this code of speech. Switching between different languages within one conversation is known as code-switching. In some parts of the world code-switching is the typical way of talking (e.g. Cheng and Butler, 1989; Poplack, 1980), and it is used widely in Lajamanu. When Warlpiri talk to each other they often switch between Warlpiri and English or Kriol within one conversation or sentence, as in Example 2, consecutive sentences from one speaker. In the examples, Warlpiri elements are shown in italics and AE/K elements are shown in plain font.

Example 2

(a) modika   *winji-rni-ngki-rla*   angkulu-*rlu*   *yijala*
    motor:car   pour-NPST-2SG-DAT   uncle-ERG   also
    'Also uncle is filling up your vehicle with fuel.'

(b) *wirnji-rni*   angkulu-*rlu*
    pour-NPST   uncle-ERG
    'Uncle is filling it up.'

(c) a   wana   fil-im-ap-i   diesel-u   *nganayi-rla*
    1SG   want to   fill-TRN-up-EPEN   diesel-EPEN   you:know-DAT
    'I want to fill up that, you know, with diesel'

(d) *nganayi-rla*   jeri   ken-*rla*   tu
    you:know-DAT   jerry   can-DAT   too
    'you know, the jerry can too.'

In Example 2, a woman in her seventies is talking to her granddaughter about filling up their vehicle with fuel. In Example 2(a) she uses a common borrowing from English, *modika*, for vehicle. Then she uses a Warlpiri verb, *winjirni* 'pour', and attaches to it a syllable -*ngki* '2sg non-subject' that in this context means 'for you', and a dative case-marker that also means non-subject, that is, 'the vehicle'. She uses an English word, *uncle*, with a Warlpiri ending attached to it, -*rlu*,[1] to mean that the uncle is doing the action of pouring the fuel. She could have chosen the Warlpiri word for uncle, *ngamirni* 'mother's brother'. In Example 2(b) some of Example 2(a) is repeated. Then in Example 2(c) and (d), the speaker switches into Aboriginal English for most of the sentence. The words *a* 'I', *wana* 'want to', *filimapi* 'fill up', *diesel* 'diesel' and *jeri ken* 'jerry can' are recognisable as being either English words or words derived from English. In this paper I will not try to explain why the speaker makes these choices (but see McConvell, Chapter 11, for a social explanation of code-switching). Rather I use this example to illustrate the fact that switching between languages is a common way of speaking in the community.

A new language

Code-switching between Warlpiri and AE/Kriol in Lajamanu has led to the development of a new way of speaking, which the community elders call Light

Warlpiri (in Warlpiri: *Warlpiri rampaku,* 'Warlpiri light/weak'). It is typical for Warlpiri speakers to talk about speaking a language in a heavy or strong way or in a light or weak way. Heavy or strong Warlpiri is Warlpiri with no words or grammar from English or Kriol, and with complex grammatical structures or kinship terminology that is used more by older speakers. Weak or Light Warlpiri is Warlpiri with some words or grammar from English or Kriol, or with some Warlpiri grammatical elements absent. In Light Warlpiri, as shown in Example 3, spoken by a 4-year-old child, verbs and word endings on verbs are from AE/Kriol and most nouns and word endings on nouns are from Warlpiri, although nouns can also be from English or Kriol. In the Light Warlpiri examples I also show elements from Warlpiri in italics and elements from English or Kriol in plain font.

Example 3

nganimpa-ng	gen	wi-m	si-im	worm-*wat*	mai	aus-*rla*
we(not you)-ERG	also	we-NF	see-TRN	worm-PL	my	house-LOC
'We also saw worms at my house.'						

In Example 3 the pronoun *nganimpa* (first-plural-exclusive) is from Warlpiri and means 'us but not including you'. The *-ng* ending says that *nganimpa* is the subject, the person who 'saw'. The next word, *gen* 'again, also' is derived from English 'again' but its meaning has changed a little, so that in Light Warlpiri it means 'also' as well as 'again'.

The next word, *wi-m* is the 'auxiliary' component. By this I mean a component which is obligatory in most sentences, which is not the verb, but which carries information about the tense of the sentence and about the subject of the sentence. *wi-m* consists of two parts, *wi* which agrees with the subject *nganimpang*, and which comes from English 'we', and the *-m*. The *-m* element refers to time. It means that the event denoted by the verb is either happening now or has already happened. It is glossed in the examples as 'NF' meaning 'non-future'. (The *-m* is probably partly derived from English *-m* as in 'I'm' and partly from Kriol and Warlpiri forms (O'Shannessy, 2005, p. 39)).

The next element in the sentence is the verb, *si* 'see' from English, but with an AE/Kriol transitive marker, *-im*, attached to it. Then *worm* is easily identifiable as an English noun but has an ending from Warlpiri, a plural marker, on it, meaning that there is more than one worm. *Mai* 'my' is clearly from English. *Aus* 'house' is also from English and has another Warlpiri ending on it, which means 'at, in' or 'on' the noun it attaches to. In this context it means 'at' or 'in' the house.

This way of talking is so different from Warlpiri and AE/Kriol that I consider it to be a new language, even though the Warlpiri people in Lajamanu consider it to be a type of Warlpiri. This type of language is called a Verb-Noun mixed language (Bakker, 2003) because of the mix of verbs from one source language (AE/Kriol) and most nouns from another (Warlpiri). A famous example of this type of language is Michif, in Canada, which combines verbs and verb endings from Cree, the Indigenous language, and nouns and noun endings from French, the colonial language (Bakker, 1994). Light Warlpiri has an additional feature, not seen in other VN-mixed languages, which is that one of its subsystems, the auxiliary system, is not exactly the same as the auxiliary systems in Warlpiri or AE/K, but is derived from them. Examples 3 and 4 show part of the auxiliary system.

Example 4

nyarrpara-wana	yu-m	bai-im	*ngula*	*Nungarrayi*
where-along	you-NF	buy-TRN	that	name

'Where did you buy that Nungarrayi?'

While Example 3 shows one auxiliary form, *wi-m*, Example 4 shows another, *yu-m*. Speakers of English know that while *yu* and *wi* are English forms, in English one cannot say *yu-m* or *wi-m*. These forms do not occur in Kriol or Warlpiri either, yet elements of their form or their function are derived from each of the source languages. (See O'Shannessy (2005) for more information on the Light Warlpiri auxiliary system). The Light Warlpiri auxiliary system is important because it is partly how we can decide whether a person is speaking Light Warlpiri or is code-switching between Warlpiri and AE/Kriol. The Light Warlpiri auxiliary system is not used in older speaker's code-switching between Warlpiri and AE/Kriol.

The language learning situation

Light Warlpiri is only spoken in Lajamanu community and is spoken by adults, under about age 30, and children. This way of talking may have developed when the 30 year olds were teenagers, and were code-switching frequently between Warlpiri and AE/Kriol when they talked to each other. Their way of speaking became so conventionalised that it became a completely new way of speaking, and its speakers also made innovations, such as the new auxiliary system. When this group of teenagers and young adults had children they talked to them in the new way, so that the children now learn this way of speaking as one of their home languages.

The other home language that children in Lajamanu learn is Warlpiri, so they are learning both Warlpiri and Light Warlpiri. The following examples show excerpts from stories told in Warlpiri, in Example 5, and Light Warlpiri, in Example 6.

Example 5

(a) *kurdu*   *ka-rla*   *yulka-mi*   *karnta-ku*   *juwingjuwing-wana*
child   PRES-DAT   cry-NPST   woman-DAT   swing-by
'The child is crying for its mother by the swing.'

(b) *jarntu*   jalpi   *ka-Ø*   *karri-mi*
dog   self   PRS-3SG   stand-NPST
'The dog is standing alone.'

(c) *kuuku-ng*   *ka-Ø-Ø*   *ma-ni*   *jarntu*
monster-ERG   PRS-3SG-3SG   get-NPST   dog
'The monster gets the dog.'   Warlpiri

Example 6

(a) *karnta-pawu-ng*   *i-m*   *pud-um*   beibi   *juwing-rla*   *juwingjuwing-rla*
woman-DIM-ERG   3SG-NF   put-TRN   baby   swing-LOC   swing-LOC
'The woman put the baby on the swing, on the swing.'

(b) *kuuku-ng*   *i-m*   *ged-im*   *jarntu*
monster-ERG   3SG-NF   get-TRN   dog
'The monster got the dog.'

(c) an   *jarntu*   *i-m*   krai
and   dog   3SG-NF   cry
'And the dog cried.'   Light Warlpiri

The diagnostic of Light Warlpiri is the use of the Light Warlpiri auxiliary forms and AE/Kriol verbs and verb endings (e.g. *i-m ged-im* 'he/she/it gets'), while the diagnostic of Warlpiri is the use of the Warlpiri auxiliary-plus-verb system (e.g. *ka-Ø-Ø ma-ni* 'he/she/it gets'). The Warlpiri auxiliary, like the Light Warlpiri auxiliary, marks both the tense and aspect of the sentence, as well as the subject, and also marks the object. *ka-Ø-Ø* marks the sentence as happening now. The absence of overt marking (expressed here as -Ø-Ø) indicates that the subject and object are both third person singular, that is, that one participant performed the action on one other participant.

When speaking Light Warlpiri speakers might use more AE/Kriol features at times and more Warlpiri features at others. As seen in Examples 4 and 5, there is a lot of overlap between Light Warlpiri and Warlpiri, because many elements in Light Warlpiri are from Warlpiri. For instance, *kuuku* is the word for monster in both languages, *jarntu* is the word for dog, and the form of the ergative case-marker is -*ng*.

From when children are born, people talk to them in both Warlpiri and Light Warlpiri and code-switch between several languages. The children's parents talk to them in Light Warlpiri, and code-switch between Light Warlpiri, Warlpiri and AE/Kriol, and their older carers talk to them in Warlpiri and code-switch between Warlpiri and AE/Kriol. Children talk to each other in Light Warlpiri. This is a very complicated picture! Example 7 shows an adult code-switching between Warlpiri and AE/Kriol.

Example 7

(a) *ya-nu-Ø-lu*   *wirlinyi*   *marnkurrpa*   *wirriya-patu*
go-PST-PERF-3PL   hunting   few   boy-PL
'A few boys went hunting.'

(b) *parlupu-ngu-Ø-Ø-Ø*   *jurlpu*
find-PST-PERF-3SG-3SG   bird
'One finds a bird.'

(c) *parlupu-ngu-Ø-Ø-Ø*   *jurlpu*   *nya-ngka*   *Bajo-ngu*
find-PST-PERF-3SG-3SG   bird   look-IMP   name-ERG
'He finds a bird, look, Bajo does.'

(d) jee   *Bajo*   im   paind-im   *jurlpu*
see   name   3SG   find-TRN   bird
'See, Bajo finds a bird.'

In Example 7, the speaker, a man about 45 years old, is telling a story from a picture stimuli to his young daughter. He speaks in Warlpiri at the start. In Example 7(a) the auxiliary elements are Ø-*lu* 'perfect-3plural', meaning that several people performed the action of going and the action has been completed. In Example 7(b) and (c), the auxiliary elements are null (represented as -Ø-Ø-Ø), and their meaning is again that the action is completed and also that one participant performed the action on one other participant, that is, the bird. In Example 7(d), the speaker switches into AE/Kriol with *jee* 'see', *im paindim* 'he finds it' and back into Warlpiri for *jurlpu* 'bird'. It is possible that he did this to use more variety of style in his speech in order to get the full attention of his 2-year-old daughter.

Table 12.1 Languages mainly spoken to children by age group of speakers

Age group	Language mainly spoken to children	With code-switching into
Adults over approximately 30 years old	Warlpiri	AE/Kriol
Adults under approximately 30 years old	Light Warlpiri	Warlpiri; AE/Kriol
Children	Light Warlpiri	

The next examples show an adult code-switching between Warlpiri and Light Warlpiri. In the examples a mother is beginning to tell a story from a picture book stimulus to her two children.

> **Example 8**
>
> (a) *nyina-ya*   *nyina-ya*   *Jakamarra*   *nya-ngka*
>   sit-IMP   sit-IMP   name   look-IMP
>   'Sit down! Sit down! Jakamarra! Look!'
>
> (b) yu   luk   *kurdu-kurdu*   na   de-m   go   shangai-*kirl*   *nya-ngka*
>   you   look   child-REDUP   DIS   3PL-NF go   slingshot-COM   look-IMP
>   'Look at these children, they're going with a slingshot, look!'

In Example 8(a), the mother gives one of the children, Jakamarra, directions in Warlpiri. Then in Example 8(b) she switches to Light Warlpiri. She gives the same direction using an AE/Kriol construction which is common in Light Warlpiri (*yu luk* 'look'), then uses the Light Warlpiri auxiliary and verb *dem go* 'they are going' when she starts to tell the story. Table 12.1 summarises the different ways people speak to children in Lajamanu.

The verb-plus-auxiliary components in each language

Two of the main languages spoken in the community, Warlpiri and Light Warlpiri, have shared elements, and there is a great deal of code-switching between languages. Does that mean that speakers code-switch between languages at random, or are there patterns in the types of code-switching that take place? Similarly, in Light Warlpiri, can elements of Warlpiri and AE/Kriol be combined at random, or are there constraints on how they are combined? In Examples 7(a), (b) and (c) above, we see that when adults speak Warlpiri they use a Warlpiri auxiliary-plus-verb component (even though sometimes the auxiliary component is null). In Example 8(b) we see that when they speak Light Warlpiri they use a Light Warlpiri auxiliary-plus-verb component. So, the question arises, do they ever use a Warlpiri verb with a Light Warlpiri auxiliary, or vice versa?

Only a small set of Warlpiri verbs occur in Light Warlpiri, and they have an AE/Kriol transitive affix attached to them, as in Example 9.

Example 9

jilkarla-ng	i-m	*pantirn*-im
thorn-ERG	3sg-NF	pierce-TRN

'A thorn pierced him/her/it.'

Note that although the verb stem *panti* 'pierce' is from Warlpiri, the overall structure of the verb, *pantirn-im* 'verb-plus-transitive marker', is from AE/ Kriol and the Light Warlpiri auxiliary, *i-m* '3sg-NF' is used. So I consider this structure to be a Light Warlpiri structure. The Warlpiri auxiliary is not used with this pattern in adult speech, nor is the Light Warlpiri auxiliary used with a Warlpiri inflecting verb. For example, sentences such as the following two examples do not occur in the adult data. (An asterisk before an example means that the example does not occur.)

Example 10

*i-m	panti-rni
3sg-NF	pierce-NPST

'He/she/it is piercing it.'
(Light Warlpiri auxiliary structure with Warlpiri verb structure.)

Example 11:

*ka-Ø	*pantirn*-im
PRS-3SG	pierce-TRN

'He/she/it is piercing it.'
(Warlpiri auxiliary structure with Light Warlpiri verb structure.)

I have no recordings in which an adult uses a Warlpiri auxiliary and a Kriol verb, or a Kriol pronoun and a Warlpiri inflecting verb. So even though adults switch between ways of talking in the one conversation, and it is possible to use certain Warlpiri verb stems with Kriol suffixes, there are some patterns that are never mixed – the overall structure of the auxiliary and verb of each language always occurs as a unit, that is, adult speakers do not switch the structure of the source language between the auxiliary and verb elements of a sentence.

The children's production of both languages is interesting. Often in bi- and multilingual environments children produce both languages from the time they first start to speak, but in this community they usually do not. The children produce Light Warlpiri from when they first start to speak, and usually produce Warlpiri later, from about 4 to 6 years old. But although they do not produce Warlpiri when they are very young, they are learning it. Later they produce both languages. Children in other multilingual situations have been documented to produce only one language at first, while developing knowledge in the other, but a situation such as the one in this community, in which most of the children follow this pattern, has not often been documented. The reason the children do not produce both languages at the same time is probably because the youngest children look to other children and their Light Warlpiri-speaking parents as models, rather than to their older carers. Some children, who spend their first 2 or 3 years much more in the company of older women than younger women, do sometimes speak in Warlpiri when they first begin to talk, but they then speak mostly Light Warlpiri when they start spending a lot of time with the other children.

The children's learning of both of these languages raises some interesting questions. Once the children produce both languages, do they speak each one in the same way that adults do, following the same patterns? For example, do they keep the structures of the auxiliary and verb systems of each one separate, or do they mix the auxiliary and verb systems together? Another interesting feature of the two languages is that both languages share one particular element – one small word ending, -ng, occurs in both languages, but when adults talk the -ng is used to different extents in each language. The question is: do the children also use this ending to different extents in the two languages? I report below on a study I conducted to answer these questions.

But first, some background on the -ng ending which is used to mark who is doing the action. It is called an ergative case-marker and it occurs on nouns in transitive sentences. A transitive sentence is one in which there are at least two participants, and one participant performs an action directly on the other. For example, 'the dog bites the bird' is a transitive sentence, because both the dog and the bird are participants and the dog performs the action of biting directly on the bird. When we say 'the dog bites the bird' in English, we don't have any word endings on the participant that performs the action (the dog), who we can refer to as the 'agent'. We know who performs the action by the order of the words in the sentence – if we said, 'the bird bites the dog', the meaning would be the opposite, that is, the bird would be the agent. But in Warlpiri an ergative case-marker gives the same information that word order gives in English. In Warlpiri, to say, 'the dog bites the bird', speakers could say:

Example 12

jarntu-ngku	ka-Ø-Ø	paji-rni	nantuwu
dog-ERG	PRES-3SG-3SG	bite-NPST	bird

'The dog bites the bird.'

The words could be in any order, as long as the auxiliary, *ka-Ø-Ø* 'present imperfective' (roughly, someone is doing something to someone now), is the second word. So all of the following sentences make sense in Warlpiri, and mean the same thing.

Pajirni ka nantuwu jarntu-ngku.
Nantuwu ka jarntu-ngku pajirni.
Jarntu-ngku ka jurlpu pajirni.
Pajirni ka jarntu-ngku nantuwu.
Nantuwu ka pajirni jarntu-ngku.

Speakers use the different word orders to present new or surprising information versus old information (Laughren, 2002; Mushin, 2005; Simpson, 2007; Swartz and Swartz, 1991).

Similarly, in Light Warlpiri, the presence of the ergative case-marker, *-ng*, shows who the agent is, and the words can be in any order, as long as the auxiliary and verb are next to each other and the verb follows the auxiliary.

Example 13

jarntu-ng	i-m	bait-im	jurlpu
dog-ERG	3SG-NF	bite-TRN	bird

'The dog bites the bird.'

All of the following word orders make sense in Light Warlpiri and mean the same thing.

Jurlpu i-m bait-im *jarntu-ng.*
Jarntu-ng jurlpu i-m bait-im.
Jurlpu jarntu-ng i-m bait-im.
I-m bait-im *jurlpu jarntu-ng.*
I-m bait-im *jarntu-ng jurlpu.*

But in Light Warlpiri the ergative marker is not always present – in adult speech it only occurs on approximately 60 per cent of agents. When it is not present, the agent can be identified from other information, for example, by knowing who the agent was in the previous sentence, or by using contextual information such as who is most likely to be the agent.

The use of the ergative marker by adults 90–100 per cent of the time in Warlpiri (O'Shannessy, forthcoming), but only 60 per cent of the time in Light Warlpiri is interesting when we recall that the children are learning both languages, and the ergative marker is only one syllable. We might wonder how well they learn about using the ergative marker. Have they tuned in to the small differences in the adult patterns in each language, or do they use a different pattern?

The study

Methodology

To answer the questions about patterns of verb-auxiliary use and about the use of the ergative marker, I recorded children and adults telling stories from picture books, and analysed their stories. I developed a set of three stimulus picture stories in which there were several agents, so that to tell the story, a noun had to be used to talk about the agent. When story-tellers produce a noun as an agent, they have the option of adding an ergative case-marker to the noun.

I asked several groups of adults, and 8–10 children in each of two age groups, mean age 7 and 9 years, to tell the stories. The children told the stories to me, and the adults told the stories to another adult who acted out the story she was hearing with toys. This was to encourage the person telling the story to talk the same way as she normally does to the person listening. I tried to get the children to tell the stories to each other and have the listener act out the stories with toys, but the method didn't work well with the children, because the speaker tended to give instructions to the other child, such as 'Put the dog in the yard'. If the children gave instructions they wouldn't need to use agent nouns, so there would not be any examples of ergative case-marking.

One difficulty working with the children was that they were not all used to telling stories in both languages. I needed to know if they used the verb-plus-auxiliary component and ergative case-marking differently in each language, so I needed to hear stories in both languages. The older children were used to performing school-type tasks in Warlpiri, which is taught in the school, but not in Light Warlpiri, which is not taught in the school. In fact, normally there is no overt interest from non-Warlpiri people in the children's speaking Light Warlpiri, but there is interest in how they speak Warlpiri. So the older children expected that the task would be only in Warlpiri, and were not used to doing an activity of this kind in Light Warlpiri. Some of the younger children were the opposite – they were not old enough to be used to performing in Warlpiri, for example at school, and were only used to speaking in Light Warlpiri. As a result, they naturally started to talk in Light Warlpiri.

To help the children to tell the stories in both languages I made short videos in which another child told a completely different story in each language, one in Warlpiri and one in Light Warlpiri. Before a child was going to tell a story in, for example, Light Warlpiri, the child would watch a short video in Light Warlpiri (while eating a sandwich, in case they were hungry and might be distracted during the task). Similarly, before telling a story in Warlpiri, they would watch a short video in Warlpiri (while eating a sandwich). Then each child was asked to speak like the child they heard in the video to tell the story from the picture book. In this way each child was cued into speaking in one language or the other. The order in which they told the stories in each language was counter-balanced so that half of the children told the stories in Warlpiri first and the other half told them in Light Warlpiri first. There was a 2-week break between story-telling sessions. These strategies were to make sure that using one language before the other did not have any effect on the kind of grammar and words used in each language.

After the children told the stories, I transcribed each story with a speaker of the language. I then broke the stories into separate clauses (the part of a sentence containing a verb, the agent and words showing who or what is affected by the verb).[2] I then counted all of the nouns which were agents, with and without ergative case-marking, and all of the sentences with either a Warlpiri verb and auxiliary, a Light Warlpiri verb and auxiliary, or a mixture of verb and auxiliary from each language in the one sentence.

Results

Verb-plus-auxiliary component

The results for mixing the verb-plus-auxiliary components of each language within one clause are reported first. As the summary in Table 12.2 shows, a total of 1,702 clauses were examined. The summary in Table 12.2 groups the clauses into groups – those produced by children with a mean age of 7 and a mean age of 9, and those in Warlpiri and Light Warlpiri stories.

Table 12.2 Children's narratives: Number of clauses with mixed auxiliary-plus-verb components

Age group	Language of story	Number of clauses	Number of clauses with mixed form in auxiliary + verb
7	Light Warlpiri	556	7
7	Warlpiri	486	3
9	Light Warlpiri	479	0
9	Warlpiri	181	0
Total		1,702	10

Table 12.2 shows that out of a total of 1,702 clauses, only 10 of them contain a mix of languages in the auxiliary-plus-verb component. These are all from children in the 7-year-old group, when they are telling a story in either Warlpiri or Light Warlpiri. Most of the time the children keep the two auxiliary-plus-verb systems separate, and are able to use the auxiliary-plus-verb system in Warlpiri in an adult-like way.

The few mixes of elements of each language that do occur are of both possible types – a Light Warlpiri auxiliary, *i-m*, with a Warlpiri verb, as in Example 14, and a Warlpiri auxiliary *kapu-Ø-Ø* 'fut-3sg-3sg', with a Light Warlpiri verb, as in Example 15.

Example 14

i-m   push-i-*ma-ni*
3sg-NF   push-EPEN-cause-NPST
'She is pushing him.'

In Example 14 the child uses the Light Warlpiri auxiliary, *i-m* '3sg-NF', with a Warlpiri verb. The Warlpiri verb he uses consists of two parts, a borrowing from English, *push*, and a bound main verb from Warlpiri, *ma-ni* 'CAUSE-NON-PAST'. Combining bound main verbs with other words is a common process of Warlpiri verb formation (Nash, 1986). The use of the verb forms here might show that the child does not have full control over the Warlpiri verb and auxiliary systems, although he uses them correctly at other times in the same narratives. An alternative is that he code-switched from Light Warlpiri to Warlpiri within the clause, that is, began to speak in Light Warlpiri, then realised he was supposed to tell the story in Warlpiri, and so switched language. Or, he might have code-switched because he wanted to provide the information about who was doing the action (*i* 'third person singular') early in the clause, so used the Light Warlpiri form, because in Warlpiri that information would need to be placed after the verb.

Example 15

kapu-∅-∅	help-im	jarntu
fut-3sg-3sg	help-TR	dog

'He/she/it will help the dog.'

Example 15, from a 6-year-old, shows that children sometimes mix a Warlpiri auxiliary with a Light Warlpiri verb form. The Warlpiri verb form that would typically have been used is *help-i-ma-ni* 'help-EPEN-CAUSE-NPST', a combination of an English or Kriol word and a Warlpiri bound main verb. It is possible that beginning the word with a form from English or Kriol led the child to use the Light Warlpiri form instead of the Warlpiri form.

In sum, when children begin to produce Warlpiri they are generally able to use the auxiliary-verb component in an adult-like way. They occasionally mix both languages within the auxiliary-plus-verb component at age 7, but there is no evidence in the data of this kind of mixing by age 9.

Ergative case-marking

I now turn to the children's use of ergative case-marking in each language. The results are summarised in Table 12.3, including results of the young adult speakers of both languages for comparison.

As Table 12.3 shows, speakers in all age groups use ergative marking in Warlpiri narratives more often than in Light Warlpiri narratives. A statistical analysis[3] of the results shows that the difference in use of ergative marking between the languages is not due to chance; we can confidently expect that the difference is always there. Conversely, the differences between age groups

Table 12.3 Number of agent nouns and percentage of ergative case-marking in Light Warlpiri and Warlpiri narratives, per age group

Age	7		9		20	
Language	Light Warlpiri	Warlpiri	Light Warlpiri	Warlpiri	Light Warlpiri	Warlpiri
Agent nouns	78	66	81	95	66	59
Percentage of ergative marking on agent nouns	58	80	44	79	65	86

within each language are only due to chance – there is no real difference in how often each group uses ergative marking on agents within one language.

As seen in Table 12.3, the 7- and 9-year-old children use ergative case-marking in Warlpiri on 80 and 79 per cent of agents, respectively, and the adults use it on 86 per cent of agents, so the children use ergative case-marking in Warlpiri about as often as the young adults do.[4] The same comparison applies to Light Warlpiri – children are adult-like in how often they use ergative marking.

Discussion

These sets of results provide considerable information about the children's language learning and language awareness. They show that the children are able to tune in to quite subtle patterns in the languages they hear. Although Light Warlpiri consists of elements from Warlpiri and elements from AE/Kriol, the children reproduce the elements in exactly the same patterns as in the speech of young adults who speak to and around them. The structures of the two source languages are never mixed within the verb-plus-auxiliary component in adult Light Warlpiri, and in the main the children do not mix them either. Up to age 7 there is a very small amount of mixing, which is consistent with research about children learning other languages – children can still make errors in their first language at ages 6 and 7 (Bowerman, 1981, 1990). By age 9 there is no evidence in the data of these elements being mixed either in Light Warlpiri or in Warlpiri.

The patterns of ergative case-marking in each language are also subtle. The same form, -*ng*, is the ergative case-marker in both languages, but in adult speech the marker is used more often in Warlpiri than in Light Warlpiri. The children are able to pick up on this pattern and reproduce it in their own speech. Their doing so demonstrates that they can identify and reproduce patterns which differ in subtle ways in each language.

The implications for the children's language learning are that even in environments in which several languages are spoken and people code-switch between them, children can identify which elements belong to which language, which elements can be mixed in certain circumstances and which may not. In addition, they can detect differences in quantities of use of particular elements, for example, in ergative case-marking, and reproduce the different quantities of use themselves. So not only do they learn two languages at home before they attend school and start learning English, they have a considerable amount of awareness of detail about the two languages they learn at home.

I have had several conversations with children aged 5 to 7 years, and have found that they can talk confidently about differences between Warlpiri, Light Warlpiri and English, for instance, giving examples of how something could be said in each language. Several of the children also talk to each other about the ways people in the community and visitors speak. One 5-year-old child told me exactly which new Warlpiri words she was learning at school, without my prompting her. While I could not claim that all the children have the same level of interest and overt awareness and can participate in these discussions, at least several children are able to do this.

All of these factors bode well for the children's future language learning. They show that if the children are motivated and engaged in the learning process and have adequate exposure to the language they are learning, they are capable of identifying and reproducing quite finely distinguished patterns. The children's abilities to speak two languages which they learn in the home have allowed us a glimpse into their levels of linguistic awareness and their linguistic analysis skills.

Notes

1. In classic Warlpiri the ergative case-marker has four forms (allomorphs): *-ngki, -ngku, -rli, -rlu.* Which form is used depends on the length and final vowel of the word it is attached to. But in Warlpiri as spoken in Lajamanu nowadays another form, *-ng,* is often used, regardless of length and final vowel of the word it is attached to.
2. For example, in 'I went to the bank and got some money', 'I went to the bank' is one clause and 'and got some money' is another.
3. Using multilevel logistic regression analysis: $p < 0.001$.
4. In Warlpiri as it is spoken in Lajamanu community, adults over the age of about 60 use ergative marking on all agents, and younger adults use it on approximately 90 per cent of agents, O'Shannessy, C. (Forthcoming). Language variation and change in a north Australian indigenous community. In James N. Stanford and Dennis R. Preston (eds), *Quantitative Sociolinguistic Studies of Indigenous Minority Languages,* Michigan State University.

References

Baker, C. (2006). *Foundations of Bilingual Education and Bilingualism.* Clevedon: Multilingual Matters.

Bakker, P. (1994). Michif, the Cree-French mixed language of the Métis buffalo hunters in Canada. In P. Bakker and M. Mous (eds), *Mixed Languages: 15 Case Studies in Language Intertwining* (pp. 13–33). Amsterdam: IFOTT.

Bakker, P. (2003). Mixed languages as autonomous systems. In Y. Matras and P. Bakker (eds), *The Mixed Language Debate: Theoretical and Empirical Advances* (pp. 107–50). Berlin: Mouton de Gruyter.

Bialystok, E. (2007). Cognitive effects of bilingualism: how linguistic experience leads to cognitive change. *International Journal of Bilingual Education and Bilingualism, 10*(3), 210–23.

Bowerman, M. (1981). Language development. In H. C. Triandis and A. Heron (eds), *Handbook of Cross-Cultural Psychology: Developmental Psychology* (Vol. 4). Boston: Allyn and Bacon.

Bowerman, M. (1990). Mapping thematic roles onto syntactic functions: are children helped by innate linking rules? *Linguistics, 28*, 1253–89.

Brauer, M. (1998). Stroop interference in bilinguals: the role of similarity between the two languages. In A. F. Healy and L. E. Bourne (eds), *Foreign Language Learning: Psycholinguistic Studies on Training and Retention* (pp. 317–37). Mahwah, NJ: Lawrence Erlbaum Associates.

Chen, H.-c. and Ho, C. (1986). Development of Stroop interference in Chinese-English bilinguals. *Journal of Experimental Psychology: Learning, Memory, and Cognition, 12*(3), 397–401.

Cheng, L. R and Butler, K. (1989). Code-switching: a natural phenomenon vs. language 'deficiency'. *World Englishes, 8*(3), 293–309.

Cummins, J. (1978). Educational implications of mother tongue maintenance in minority-language groups. *The Canadian Modern Language Review, 34*(3), 395–416.

Cummins, J. (1991). Conversational and academic language proficiency in bilingual contexts. *Association Internationale de Linguistique Review, 8,* 75–89.

Daniels, K., Toth, J. and Jacoby, L. (2006). The aging of executive functions. In E. Bialystock and F. I. M. Craik (eds), *Lifespan Cognition: Mechanisms of Change* (pp. 96–111). New York: Oxford University Press.

Dijkstra, T., Grainger, J. and van Heuven, W. J. B. (1999). Recognition of cognates and interlingual homographs: the neglected role of phonology. *Journal of Memory and Language, 41*(4), 496–518.

Gollan, T. H., Forster, K. I. and Frost, R. (1997). Translation priming with different scripts: masked priming with cognates in Hebrew–English bilinguals. *Journal of Experimental Psychology: Learning, Memory, and Cognition, 23*(5), 1122–39.

Gollan, T. H., Montoya, R. I. and Werner, G. (2002). Semantic and letter fluency in Spanish-English bilinguals. *Neuropsychology, 16*(4), 562–76.

Haritos, C. (2002). A developmental examination of memory strategies in bilingual six, eight and ten year olds. *International Journal of Bilingual Education and Bilingualism, 5*(4), 197–220.

Hermans, D., Bongaerts, T., De Bot, K. and Schreuder, R. (2003). Producing words in a foreign language: can speakers prevent interference from their first language? *Bilingualism: Language and Cognition, 1*(03), 213–29.

Hudson, J. (1983). *Grammatical and Semantic Aspects of Fitzroy Valley Kriol. Work Papers of SIL-AAB, Series A,* (Vol. 8). Darwin: Australian Aborigines Branch, Summer Institute of Linguistics.

Lanza, E. (1997). *Language Mixing in Infant Bilingualism: A Sociolinguistic Perspective* (second edn). Oxford: Oxford University Press.

Laughren, M. (2002). Syntactic constraints in a 'free word order' language. In M. Amberber and P. Collins (eds), *Language Universals and Variation*. Westport, CT: Praeger.

Laughren, M., Granites, R. J., Hale, K. and Hoogenraad, R. (1996). *A Learner's Guide to Warlpiri*. Alice Springs, NT: IAD Press.

Malcolm, I. G. and Kaldor, S. (1991). Aboriginal English: an overview. In S. Romaine (ed.), *Language in Australia* (pp. 67–83). Cambridge: Cambridge University Press.

McLeay, H. (2003). The relationship between bilingualism and the performance of spatial tasks. *International Journal of Bilingual Education and Bilingualism, 6*(6), 423–38.

Munro, J. M. (2004). 'Substrate language influence in Kriol: the application of transfer constraints to language contact in northern Australia'. Unpublished PhD thesis, University of New England, Armidale, NSW.

Mushin, I. (2005). *Second Position Clitic Phenomena in North-Central Australia: Some Pragmatic Considerations*. In Proceedings of the 2004 Conference of the Australian Linguistic Society. Sydney: Australian Linguistic Society.

Nash, D. (1986). *Topics in Warlpiri Grammar*. New York: Garland Publishing Inc.

O'Shannessy, C. (2005). Light Warlpiri: a new language. *Australian Journal of Linguistics, 25*(1), 31–57.

O'Shannessy, C. (Forthcoming). Language variation and change in a north Australian indigenous community. In James N. Stanford and Dennis R. Preston (eds), *Quantitative Sociolinguistic Studies of Indigenous Minority Languages*, Michigan State University.

Poplack, Shana (1980). Sometimes I'll start a sentence in Spanish y termino en Espanol. *Linguistics* 18: 581–618.

Ransdell, S., Barbier, M.-L. and Niit, T. (2006). Metacognitions about language skill and working memory among monolingual and bilingual college students: when does multilingualism matter? *International Journal of Bilingual Education and Bilingualism, 9*(6), 728–41.

Ross, E. (1999). *Warlpiri Triangle Report*. Paper presented at the Warlpiri Triangle, Willowra, NT.

Sandefur, J. (1991). A sketch of the structure of Kriol. In S. Romaine (ed.), *Language in Australia* (pp. 204–12). Cambridge: Cambridge University Press.

Simpson, J. (2007). Expressing pragmatic constraints on word order in Warlpiri. In A. Zaenen, J. Simpson, T. H. King, J. Grimshaw, J. Maign and C. Manning (eds), *Architecture, Rules and Preferences: Variations on Themes by Joan W. Bresnan* (pp. 403–27). Stanford, CA: CSLI.

Swartz, S. M. and Swartz, S. M. (1991). *Constraints on Zero Anaphora and Word Order in Warlpiri Narrative Text*. Darwin, NT: Summer Institute of Linguistics.

van Heuven, W. J. B., Dijkstra, T. and Grainger, J. (1998). Orthographic neighborhood effects in bilingual word recognition. *Journal of Memory and Language, 39*(3), 458–83.

Unravelling languages: multilingualism and language contact in Kalkaringi

13

Felicity Meakins

Newcomers to Aboriginal communities in the Northern Territory are often struck by the range of languages spoken, and the ease with which people switch between languages. It can be a daunting experience trying to understand and operate within this language environment. This chapter will describe the range of languages and linguistic practices used in one community, Kalkaringi. In Kalkaringi, older people continue to speak a traditional language (Gurindji), and younger speakers speak a new youth variety (Gurindji Kriol) which is built from Gurindji and Kriol elements. Warlpiri is also spoken by many people and English is the main language of non-Indigenous institutions. In addition, people switch and mix these languages in various ways. Although the picture is very complex, this paper will show that there are clear patterns of language use. Understanding the patterns can help people working in the communities make sense of these complex environments.

Introduction

A person working in an Aboriginal community in the Northern Territory (NT) might hear people speaking in a variety of ways. Frequently people speak more than one language, and the use of multiple languages in conversation is common. Most often the community languages are combined in various ways when people are talking with each other. It can be a confusing experience for a newcomer trying to decipher and make sense of this type of language environment. This chapter is a case study of the range of languages and linguistic practices used in one community, Kalkaringi (NT).[1] The traditional language of Kalkaringi and the surrounding area is Gurindji. However the language environment of this region is a complex situation of languages influencing each other and people switching between these languages. Although this chapter describes only one Aboriginal community, the language situation here is typical of many communities in northern Australia.

Older people at Kalkaringi continue to speak a traditional language (Gurindji), however younger people speak a new youth variety (Gurindji Kriol) which systematically combines elements of Gurindji and Kriol. Some Warlpiri is also spoken; English is the main language of the school, clinic and other government facilities; and Kriol is spoken by Aboriginal visitors. In addition, people rapidly switch between these languages in various ways. Although the picture is very complicated, this chapter shows that there are clear patterns of language use. Understanding these patterns can help people working in this and similar NT communities make sense of these intricate linguistic environments.

This chapter begins the way a newcomer to Kalkaringi would find themselves – diving straight into a conversation between community members. Three languages are used in this conversation: Gurindji, Kriol and Gurindji Kriol; and switches between these languages occur between speakers, between sentences spoken by the same speaker, and within sentences. This excerpt of conversation paints a complex picture of the language practices found at Kalkaringi. The following sections provide some tools for untangling these complexities. First, I describe the languages which are spoken at Kalkaringi: Gurindji, Warlpiri, English, Kriol and Gurindji Kriol; followed by a description of the types of language mixing strategies used by speakers. This description of Kalkaringi can be placed within the broader context of multilingualism and language contact around the world (McConvell, Chapter 11).

The conversation from the first section is supplemented by further examples of speech from around 60 hours of video recordings of conversations and stories.[2] All the examples of speech include three lines of text. The first line is the speaker's sentence, transcribed as it was said. The second line contains a break-down and translation of the words and suffixes. The suffix meanings are contained in the List of Abbreviations (p. vii). Finally the third line is an

English translation. I have used the standard spelling systems of Gurindji, Kriol and English. All Gurindji words in the speech and translation lines are italicised, and the Kriol words are in plain font. Occasionally I draw attention to some feature of the speech using bold font. All names have been changed to maintain the anonymity of the speakers.

A typical intergenerational conversation among Gurindji people

The following example is a snapshot of a typical intergenerational conversation between 40-year-old and 20-year-old women from Kalkaringi. This conversation was recorded in the nearby Ngarinyman community of Yarralin on an overnight trip from Kalkaringi in August 2005. The first topic of conversation is about where another group of people have gone fishing (a–e). The second excerpt is a discussion about the type of ashes that are used to flavour chewing tobacco and where to find it around Yarralin (f–j). The speakers are Sue who is 19 years old, Kath (21 years), Irma (48 years) and Fiona (43 years). The women have close relationships with each other. Fiona and Irma are sisters. Kath is the adopted daughter of Fiona, and she also calls Irma 'mother'. Sue calls both Fiona and Irma 'sister' because her adopted mother was the sister of the mother of Irma and Fiona.

Example 1: Fishing conversation excerpt

(a) Sue: Kylie-mob　　weya　dei　bin　gon　bij-in-bat?
Kylie-GROUP　　where　they　PST　go　fish-ing-ing
'Kylie and that lot – where did they go fishing?'

(b) Irma: *marntaj*　wi　kan　*liwart*　hiya　wi　*ngurra*　*nyawa-ngka-rni.*
ok　　we　can　wait　here　we　camp　this-LOC-ONLY
'OK we can *wait* here, we'll *camp right here.*'

(c) Fiona: *wanyjika-warla*　*nyila*　*ngu-lu*　*ya-ni?*
where-FOC　　that　CAT-they　go-PST
'Where did they go?'

(d) Kath: dei　neba　tok　*ngayiny*　dei　bin　jus　tok　'ai- mgon bij-in'.
they　never　talk　me-DAT　they　NF　just　talk　'I-　NF go　fish-ing
'They didn't talk *to me*, they just said 'I'm going fishing'.'

(e) Fiona: wal　　*yangki*　*pa-rra*　*nganayirla?*
well　　ask　hit-IMP　whats.it.name
'Well *ask whats-his-name.*'

(Continued)

Example 1: Fishing conversation excerpt—Cont'd

Ashes conversation excerpt

(f) Kath: | milktin-*ta* | rait | ful | *kawurn-ma,* | *kuya-ny* | na | wait-wan-*walija.* |
| milk.tin-LOC | right | full | ashes-DIS | thus-NOM | now | white-NOM-PAUC |

'There's loads of *ashes in* the milk tin, *lots of that* white stuff now.'

(g) Irma: | *wanyjika-warla* | dei | ged-im-bat | *kawurn?* |
| where-FOC | they | get-TRN-ing | ashes |

'*Where* are they getting *ashes* from?'

(h) Kath: | hiya | la | Lingara Road-*ta* | jamweya | dei | bin | ged-im-bat. |
| here | on | Lingara Road-LOC | somewhere | they | NF | get-TRN-ing |

'Here *on* the Lingara road, they've been getting it.'

(i) Kath: | dei | bin | ged-im-bat | *Kiwala*-mob-*tu-ma.* |
| they | NF | get-TRN-ing | NAME-GROUP-ERG-DIS |

'They got it, Kawurla and that lot.'

(j) Irma: | *ngu-lu* | *manku* | na | *purinyjirri-ngka* | na | ib | dei | kom. |
| CAT-they | get-FUT | now | afternoon-LOC | now | if | they | come |

'*They can get it in the afternoon,* if they come back in time.'

In this conversation, the older women, Irma and Fiona speak Gurindji and Gurindji Kriol, and switch between these languages. For example, in Example 1(c) and (e) Fiona speaks only Gurindji when asking where a group of people have gone fishing. Irma uses Gurindji Kriol in (b) to suggest that they wait for the group and camp overnight. Their daughter, Kath speaks Gurindji Kriol predominantly, for example in Example 1(f) when she describes where to find some ashes. However she also alternates between Kriol and Gurindji Kriol. The speech of Sue is very similar to Kath. An example of her use of a Kriol-only sentence is in Example 1(a).

Both the older and younger women also change between languages in various ways, which is called 'code-switching' (see also McConvell, Chapter 11). Switching can occur between speakers of different generations. For example in Example 1(c) Fiona asks Kath where some people have gone in Gurindji. Kath replies in Gurindji Kriol in Example 1(d) and Fiona follows with a command in Gurindji. Switching also occurs within a sentence. In Example 1(j) Irma tells Kath when some other people can collect ashes. She begins in Gurindji and then switches to Kriol halfway through. Another pattern of switching is slotting a single word or suffix into a sentence of a different language, also called 'insertional code-switching'. For instance in Example 1(e) Fiona uses a Kriol discourse marker *wal* (well) in an otherwise Gurindji sentence. Kath also uses this mixing strategy in Example 1(d), (h) and (i), however these sentences represent a more fixed form of mixing, Gurindji Kriol. The differences between Gurindji Kriol and code-switching between Gurindji and Kriol will become clearer later.

The different use of language by all of these speakers illustrates the complexity of the language situation at Kalkaringi. The following sections will tease out the different languages and mixing strategies used in the conversation and others. I begin with a description of the languages spoken at Kalkaringi.

The languages spoken at Kalkaringi

Although the traditional language of Kalkaringi is Gurindji, a number of languages are spoken by the Gurindji people. The main languages in this mix are Gurindji and the youth variety of Gurindji, Gurindji Kriol. Kriol, Aboriginal English and Standard Australian English are also found, along with a neighbouring language, Warlpiri, though their use is less frequent. A lot of crossover exists in the sounds, grammar and vocabulary of these languages. Gurindji Kriol is the most radical amalgam of these languages, combining equal elements from the grammar and vocabulary of Gurindji and Kriol. The Aboriginal English spoken at Kalkaringi is influenced by the Gurindji sound inventory and some grammar. Finally Kriol, though it probably originally came from Ngukurr (Munro, 2000), also contains grammatical structures which later developed under the influence of Gurindji.

In the following section, I describe the function and structure of each of these languages. Their function, within the context of language mixing, is examined afterwards.

Gurindji

Domain of use

Gurindji is closely related to the neighbouring languages Bilinarra, which is spoken at Pigeon Hole (Nordlinger, 1990), and Ngarinyman, which is the traditional language of Yarralin (Jones and Campbell, Chapter 8). Linguistically, it is more distantly related to Warlpiri (O'Shannessy, Chapter 12). The northernmost Warlpiri-speaking community is Lajamanu, which is only 120 km away. Gurindji is an endangered language, with only 60 full speakers remaining in 2001 (Lee and Dickson, 2002), though a lot of its vocabulary and grammar is preserved in the youth language, Gurindji Kriol (Meakins, 2007).

Gurindji is rarely spoken monolingually, that is, without switching into another language. Even then it is only spoken monolingually by older people. This situation is common across much of Australia, and indeed in other colonised countries where introduced languages have replaced the Indigenous languages as the main language. These languages are increasingly spoken only by older people and they are not passed onto the next generation. Examples of monolingual Gurindji were shown in Example 1(c), (e) and (h). Language mixing is not a new language practice at Kalkaringi. Code-switching between Gurindji and Kriol was observed in the mid-1970s, and it is likely that code-switching between traditional Australian languages was a common social practice even before colonisation (McConvell, 1985; 1988; Chapter 11).

Although Gurindji is spoken among older people, when they speak to younger people, particularly children, they tend to use more Kriol. This practice of using Kriol with children is a common phenomenon reported across northern Australia. Gurindji people under the age of 35 years do not speak Gurindji monolingually with a high degree of proficiency. Younger speakers are not able to use the Gurindji inflecting verb and bound pronoun systems (see the section on Structure). However they do use Gurindji noun phrases and an extensive range of Gurindji suffixes in the youth language, Gurindji Kriol. Despite their limited use of monolingual Gurindji, their level of passive knowledge seems to be high; that is, young people have little trouble understanding what older people say to them.

Structure

Gurindji is a fairly typical member of the Pama-Nyungan language family. This family of languages extends across most of Australia, with the exception of Arnhem Land. The grammar of Gurindji is very different from English, as I will show through a discussion of Example 2.

Example 2

kirrawa	ngu-lu-ø	pangkily	pa-ni	ngarlaka-la	kajirri-walija-lu
goanna	CAT-they-it	hit.head	hit-PST	head-LOC	women-PAUC-ERG

'A number of old women hit the goanna on the head.'

The first thing an English speaker might notice about this sentence is that the patient ('the goanna' in this case) appears at the beginning of the sentence and the agent ('the group of old women') is at the end of the sentence. This is the opposite of English. In fact, in Gurindji, these actors may appear in just about any position in the sentence. Word order is determined by which actor the speaker wants to emphasise. For example, in Example 2, the speaker highlights 'the goanna' in this sentence by placing it at the front of the sentence. Word order in English is fixed because it is used to show who is doing what to whom. The agent is generally found before the verb in an English sentence (subject position), and the patient is placed after the verb (object position). In Gurindji case suffixes are used to indicate who the agent and patient are. For example, in the sentence above, an ergative suffix *-lu* tells us that the group of old women is the agent. The lack of a suffix on *kirrawa* (the goanna) indicates that it is the patient. Gurindji is similar to Warlpiri, in this respect. O'Shannessy (Chapter 12) discusses word order and the ergative suffix for Warlpiri and Light Warlpiri.

Gurindji has many other types of suffixes. For example, Gurindji also uses spatial suffixes where prepositions would be found in English. Thus in Example 2, a locative *-la* is suffixed to *ngarlaka* (head) to show where the group of women hit the goanna '*on* the head'. Gurindji also has other suffixes which can change the meaning of a noun. The paucal suffix *-walija* in the example above changes the number of women from one to a small group. Suffixes may also change a noun into an adjective or a different type of noun. A couple of commonly used suffixes are *-murlung* (lacking), for example, *langa-murlung* (meaning 'dumb' or literally 'without ears'), and *-kaji* (agentiser), for example, *langa-kaji* (meaning 'an otoscope' or literally 'the thing that relates to ears').

Another large group of suffixes are pronouns. Unlike English, Gurindji uses pronominal suffixes rather than free words; thus *-lu* (they) in Example 2 which attaches to an element called the 'catalyst' has no meaning of its own. The pronoun 'it' has no form. Another feature of Gurindji is the use of both a noun and a pronoun to refer to the agent. In English, either a pronoun or a noun is used, but rarely both. In Gurindji, a pronoun suffix is always present, however nouns are optional. The speaker could have said this sentence without the 'goanna' or 'old women' nouns, and it would have still been grammatical.

Finally, the Gurindji compound verb structure is made up of an inflecting verb and a coverb. The inflecting verb provides most of the tense, aspect and mood information, and the coverb takes most of the semantic load of the verb compound. In Example 2 above, *pani* (have hit) is the inflecting verb which is a past perfect form of 'hit'. The co-verb *pangkily* (hit on the head) provides more information about where the women hit the goanna. Inflecting verbs may be used on their own, or in combination with coverbs, which carry additional meaning.

Warlpiri

The only other traditional language which is regularly spoken in Kalkaringi is Warlpiri. Warlpiri is the only language in this region which remains strong, although it is endangered in regional and world terms. In general the grammar is very similar to Gurindji; see Laughren and Hoogenraad (1996) and O'Shannessy (Chapter 12) for more information. Warlpiri is spoken at Lajamanu also in conjunction with Kriol, Aboriginal English and a mixed language, Light Warlpiri (O'Shannessy, 2005; Chapter 12). Many Warlpiri people speak Warlpiri among themselves at Kalkaringi. However younger speakers who grew up at Kalkaringi generally do not speak Warlpiri fluently. Nonetheless they mark their Warlpiri identity through the use of some commonly borrowed nouns. For example in Example 3 the 23-year-old speaker inserts the Warlpiri word for tree, *watiya*, into a Gurindji Kriol sentence.

Example 3

nyila-nginyi-ma	i-m	baldan	na	*nyawa-ma*	*nyawa-ngka*	**watiya**-*ngka*.
that-ABL-DIS	he-NF	fall.over	now	this-DIS	this-LOC	**tree**-LOC

'*After that, this one* fell over the **tree** *here*.'

Other Warlpiri words have come into common usage among younger Gurindji people. For example, the Warlpiri numeral 'one', *jinta*, has gained some currency. It is now used more often than the related Gurindji word, *jintaku*. A shorter-lived Warlpiri fashion among the 5–10-year-olds in 2005 was the Warlpiri word for 'water', *ngapa*. This group was aware of the word's language origin, and have since reverted back to the Gurindji word *ngawa*.

English

Standard Australian English and Aboriginal English are not dominant languages in Kalkaringi. English is generally only heard at the school, which is an English-medium-of-instruction school, at the clinic, council office and in other places where interactions with *kartiya* (non-Indigenous people) are common. English is rarely used in the home, though younger people do use English to imitate television personalities or school teachers, usually to comic effect. For example, in Example 4 below, Sue and Sonya are playing with Sue's 2-year-old son, pretending to be doctors. Sue (18 years) begins speaking in Gurindji Kriol, and switches to Aboriginal English in Example 4(b). Sonya (14 years) follows with a list of instructions for the patient, which she says in English with an American accent. In this sequence they are laughing as they re-enact their previous experiences at the local clinic and mimic American television shows.

Example 4

(a) Sue:

janga	Clayton	*janga*	*nyuntu*	*janga.*
sick	NAME	sick	you	sick

'You're sick Clayton, sick, you're sick.'

(b) Sue: go back home you very hot Clayton.

(c) Sonya: you need to go home relax have some cup of tea . . . you got it?

Kriol

Domain of use

Two of the languages which are spoken in Kalkaringi are the result of contact between other languages. The first of these contact languages is Kriol which is an English-lexifier creole language (Wigglesworth and Simpson, Chapter 1). The other, discussed below, is Gurindji Kriol.

Kriol is spoken by younger Gurindji people but again rarely without some mixing with Gurindji. For example, in Example 1(a) Sue uses a Kriol-only sentence to ask where a group of people have gone. Example 5 is another example of a monolingual Kriol utterance from a conversation between two 20-year-old Gurindji women travelling in a government car near Kalkaringi.

Example 5

yeah	ai	garram	jumok	bat	wi	not	alaud	tu	jumok la motika.
yes	I	have	cigarette	but	we	not	allowed	to	smoke in car

'Yeah I have a cigarette but we're not allowed to smoke in the car.'

Though Kriol is rarely spoken monolingually, it is used with other Aboriginal people in the nearest service centre, Katherine, or is spoken to Kriol-speaking visitors in Kalkaringi. Gurindji people usually have little trouble replacing Gurindji words and suffixes with equivalent Kriol words.

Grammar

Grammatically, Kriol is similar to English in its paucity of morphology, that is, prefixes and suffixes. The formation process of Kriol involved fusing much of the grammar and lexicon of English with the phonology and semantics of the traditional languages of the Ngukurr area. Aspects of Gurindji grammar influenced Kriol later when it developed further in the Kalkaringi area. Below is an example of a Kriol sentence. It can be compared with the Gurindji example in Example 2. What follows is a brief description of the grammar of Kriol. For fuller descriptions see Sandefur (1979) and Munro (2004).

Example 6

det	olgamen-mob	dei	bin	kil-im	det	guana	langa	hed
the	old.women-GROUP	they	PST	hit-TRN	the	goanna	on	head

'The group of old women hit the goanna on the head.'

Kriol is similar to English in that it distinguishes the agent ('the group of old women') and the patient ('the goanna') using word order. The agent comes before the verb and the patient occurs after the verb (Munro, 2004, p. 117). The Kriol noun phrase consists of a noun often accompanied by an adjective or a determiner such as *det* ('the' from 'that') in Example 6 above or a demonstrative such as *darran* ('that' from 'that one'). Also like English, Kriol nouns only take a few suffixes, such as -*mob* (group) in the example above. Nouns can also co-occur with pronouns, which is more similar to Gurindji than English. So in Example 6 both the noun 'the group of old women' and 'they' refer to the same agent.

Like Gurindji, the Kriol verb phrase often consists of two words – a function word which marks tense and aspect, and the verb itself which carries the meaning. For example, in Example 6 there are two parts to the verb – the verb itself, *kilim* (hit), which is preceded by the past tense marker *bin* (from 'been'). Other markers which modify the verb may be aspect markers, for example, *mait* (might), *garra* (have/got to) (Munro, 2004, p. 87). Verbs can take a small number of suffixes. For instance, verbs which have an agent and a patient such as *kilim* (hit) in Example 6 are marked with a transitive suffix -*im* which is derived from the third person pronoun 'him' (English) or 'im' (Kriol) (Meyerhoff, 1996).

Finally Kriol has a prepositional phrase, similar to English which is used to describe location in time and space. The Kriol prepositional phrase consists of an adverbial particle, preposition and noun phrase. Prepositions head the Kriol prepositional phrase, as in Example 6 where *la* (from 'langa' and from 'along a') heads a phrase describing where the group of old women are hitting the goanna. *La* or *langa* has a large range of meanings, covering the English prepositions *towards, in, on, under, over, beside* etc. Other Kriol prepositions include *brom* (from), *garram* ('with', from 'got') and *bo* (for), which have slightly different forms in different areas.

Gurindji Kriol

Domain of use

The other contact language spoken in Kalkaringi is the youth language, Gurindji Kriol. It combines the Kriol verb grammar with the Gurindji noun grammar. This mixed language looks a lot like and probably found its historical roots in code-switching (McConvell and Meakins, 2005); however it has stabilised into an autonomous language, that is, the patterns of the mix are now fixed and speakers use the Gurindji and Kriol elements in ways which differ from their use in the source languages. Gurindji Kriol also no longer represents code-switching because its speakers are not proficient speakers of Gurindji (Meakins, 2007). Gurindji Kriol is now the main language of Kalkaringi and is spoken by everyone under the age of about 35 years. For example, Kath uses Gurindji Kriol in Example 1(j) when she describes where the ashes for chewing tobacco are kept. Younger speakers often switch between Gurindji Kriol and Kriol, and older speakers switch between this youth language and Gurindji.

Gurindji Kriol has a low social status in Kalkaringi compared with Gurindji. For starters, this youth language has no name. The term 'Gurindji Kriol' was created during a language workshop facilitated by Erika Charola (2002). In fact this language is usually called Gurindji, and Kalkaringi people generally describe it in terms of the loss of Gurindji, rather than the creation of a new language. For example, older people complain that the younger generations do not speak Gurindji correctly. This can make it difficult for Kalkaringi organisations to get translations of resources. Speakers are generally anxious about their performance, and often attempt to produce traditional Gurindji, or refer organisations to older Gurindji speakers for translation. In fact it is often better to have resources translated into Gurindji Kriol because this is the main language of the community now.

Grammar

Due to its systematic combination of Gurindji and Kriol grammar and vocabulary, Gurindji Kriol is best described as a mixed language, which is a type of contact language. Contact languages often arise when people speaking different languages are in social contact with one another, and when one group dominates another. Gurindji Kriol fits into the category of V(erb)–N(oun) mixed languages, a rare subclass of mixed languages. Most mixed languages combine the grammar of one language with the vocabulary of another language. For instance, Angloromani, spoken by the Rom in England combines the grammar of English with some lexicon from Romani (Boretzky and Igla, 1994), and Media Lengua, spoken by the Quechuan Indians in Ecuador mixes a Quechuan grammar with Spanish words (Muysken, 1997).

Very few examples of a V–N mixed language have been identified in the world (Bakker, 2003). The most widely discussed is Michif which is spoken in Canada. It has a structural and lexical split between the verb (Cree) and noun systems (French) (Bakker, 1994). Closer to home, another mixed language, Light Warlpiri, is spoken by younger people at Lajamanu. Like Gurindji Kriol, the traditional language, in this case Warlpiri, provides the noun phrase structure and Kriol dominates the verb phrase structure (O'Shannessy, 2005; Chapter 12). In the case of Gurindji Kriol, Kriol contributes much of the verb phrase structure including the tense, aspect and mood systems, and Gurindji supplies the noun structure including case and derivational morphology.

In terms of vocabulary, Gurindji Kriol is quite mixed. Nouns are derived from both Gurindji and Kriol, and the same is true of verbs. In Gurindji Kriol 35 per cent of words are from Kriol, 28% per cent from Gurindji, and the remaining 37 per cent are synonymous forms drawn from both languages. For example, Gurindji Kriol speakers always use the Gurindji word for 'child', *karu*, and never the Kriol word, *biginini*. Similarly, they always use the Kriol word for 'hit', *kilim* and never the Gurindji word *panana*. Synonymous words from Gurindji and Kriol may be used interchangeably, depending on a number of social factors including group identification and the age of the hearer. For example, the Gurindji word for 'jump', *tipart*, may be chosen if the speaker is addressing an older person, whereas the Kriol form *jam* may be used in conversation with peer groups or younger people (Meakins and O'Shannessy, 2005, p. 45).

I will not go into detail about the grammar and vocabulary of Gurindji Kriol. The descriptions of Gurindji and Kriol above should provide enough information to understand the structure of the mixed language. Example 7 demonstrates the grammatical relationship between Gurindji Kriol and its source languages. In this example, the core verb phrase structure *i bin kilim* (*im*) (she hit it) is drawn from Kriol while the noun phrase, including case marking, are from Gurindji.

Example 7

det	olgamen	[i	bin	kil-im]	det	guana	langa	hed
the	old.women	she	PST	hit-TRN	the	goanna	on	head

[det	*kajirri-ngku*]	[i	bin	kil-im]	[det	guana	*ngarlaka-ngka*]
the	woman-ERG	she	NF	hit-TRN	the	goanna	head-LOC

[*kajirri-lu*]	*ngu-ø-ø*	*pangkily*	*pa-ni*	[*kirrawa*	*ngarlaka-ngka*]
woman-ERG	CAT-she-him	hit.head	hit-PST	goanna	head-LOC

'The old woman hit the goanna on the head.'

The following example is more extended and typifies the mixed character of Gurindji Kriol. This excerpt is from a 20 year old using a picture book, *Frog, Where Are You?* (Mayer, 1969),[3] to tell a story. It begins from where the boy has climbed onto the back of the deer.

Example 8

karu	i-m	top	la	im	*kankula*	diya-*ngka*.
child	he-NF	be	on	it	up	deer-LOC

'The *child* is sitting *on top of* the deer.'

i-m	teik-im	*rarraj*	det	*karu-ma*	*nyanuny*	*ngarlaka-ngka*.
he-NF	take-TRN	run	the	child-DIS	its	head-LOC

'It took the *child running on its head*.'

det	diya-*ngku*	i	bin	*jak*	im	na	*karu*	an	*warlaku*	kanyjurra-k.
the	deer-ERG	it	NF	make.fall	him	now	child	and	dog	down-ALL

'The deer threw the *child* and the *dog off the cliff*.'

tubala	baldan	*kujarrap-pa-rni*	*karu*	an	*warlaku*	ngawa-ngkirri	*jirrpu*.
those.two	fall	pair-PA-ONLY	child	and	dog	water-ALL	dive

'Those two, *the pair of them*, the *child* and *dog* fell down, *plunging into the water*.'

In this example, the verb frame is Kriol with basic meaning verbs *teikim* (take), tense marking *bin* (non-future) and transitive marking *-im* all derived from this language. The structure of the NP is predominantly Gurindji. Present is Gurindji inflectional morphology including case marking, for example, ergative *-ngku/-tu*, locative *-ngka/-ta*, allative *-ngkirri*; and dative pronouns, for example, *nyanuny* (his/her/its). Also present from Gurindji is discourse marking *-ma* and some derivation morphology *-rni* (only). Lexically, there is a mix between Kriol and Gurindji with some verbs derived from Kriol, *teikim* (take) and *baldan* (fall), and others from Gurindji *rarraj* (run) and *jirrpu* (dive). Similarly nouns from both languages are present – *diya* (deer) is from Kriol; and *karu* (child) and *ngawa* (water) from Gurindji.

Language mixing in Kalkaringi

The main point of the previous section was to give a general idea of the social domain and grammar of each of the languages spoken at Kalkaringi. A common theme which has emerged is the rarity with which only one language is used both on the sentence level and certainly within conversation. Language mixing in the form of *code-switching* is the most common language practice. It can occur between speakers where one person speaks one language and the other person speaks another language. It can also occur within one speaker's sentence. Code-switching by one speaker occurs as *insertional* and *alternational* code-switching (Muysken, 2000), as discussed in McConvell (Chapter 11).

First, speakers do not necessarily speak to each other using the same language. Sometimes one speaker may accommodate for another speaker. For example, an older speaker may use Gurindji Kriol instead of Gurindji to fit in with a younger speaker's style. A younger speaker may accommodate to an older speaker in particular situations, for example, when she is attempting to ask for money or to elicit a favour which might be stretching the bounds of kinship obligations. But it is also quite common for speakers to maintain their own speech style in the course of a conversation. An example of an older person speaking Gurindji and a younger person replying in Gurindji Kriol was provided in the first example (Example 1(c)–(e)). The following exchange (Example 10) is another example which comes from a conversation about fishing between a 54-year-old woman (Clair) and her 19-year-old daughter (Ann) at Pawuly, a popular fishing spot. In this case, one speaker is associated with one language, and code-switching occurs between speakers. Ann begins in Kriol, and Clair replies in Gurindji.

Example 9

Ann: jak-im   yu   rait.
     throw-TRN   you   right
     'You're right to throw it now.'

Clair: *kula*   *yikili*   *ngu-rna*   *yu-warra.*
       not   far   CAT-I   put-IMP
       '*I won't throw it too far.*'

As discussed in McConvell (Chapter 11) one form of language mixing which occurs within one speaker's utterance is *insertional* code-switching. Insertional code-switching occurs when one language is embedded within another. It often involves a speaker inserting a word from one language into the sentence of another language (Muysken, 2000). In Kalkaringi older speakers use either Gurindji or Kriol as their base language, and younger speakers, only Kriol, if they are code-switching. In Example 10 the 39-year-old speaker uses the Kriol/English noun *kap* (cup) within a Gurindji sentence. Example 11 is an example of a 23-year-old speaker inserting Gurindji words, *ngaji* (God, originally father) and *kankula* (up) into a Kriol sentence. This sentence is considered code-switching rather than Gurindji Kriol, because the speaker uses Kriol elements, such as the preposition *la* (on), which are not found in Gurindji Kriol.

Example 10

ngu-rna	*yuwa-ni*	**kap**-*kula*.
CAT-I	put-PST	cup-LOC

'I put it in the **cup**.'

Example 11

ngaji	bin	put-im	deya	luk	*kankula*	la	det	hil	jeya.
god	NF	put-TRN	there	look	up	on	the	hill	there

'*God* put (the donkeys), look, *up* on the hill there.'

Alternational code-switching (where a language is not nested within another language to the same extent as insertional code-switching) is also commonly used to mix Gurindji, Kriol and Gurindji Kriol. In most cases, an utterance begins with a clause in one language and finishes in another (Muysken, 2000). In Example 12, Irma (46 years) directs Selina to tell a story to her grandson, beginning in Gurindji and later switching to Gurindji Kriol. In Example 13 Linda (19 years) is describing what a water goanna is doing at Kalkarriny (another popular fishing place) to her friends. She begins in Gurindji Kriol and then switches halfway through to Aboriginal English.

Example 12

Selina	*jarrakap*	*ma-nyja-rla*	*nyila-wu*	*karu-wu*	Timo-*wu*/
NAME	talk	talk-IMP-to.him	that-DAT	child-DAT	NAME-DAT/
yu	yurrk	la	im.		
you	tell.story	to	him.		

'SO talk to that kid Timo, you tell him a story.'

> ### Example 13
>
> | i-m | *wirl-karra* | i-m | *wirlk* | im | / | that's | why | he bin come back this side |
> |-----|-----------|-----|-------|-----|---|--------|-----|-----------------------------|
> | it-NF | pull-ing | it-NF | pull | it | | | | |
>
> 'It (the water current) is *dragging* it (the goanna), that's why it came back to this side.'

Conclusion

The number of languages and types of mixing strategies found at Kalkaringi can be placed within the broader context of other Aboriginal communities and the world in general. To begin with, multilingualism is standard within Aboriginal communities and is the world-wide norm, more generally. It is common for people to speak more than one language when they are in close proximity with other language groups. Marriage between groups, shared cultural practices and experiences, and population movement also promote the sort of multilingualism which is found in northern Australia and the rest of the world. Often two or more languages can exist side-by-side without them having any effect on each other. Populations in close proximity will speak both languages, perhaps to varying degrees of proficiency, and code-switch between these languages. Code-switching is not seen as a sign of linguistic weakness for either language, merely a language practice which promotes a multilingual identity. Dutch and French in Brussels is a good example of this type of co-occurrence where speakers fluidly shift between languages. Though speakers may identify more with Dutch or French, the code-switching also constructs a specific Brussels identity which separates them from other Belgians (Treffers-Daller, 1994).

Not all situations of multilingualism are stable, however. Language endangerment and death is also an increasingly common characteristic of the world's languages. Of the 6,000 languages spoken today, perhaps only half to one-tenth will be spoken by the end of the twenty-first century (Krauss, 1992). Indigenous languages in colonised countries have fared particularly badly. For example, in Australia most of the original 250 Aboriginal languages are no longer spoken or are highly endangered, with only languages in Arnhem Land and the desert regions showing signs of strength (McConvell and Thieberger, 2001). Similar situations are reported in other heavily colonised areas such as North and South America and Africa.

Language dominance can also have other consequences. Many languages are the product of colonisation, and of languages coming into contact with each other or dominating other languages. Creole languages are the result of colonial powers bringing together disparate groups of people often in slavery. In the case of Kriol in northern Australia, children from different language backgrounds were separated from their families and brought together with only English and a cattle station pidgin as a *lingua franca*. Around 500 creole languages exist, from other English-based creoles such as Jamaican and Hawai'i Creole and Tok Pisin in Papua New Guinea, to French-based creoles such as the ones spoken on Mauritius and Haiti.

Another result of language contact is a much more equal mixing of languages. These languages, called 'mixed languages', are much more unusual than creoles. They are the product of only two languages coming into contact. Sometimes they reflect the mixed identity of the speakers, as in Michif where the speakers were the children of Cree mothers and French buffalo-herding fathers in Canada (Bakker, 1997). Mixed languages can also arise from people reclaiming their traditional language. For the Rom in England, mixing large amounts of Romany vocabulary with an English grammar created a language which is unintelligible to English speakers. Angloromani both strongly marks the identity of the speaker, and functions as a secret language.

The language ecology of Kalkaringi is perhaps extraordinary on a world scale given the presence of all these language contact processes – multilingualism, code-switching and contact languages. Some of these languages and linguistic practices of the Gurindji people are very old including the use of Gurindji, Warlpiri, and code-switching between these and other languages. However some features of Kalkaringi's language environment are the result of colonisation and corresponding shifts of identities and practices. The use of Kriol as a language itself and within the youth language, Gurindji Kriol is a relatively new phenomena and perhaps part of a pan-Aboriginal identity across northern Australia which only became relevant post-colonisation. The Gurindji element of Gurindji Kriol helps maintain a strong sense of Gurindji identity for young Gurindji people. The result of this fusion of new and old languages and different mixing styles makes for a fascinatingly complex language environment.

The degree of multilingualism and language mixing found in Kalkaringi can be quite daunting for newcomers, especially monolingual English speakers who are not equipped to understand the intricacies of how people operate in more than one language. It can appear as if Gurindji people, and indeed Aboriginal people in similar north Australian communities, have little control over their linguistic repertoire and mix languages randomly. The aim of this chapter has been to demonstrate that the knowledge and function of languages within multilingual contexts, such as Kalkaringi, is a systematic and highly skilled enterprise. This use of multiple languages grounds speakers in different spheres of identity. Gurindji links its speakers to the immediate family and kin group, with Kriol an in-group marker for north Aboriginal people. Finally the use of English anchors speakers within the broader Australian community. The systematic mixing of all of these languages expresses a simultaneous sense of belonging in all of these social spheres.

Notes

1. When I refer to Kalkaringi, I include Daguragu which is a settlement 8 km away. These communities were set up separately historically, however they operate as a single entity in terms of kin relations and administration. In fact all of the data was collected with Daguragu people. However the name 'Kalkaringi' is more familiar and more often used to refer to both settlements.
2. This work was funded by the Aboriginal Child Language Acquisition project and Melbourne University: http://www.linguisitics.unimelb.edu.au/projects/ACLA/index.html. Many fruitful discussions about the language environment of similar Aboriginal communities have come out of this project. Many thanks especially to Patrick McConvell, Jane Simpson, Carmel O'Shannessy and Samantha Disbray.

   Many Daguragu families were involved in these recordings, including Samantha Smiler Nangala-Nanaku and her family; Ronaleen and Anne-Maree Reynolds Namija, Curley Reynolds Nimarra and their family; Cassandra Algy Nimarra, and Ena, Frances and Sarah Oscar Nanaku; Cecelia Edwards Nangari; and Rosy, Lisa and Leanne Smiler Nangari. In particular, Samantha Smiler, Ronaleen Reynolds and Sarah Oscar were instrumental in organising recording sessions, helping me turn these recordings into written transcripts, and teaching me Gurindji and Gurindji Kriol.
3. This is a book which has been widely used in linguistic research to elicit narratives, particularly with children.

References

Bakker, P. (1994). Michif, the Cree-French mixed language of the Métis buffalo hunters in Canada. In P. Bakker and M. Mous (eds), *Mixed Languages: 15 Case Studies in Language Intertwining* (pp. 13–33). Amsterdam: IFOTT.

Bakker, P. (1997). *A Language of Our Own: The Genesis of Michif, the Mixed Cree-French Language of the Canadian Métis.* Oxford: Oxford University Press.

Bakker, P. (2003). Mixed languages as autonomous systems. In Y. Matras and P. Bakker (eds), *The Mixed Language Debate: Theoretical and Empirical Advances* (pp. 107–50). Berlin: Mouton de Gruyter.

Boretzky, N. and Igla, B. (1994). Romani mixed dialects. In P. Bakker and M. Mous (eds), *Mixed Languages: 15 Case Studies in Language Intertwining.* Amsterdam: IFOTT.

Charola, E. (2002). 'The verb phrase structure of Gurindji Kriol'. Unpublished Honours thesis, University of Melbourne, Melbourne.

Krauss, M. (1992). The world's languages in crisis. *Language, 68*, 4–10.

Laughren, M. and Hoogenraad, R. (1996). *A Learner's Guide to Warlpiri: Tape Course for Beginners.* Based on a tape course prepared by Kenneth Hale and Robin Japanangka Granites. Alice Springs, NT: IAD Press.

Lee, J. and Dickson, G. (2002). *State of Indigenous Languages of the Katherine Region.* Katherine: Diwurruwaurru-jaru Aboriginal Corporation.

Mayer, M. (1969). *Frog, Where Are You?* (1994 edn). New York: Dial Books.

McConvell, P. (1985). Domains and codeswitching among bilingual Aborigines. In M. Clyne (ed.), *Australia, Meeting Place of Languages.* Canberra: Pacific Linguistics.

McConvell, P. (1988). Mix-im-up: Aboriginal code switching, old and new. In M. Heller (ed.), *Codeswitching: Anthropological and Sociolinguistic Perspectives* (pp. 97–149). Berlin: Mouton de Gruyter.

McConvell, P. and Meakins, F. (2005). Gurindji Kriol: a mixed language emerges from code-switching. *Australian Journal of Linguistics, 25*(1), 9–30.

McConvell, P. and Thieberger, N. (2001). The state of Indigenous languages in Australia. *Australia: State of the Environment.* Second Technical Paper Series No.2 (Natural and Cultural Heritage). Canberra: Environment Australia.

Meakins, F. (2007). 'Case-marking in contact: the development and function of case morphology in Gurindji Kriol, an Australian mixed language'. Unpublished PhD thesis, University of Melbourne, Melbourne.

Meakins, F. and O'Shannessy, C. (2005). Possessing variation: age and inalienability related variables in the possessive constructions of two Australian mixed languages. *Monash University Linguistics Papers, 4*(2), 43–63.

Meyerhoff, M. (1996). Transitive marking in contact Englishes. *Australian Journal of Linguistics, 16*(1), 57–80.

Munro, J. (2000). Kriol on the move: a case of language spread and shift in Northern Australia. In J. Siegel (ed.), *Processes of Language Contact: Studies from Australia and the South Pacific.* Saint-Laurent, Quebec: Fides.

Munro, J. (2004). 'Substrate language influence in Kriol: the application of transfer constraints to language contact in northern Australia'. Unpublished PhD thesis, University of New England, Armidale, NSW.

Muysken, P. (1997). Media Lengua. In S. G. Thomason (ed.), *Contact Languages: A Wider Perspective* (pp. 365–426). Amsterdam: John Benjamins.

Muysken, P. (2000). *Bilingual Speech: A Typology of Code-Mixing.* Cambridge: Cambridge University Press.

Nordlinger, R. (1990). 'A sketch grammar of Bilinara'. Unpublished Honours thesis, University of Melbourne, Melbourne.

O'Shannessy, C. (2005). Light Warlpiri: a new language. *Australian Journal of Linguistics, 25*(1), 31–57.

Sandefur, J. R. (1979). *An Australian Creole in the Northern Territory: A Description of Ngukurr-Bamyili Dialects (Part 1)*. Work Papers of SIL-AAB, Series B, Vol. 3. Darwin, NT: Australian Aborigines Branch, Summer Institute of Linguistics.

Treffers-Daller, J. (1994). *Mixing Two Languages: French-Dutch Contact in a Comparative Perspective*. Berlin: Mouton de Gruyter.

Authors index

Languages index

Places index

General index